Photography's Materialities

# Photography's Materialities

## Transatlantic Photographic Practices over the Long Nineteenth Century

*Edited by*
*Geoff Bender and Rasmus R. Simonsen*

LEUVEN UNIVERSITY PRESS

Published with support from the William L. Haines Fund and a Faculty Development Award from the State University of New York, College at Cortland.



ISBN 978 94 6270 268 4
eISBN 978 94 6166 376 4
https://doi.org/10.11116/9789461663764
D / 2021/ 1869 / 15
NUR: 652

Typesetting: DOGMA
Cover design: Daniel Benneworth-Gray
Cover illustrations: Clockwise, left to right: *Cystoseira Granulata* by Anna Atkins (1843); *Fuß eines 17 Jährigen Jünglings* by Josef Maria Eder and Eduard Valenta (1896); *Aesculapian Snake* by Josef Maria Eder and Eduard Valenta (1896); *Mission Santa Barbara, Rear View* by Carleton Watkins (1876)

GPRC
Guaranteed
Peer Reviewed
Content
www.gprc.be

# Table of Contents

# Acknowledgements

Two of the essays in this collection have been previous published, in slightly different forms. We are grateful to the *Edith Wharton Review* for their permission to republish Mary Marchand's "'Every Object Leaves a Trace': Edith Wharton and the Forensic Imagination" and to Taylor & Francis, Ltd., for their permission to republish Kris Belden-Adams's "Composita, the 'Mascot' of the Class of 1886: A (Fictional) Picture of 'Real' Victorian-era College Sisterhood and Social-Caste Expectations."

# Introduction: Photography's Materialities

Geoff Bender and Rasmus R. Simonsen

There is little dispute that photography is a material practice, and that the photograph itself is ineluctably material. And yet, "matter," "material," "materiality," as terms of inquiry, possess remarkable shape-shifting power, making these assertions less self-evident than they might at first appear. To take a few illustrative examples: In *Photography: The Unfettered Image*, Michelle Henning emphasizes turn-of-the-century photography's "materiality by examining photography's dependence on the global trade in chemical and animal products" (2018: 85). Here, photography's materiality is defined by its modes of production, distribution, and circulation. Henning's approach is, methodologically, in the vein of historical materialism, for which Marx was the great progenitor.

In contrast, Daniel Rubinstein and Katrina Sluis, in their influential essay, "The Digital Image in Photographic Culture," insist that "the materiality of the digital image is not to be found in its indexical adherence to objects in the world, or in signifying and iconic schemas," as is thought to be the case with analog photographs, but instead in the "algorithmic processes that operate on the raw data collected by the light-sensitive sensors in a camera" (2013: 27). The study of digital photography's materiality, in this altered angle of approach, stresses the ontology of the image instead of the economics of its production – an ontology emphasizing "algorithmic processes" rather than the physical components that make those processes possible in digital photography: lithium batteries, silicon chips, photo-litho circuits, and so on. In a manner more dematerialized than obviously material, Rubinstein and Sluis identify the digital photograph's being, not its instrumentality in or commodification by the global marketplace, as the defining feature of its material heft. They thus approach Graham Harman's phenomenological, paradoxically materialist sense of "immaterialism:" moments of symbiosis among entities that "mark genuine points of irreversibility" (2016: 48).

In yet another methodological shift, Elizabeth Edwards argues, in her enduringly important essay, "Material Beings: Objecthood and Ethnographic Photographs," that a photograph's "materiality is closely related to [its] social biography," which is to say that a photograph "cannot be fully understood at any single point in its existence but rather should be understood as belonging in a continuing process of meaning, production, exchange and usage" over its life cycle (2002: 68).[1] Like Rubinstein and Sluis, Edwards is concerned with the being of the photograph. And like Henning, she is concerned with its production. But her concerns are those of an anthropologist, not a phenomenologist, and not a Marxist per se. Her approach brings with it a different set of questions, which, in turn, constitute a different materiality as an object of study. Methodology, as much as or more than academic discipline, makes the matter of Edward's (and Rubinstein and Sluis's, and Henning's) academic work.

Thus, while each example of the materiality of photography cited above is compelling in its own way, there is little substantive overlap between the authors' respective inquiries, making a broader sense of "materiality" and its cousins, "material," "materialist," and "materialism," difficult to achieve. And while scholarly collections organizing "materialist" approaches to an array of topics abound,[2] few pull together multiple methodologies in a single volume, under one elastic rubric.[3] Hence, the purpose of this book: to foster a conversation broad enough to encompass the contributions of a range of disciplines – including art history, cultural studies, literary studies, visual rhetoric, and philosophy – and methodological approaches, all of which take photography's materiality on separate but related terms. Our strategy of assemblage, then, aims toward this broader sense of materiality's potentials.[4]

To suggest our theme's amplitude, from the outset, we yield to the pressure of a necessary plural. And so our title, *Photography's Materialities*, which signals our book's primary argument: that a materialist study of photographs and photographic practices requires the close proximity of incompatible definitions and approaches, methodologies that might struggle to sit side by side, though they can and should. Indeed, if materialist study is to remain vibrant, they must, for the fertile exchange such juxtapositions enable. And while our book cannot envelop all the implications suggested by this complexity, it nevertheless seeks to advance the discussion, as much by implication as by argument, over a series of essays that explore materialities' capacious range within the remarkably interdisciplinary field that photography studies has proven to be.

## The Book's Purview

Temporally, *Photography's Materialities* is a book focused on the medium's origins and early industrialization in the 19th century, when photographs and photographic practices swelled to become ubiquitous elements of middle-class life. We agree with Geoffrey Batchen's assertion that "[a]n awareness of the physicality of the photograph is an unavoidable feature of photography's earliest processes," when photographic objects, including tintypes, ambrotypes, and daguerreotypes, had distinct kinds of "volume, opacity, tactility, and a physical presence in the world" (1997: 2). *Photography's Materialities* is intrigued by the development of such physical presences, even as the physicality of presence is frequently called into question, during a period when photographic practices, and photographs themselves, first exerted their influence on culture and long before they seemingly evaporated into the invisibility of electronic files.

Geographically, *Photography's Materialities* is transatlantic in scope. Photography's first flourishing was, after all, a phenomenon that required the cooperation and mutually constitutive pressure of cultural and national forces that spanned countries and continents. Elizabeth Anne McCauley compellingly recounts, for example, how daguerreotype technology was appropriated by and then grew independently in U.S. contexts, even while Parisian approaches had moved on to collodion-on-glass negatives and albumen prints, a technological shift that produced "the single most important and necessary ingredient for the Parisian photographic takeoff" (1994: 3). Such contrastive (yet related) technologies frequently belied just how interlinked continents and cultures were in the development of photography's material practices. Take, for example, the presence of an École de Beaux Arts sensibility in Thomas Eakins's *plein-air* photographs of American swimmers, or Jacob Riis's Danish notion of family framing his depictions of New York City tenements, or British anthropology's objectivism shaping F. Holland Day's nude portraits of African American men. It has become something of a truism in cultural studies to see the "domestic" and "foreign" in "profound interrelation," as John Carlos Rowe has asserted, in the construction of national boundaries (2000: 4). The same could be argued about cultural boundaries, whose delimitations are not well understood until the material on both sides of the dividing line is understood.

Within this spatio-temporal matrix, *Photography's Materialities* works to draw together and build on several crucial strands of current photography scholarship. They include the Materialities of Process and Product, Material Instrumentality, and Human-Posthuman Materialities. Although these categories are necessarily porous, as the topics they organize are deeply interconnected, they are yet designed to build on one another, from a focus on the elemental to the intermedial to the wide-spanning speculative networks that photography studies can reveal.

## The Book's Parts

The first section of our book, Materialities of Process and Product, builds on the work of scholars who emphasize art's elemental stuff. Books such as *The Making of English Photography: Allegories* (2006) by Steve Edwards, *The Lumiere Autochrome: History, Technology and Preservation* (2013) by Bertrand Lavédrine and Jean-Paul Gandolfo, *Synthetic Worlds: Nature, Art and the Chemical Industry* (2005) by Ester Leslie, and *Color in the Age of Impressionism* (2017) by Laura Anne Kalba all take seriously the significance of the constituents of art objects, whether they be albumen, gelatin, or a spectrum of synthetic colors, respectively. Either overtly or implicitly, these authors respond to Patrick Maynard's trenchant observation that "what has for the longest time, and most obdurately, stood in the way of our understanding photography is the assumption that photography is essentially a depictive device and that its other uses are marginal" (1997: 24). Photography's "other uses" are central to this section. We follow Peter Geimer's valuable insight that "the irreducible materiality of photography requires us to examine not just the finished product – the isolated and fixed picture – but also, and no less closely, the process of its generation; to study not just visibility, but also the rendering-visible" (2018: 7). To deepen our understanding of the "rendering-visible," we turn to what Tina M. Campt has called the "thingyness" of the photograph, where thingyness defines an embodied visuality, reliant on the interplay of the "technical, material, and cultural processes of conjuring and fixing" to produce and secure a photographic image (2012: 128; emphasis original).

In the 19th century, few "conjuring and fixing" agents were more potent than compounds of salt. Among their many vital uses in photographic practices, silver salts were essential fixative agents for prints made from silver gelatin dry plates, the medium artists such as Paul Géniaux (1873–1929) relied on to make enduringly indispensable work. In her study of Géniaux for this volume, Maura Coughlin observes that the photographer not only relied on salt to make the image stick, but also took the harvesting of a different kind of salt, sea salt from along the Brittany coast, as crucial subject matter. Géniaux's choice of imagery thus provided material comment on the process of photographic development. The thingyness of

Géniaux's photos, particularly his *Marais Salants de Billiers* (c. 1900), consequently became doubly reinforced via the image of salt being gathered in combination with the matter binding the print on which the image relied. To develop her argument, Coughlin combines a careful account of the physical processes required for this double comment with ecocritical theory to demonstrate how Géniaux "gathered up the world around him" to locate the world in his work, as Coughlin says.

Coughlin's examination of the role of salt as both image and fixative in Géniaux's work sets the terms, in the next chapter, for Jacob W. Lewis's exploration of an analogous element in photogravure: bitumen, which was essential to this photo-printing process. Beginning with a brief history of the naissance of photogravure, Lewis proceeds to trace its development in the work of such early pioneers as Charles Nègre (1820–1880), Hippolyte Fizeau (1819–1896), Abel Niépce de Saint-Victor (1805–1870), and Honoré d'Albert Luynes (1802–1867). This survey leads to a deeper exploration of Nègre's photogravures of the Syrian landscape, in particular his pictures of bitumen mines. Arguing that images can "at times" be inextricable "from the substances and materials that make them," Lewis shows how Nègre's photogravures, like Géniaux's photographs of salt harvesting, match image with constitutive substance, making the print's material the subject of its latent content. Lewis calls the sharpening material awareness that ensues an example of how the "material unconscious" is revealed. The material unconscious, Lewis theorizes, describes our generally latent awareness of the stuff of the world. The concept is cousin to Walter Benjamin's "optical unconscious:" a sense of the visual world as more than the eye can see, either because it's too fast, too far, or too small, made explicit by the camera's superhuman eye (2008: 37). At the moments when the material unconscious is revealed, Lewis continues, image and substance lose their distinct boundaries to become "as viscous...as the bitumen bubbling up on the shores of the Dead Sea."

Departing from these fundamental elements, our next section, Material Remediations, looks not at how a photograph is composed, but instead at one form of work it performs once manifest in the world: the intermedial labor of photographs. "Intermedial," here, denotes that which "appropriates the techniques, forms, and social significance of other media and attempts to rival or refashion them in the name of the real" (Bolter and Grusin, 1999: 65). Such complex tasks of appropriation make the photograph "heterogeneous from the outset," as Rosalind E. Krauss has noted (1999: 294). Taking and refashioning "techniques, forms, and social significance," the intermedial photograph assumes what Elizabeth Edwards calls "new identities" as it translates other media into its own terms and transitions visual content from one context to another (2012: 227). Indeed, the photograph can be so adept at translation that Raphaël Pirenne and Alexander Streitberger have called photography "the very heart of intermediality" (2013: xvii). We would add that, as such intermedial labor is work done in the world with the stuff of the world, photography's intermedial role is material to the core.

The intricate roles of the intermedial photograph are explored, first, in Mary Marchand's study of the "forensic imagination" in Edith Wharton's *House of Mirth* (1905), a book peculiarly reliant on Alphonse Bertillon's method of crime scene photography for its visual contents. In this chapter, Marchand conceives of Bertillon's photographs as translators of physical objects, which gain "cohere[nce] by virtue of their association with the crime" – an association that the crime scene photograph fixes in space. It is this associative link that enables such photographed objects to speak as "the most reliable witnesses to an event," more dependable, it was thought, than human witnesses in the assignment of culpability. Objects of evidence in *The House of Mirth* are, in Marchand's view, analogues of Bertillon's crime scene photos. Photographically rendered, these objects are made to speak in unison, as in a Bertillon tableau. Such an elevation of objects into evidence establishes what Eyal Weizman has called an "object-oriented juridical culture" (2010: 14), a culture, Marchand claims, that is reliant on "thing power" in the way Jane Bennett defines it: that "strange ability" of nonhuman objects "to exceed their status as objects and to manifest traces of independence or aliveness...outside of our own experience" (2010: xvi). In Marchand's essay, the thing power of objects depends on the photograph to translate material across markedly different contexts, so as to make Wharton's photographic imagery articulate a vitality commensurate with the things rendered by Bertillon's telltale lens.

Marchand's interest in the photographic mediation of the crime scene becomes the palimpsest, in the following chapter, for Rasmus R. Simonsen's exploration of photography's intermedial role in Thomas Eakins's visual economy of queer desire. Of the 800 or so photographs in Eakins's oeuvre, none were more striking than the eight platinum prints that served as studies for *Swimming* (c. 1883–85), perhaps Eakins's most famous painting. These prints mediated the scene of the swimming hole, where Eakins took his art students to pose for him. They were then, in turn, remediated into the oils of Eakins's finished work. Of central significance in this series is the transfiguration of Eakins's student, J. Laurie Wallace, whose photographed body metamorphoses into that of a second art student, Jessie Godley, in Eakins's painting. The resemblance of Wallace's and Godley's pose is uncanny when compared. Within the Latourian frame of Simonsen's analysis, they establish two nodes in a "queer network of attachments," cutting across time barriers to touch in a parallel visual space. This touch leaves Wallace as a photographic trace on Godley's painted form. Consequently, the intimacy between Eakins and Wallace, obvious in the photograph, returns reconfigured in Eakins's regard for Godley as the network of attachments expands. Simonsen relies here on Bruno Latour's assertion that in complex networks "*there exist translations between mediators*" which "*generate traceable associations*" across time and space (2005: 108; emphasis original). Simonsen maps these associations to bring out photography's intermedial presence, which otherwise lingers invisibly in a visual network more densely layered than a finished painting, taken on its own, might reveal.

Simonsen's interest in the ways media revise materiality is sustained, in a shifted context, by Christa Holm Vogelius's exploration of Jacob Riis's work of visual-verbal social criticism, *How the Other Half Lives: Studies Among the Tenements of New York* (1890). Vogelius focuses here on the dense and layered processes of mediation and revision that occur across borders, showing, for example, how Riis's Danish childhood traverses the boundaries of nation and time to cast his concept of the American project in markedly Danish terms. Riis's study of New York City tenement life is consequently polyvocal, composed of varying linguistic registers belonging to a range of lived experiences. These registers translate or remediate Riis's half-tone photographs through the linguistic frame they construct. Reciprocally, these photographs picture Riis's verbal discourse so as to render them visual prose images – one version of what W. J. T. Mitchell has called "imagetexts" (1994: 89). The materiality of each medium, in other words, is constituted by its complement. The media require each other both to be and to mean in particular ways. Vogelius analyzes the ontology of these mutually constituted visual-verbal objects to explain anew how they work as a multimedial political project that was powerful in its time. She thus affirms Ariella Azoulay's important assertion – that "the ontology of photography is, fundamentally, political" (2012: 14) – even as she points out the dependency of both politics and ontology on the imagetext's intermedial relations.

Essays in the third section of the collection, Human-Posthuman Materialities, engage with the posthuman or nonhuman turn in the academy, a shift to what some have called the 'new materialism."[5] To one degree or another, these essays worry, with Stacy Alaimo, Susan Hekman, Richard Grusin, and others, about the limiting consequences of linguistic-turn methodologies that conceptualize knowledge of human phenomena as the result of linguistic models of understanding. They argue, instead, that linguistic-turn methodologies can "foreclose attention to lived, material bodies and evolving corporeal practices" (Alaimo and Hekman, 2008: 3) – that, in other words, matter has other ways of knowing and being known besides such theoretical frameworks as discourse analysis and social constructionism, which privilege the human. Because limited to human language models, such theories are inevitably "stripping the nonhuman world of agency" (Grusin, 2015: x) and its material heft. Latour's concept of a broad disbursement of agency across human and nonhuman networks alike appeals here. In such networks, human and nonhuman actors or "actants" work in conjunction and are, as Latour puts it, "modified, transformed, perturbed, or created" through mutual interaction (1999: 122).[6] These actants demonstrate relations defined by what Timothy Morton calls "interobjectivity" (2013: 82) in a universe where the human has been decentered and subjectivity replaced. The human exceptionalism intrinsic to discourse analysis and social construction consequently yields to what Levi R. Bryant describes as the "democracy of objects" (2011: 19). Such a democratic ontological flattening, arranged as "a network of actants made up of human and nonhuman parts" alike, defines what James L. Hevia has famously called the "photography complex" (2009: 81).

While post- or nonhuman studies opens up exciting new analytical opportunities in photography scholarship, essays in this section are mindful of new materialism's wary reception in some quarters of the academy. Scholars like Kyla Wazana Tompkins have posed important challenges to new materialism's premises, arguing that while some of the ecological ramifications of interconnectedness are crucial for humans "quickly headed towards and in fact already mired in ecological disaster," new materialism, in its most socially unaware forms, can be guilty of "suppress[ing] the question and problem of difference" among human beings (2016). With such suppression comes potentially disastrous consequences for the 'non-white minoritarian subject and indeed history itself" (Tompkins, 2016). Is it possible, then, to move in post- or nonhuman directions in a way that articulates human concerns – especially of those who have been historically marginalized by racism, sexism, classism, and homophobia – differently and perhaps, in some respects, better? The chapters that follow tread carefully in regard to this question, aiming to assert post- or nonhuman claims that can yet encompass, or at least gesture towards, very human crises of social justice that linguistic-turn epistemologies have sought to expose and critique for decades.

Our conversation begins with Kris Belden-Adams's exploration of the composite photograph, aptly named *Composita*, which sits on the very line between human and posthuman. The picture, depicting no specific human subject, is instead composed of the combined portraits of Smith College's graduating class of 1886. The graduate, here, has been translated to a statistical norm, an ideal average, through a visual model developed by eugenicist Francis Galton (1882–1911) in his attempt to depict "an imaginary figure possessing the average features of any group" (Galton, 1879: 132–133) so as to get at the truth revealed through that average. Composite photographs are, in Galton's words, "better looking than their components" – the individual portraits that blended together to make the composite – "because the averaged portrait of many persons is free from the irregularities that variously blemish the looks of each of them" (Galton, 1879: 135). The composite portrait of Smith's class of 1886 thus aimed at a typicality that was, at the same time, superhuman: the perfect image of a privileged class. However, Belden-Adams persuasively argues that such a face of hybridized unanimity profoundly belies the reality of the portrait sitters' lives, which were "anything but cohesive when it came to [a] willingness to assume the duties expected of them after graduation," especially "when faced with the freedoms granted to them by their education and the rise of the suffrage and New Woman movements." The fiction of the composite photograph, then, failed to arrive at some deeper statistical truth, let alone a superhuman materialization of the Smith woman. Rather than vindicating the evidence of a collective physiognomy, *Composita* proves to be nothing more than visual trickery, as characterologically deceiving as it was statistically flawed, in spite of its eugenic claims to the contrary.

Belden-Adams's complex analysis of *Composita* relies on the question of agency – specifically, the degree to which human objects, the portraits of Smith College graduates, can act together to compose the posthuman composite figure. This question of the agency of images is revisited in new terms in the following chapter, which posits material agency as a set of networked operations enacted both within and exterior to a photograph's visual frame. Specifically, Geoff Bender uses Latourian network theory to explore the intricate intersections of race, gender, and sexuality in F. Holland Day's (1864–1933) photographic portrait of J. Alexandre Skeete (1874–1937?) entitled *An Ethiopian Chief* (1897). The photograph features a nearly nude African American model, Skeete, seated facing the camera, eyes closed. Bender argues that the arresting rhetorical effect of the photograph is the consequence of a convergence of networks working at cross-purposes. On one hand, *An Ethiopian Chief* exoticizes Skeete by drawing on the visual fields of 19th-century anthropology and lynching photography, making Skeete's portrait both deeply erotic and paradoxically safe for a white spectator's long look through strategies of objectification. At the same time, Day's portrait of Skeete bears an uncanny resemblance to the Antinous bas-relief, thought an epitome of classical masculinity to 19th-century mainstream audiences and a subject of particular interest to the emerging queer communities of the time. Such a classicizing move thus both ennobles and quietly queers Skeete's body, further complicating this already socially fraught portrait.

Against the agencies of these race-, gender-, and sexuality-specific networks, all seeking, in different ways, to master Skeete's body, Skeete deploys what Tina M. Campt has called "the black grammar of fugitivity" (2017: 11) by simply closing his eyes to the white spectator's appropriating gaze. In so doing, he refuses the code of Jim Crow, which would demand a deferential look away, without the outright defiance of a returned stare. Skeete thus draws on a fourth visual network characterized by a black diasporic will to futurity. The consequence is what visual rhetorician Laurie Gries calls "a single multiple image" (2015: 301) – a portrait whose agential conflict leaves it locked in unresolvable rhetorical tension.

The next essay in this section transitions us from the materiality of Latourian networks to the startling stuff of ectoplasm, the substance departed souls were said to exude to verify their existence in 19th-century spirit photographs. Proponents of this photographic genre, Tom Gunning reminds us, "did not view" the spiritualist movement that drove it "as a faith, but rather as a metaphysics founded on empirical inquiry" (2008: 59), making ectoplasm not as much a technological wonder as a belated expression of material human presence. In his essay, Zachary Tavlin seizes the epistemic blurring of the living with the dead, concrete materiality with spiritualist empiricism, to frame the viewing of spirit photographs as an interobjective encounter. Tavlin relies here on Bryant's efforts "to think the being of objects unshackled from the gaze of humans in their being for-themselves" – an unshackling that means 'no object can be treated as constructed by another object" (2011: 19). Objects, including humans and spirit photographs, therefore behold each other as ontological peers. Spirit photographs thus provide, Tavlin argues, crucial 19th-century examples 'not just of deceit but of the desire for art to glimpse the very things we have been trained to disavow." Art consequently opens the spirit world as a concrete presence with its own ectoplasmic reality, bestowing a disorienting form of posthuman life on human objects who view it with interobjective humility.

Philosopher David LaRocca concludes this section's extended meditation on the problems and possibilities of interobjectivity with an essay that brings Anna Atkins's (1799–1871) 19th-century cyanotypes in close conversation with John Opera's 21st-century counterparts. LaRocca builds his analysis in response to the premises that Object-Oriented Ontologist Ian Bogost develops in his work of speculative realism, *Alien Phenomenology* (2012). There, Bogost posits "what it's *like* to be a Foveon digital image sensor" (2012: 72; emphasis original), working to speculate beyond human-centric perspectives in order to better understand how nonhuman objects might perceive the world. LaRocca extends and critiques Bogost's speculations by exploring an antecedent to the Foveon image sensor, the cyanotype, photography's first – and enduringly light sensitive – contact print. Cyanotypes, like Foveon image sensors, provide us with a new way of thinking about nonhuman objects, not because they "see," as Foveon image sensors see, but rather because they embody a dynamic life that depends on darkness for long life. When exposed to light, cyanotypes or the life of the cyanotype fades over time. However, as LaRocca notes, these prints also "regenerate" when returned to dark spaces, environments where they in a sense resurrect. John Opera's deployment of a process analogous to that of Atkins translates this 19th-century photographic life cycle into contemporary terms to elaborate further the ontological breadth of nonhuman, visually oriented things.

The cyanotype's remarkable elasticity over time reminds us that the image itself is also potentially infinitely pliable – a property that Christopher Pinney well captures when he writes: "If an image that appears to do a particular kind of work in one episteme is able to perform radically different work in another, it appears inappropriate to propose inflexible links between formal qualities and effect" (2003: 3). What's left of the photographic image, Pinney suggests, is nothing but a plurality that straitens into singularity with each given view. And a photo is, of course, much more than its image. It's also the stuff and the practices entailed in that image's making and remaking over time and shifting contexts. It's both representation and what representation is composed of, even or especially "at the very moment," as Georges Didi-Huberman says, "that it agrees to strip itself bare, to suspend itself and exhibit its flaw" or its fault lines, those places where representation cracks open to give itself over to the non-representational material beneath (2005: 194). Peter Geimer describes such a transition as the "shattering of the photographic plate" to expose "what was hitherto invisible:" the photograph's "vitreous existence" (2018: 7) – an existence not dependent on the photo object alone, but also on the networks that render it relationally, including the networks established by our own engagement. "[E]verything we do or say" about photographs, Costanza Caraffa writes, "will make a further contribution to their formation and transformation" (2019: 16). That which is material, then, is far from being merely concrete. Likewise, materialist methods of interpreting photographs and photographic practices, to keep the materialities of photography vibrant, must be similarly multiple, contradictory, and idiosyncratic so as to address the range that the photographic embodies. Such, at least, is the aim and argument of this volume. So, welcome to the 19th-century photographs that follow, reconstituted not just by the novel materialist readings offered here, but also, when you look at them, by you, these photos' latest interlocutor.

## Notes

1 In her study of photographic collections, Edwards has since moved away from this biographical model because, as she and Christopher Morton argue, "the history of the photographic object [unfolds] within a network of multiple originals" (2015: 9). When focusing on a photographic collection, shifting scholarly focus from a single work's unique journey to the "network of multiple origins" makes a particular kind of sense. And yet, even as the biographical model has undergone enormous scrutiny in the social sciences over the past few decades (see, for example, the literature review by Hahn and Weiss, 2013), its legacy endures, likely because an individual object's lifespan still matters, regardless of the number of copies that exist elsewhere. See, for example, Costanza Caraffa's essay, "Photographic Itineraries in Times and Space: Photographs as Material Objects" (2020), where the "itineraries" in her title elaborate, rather than replace, the structure of a photographic lifespan.

2 Of the many available titles, see for example Peter G. Johansen and Andrew M. Bauer (eds.), *The Archaeology of Politics: The Materiality of Political Practice and Action in the Past* (2011) (archaeology), Petra Lange-Berndt (ed.), *Materiality: Documents of Contemporary Art* (2015) (art/art history), and Daniel Miller (ed.), *Materiality* (2005) (anthropology).

3 For an important exception, see Paul Graves-Brown (ed.), *Matter, Materiality and Modern Culture* (2012).

4 Our concept of "assemblage" is, of course, indebted to Deleuze and Guattari, who conceive of the assemblage as a structure "necessary for the unity of composition enveloped in a stratum" that, at the same time, enables "the relation between...strata" so that relation may be "organized rather than random" (1987: 71).

5 On the distinction between the "posthuman" and the "nonhuman" turn, Richard Grusin has written: "Unlike the posthuman turn with which it is often confused, the nonhuman turn does not make a claim about teleology or progress in which we begin with the human and see a transformation from the human to the posthuman, after or beyond the human.... The nonhuman turn, on the other hand, insists (to paraphrase Latour) that 'we have never been human' but that the human has always coevolved, coexisted, or collaborated with the nonhuman – and that the human is characterized precisely by this indistinction from the nonhuman" (2015: ix-x). As Grusin acknowledges, however, the best posthuman analyses avoid the simplistic teleology that "post" implies, making "post-" and "non-" prefixes somewhat interchangeable, as they are in the paradigmatic description below.

6 Latour often opts for "actant" over "actor" because, as he says, "the word 'agent' in the case of nonhumans is uncommon," making "actant" the preferred term to underscore the agency each linked thing exerts and receives from other linked things in a network (1999: 180). Latour is not consistent in his use of "actant," however, perhaps because the notion of agency is built into "actor" and so cannot be easily shaken off. For similar reasons, we, too, prefer the latter to the former term.

## Bibliography

Stacy Alaimo and Susan Hekman, eds., *Material Feminisms* (Bloomington, IN: Indiana University Press, 2008).

Ariella Azoulay, *Civil Imagination: A Political Ontology of Photography*, trans. Louise Bethlehem (London: Verso, 2012).

Geoffrey Batchen, *Photography's Objects* (Albuquerque, NM: The University of New Mexico Art Museum, 1997).

Walter Benjamin, *The Work of Art in the Age of Its Technological Reproducibility, and Other Writings on Media*, eds. Michael W. Jennings, Brigid Doherty, and Thomas Y. Levin, trans. Edmund Jephcott, Rodney Livingstone, Howard Eiland, and Others (Cambridge, MA: Harvard University Press, 2008).

Jane Bennett, *Vibrant Matter: A Political Ecology of Things* (Durham, NC: Duke University Press, 2010).

Ian Bogost, *Alien Phenomenology, or What It's Like to Be a Thing* (Minneapolis: University of Minnesota Press, 2012).

Jay David Bolter and Richard Grusin, *Remediation: Understanding New Media* (Cambridge, MA: MIT Press, 1999).

Levi R. Bryant, *The Democracy of Objects* (Ann Arbor: Open Humanities Press, 2011).

Tina M. Campt, *Image Matters: Archive, Photography, and the African Diaspora in Europe* (Durham, NC: Duke University Press, 2012).

Tina M. Campt, *Listening to Images* (Durham, NC: Duke University Press, 2017).

Costanza Caraffa, "Objects of Value: Challenging Conventional Hierarchies in the Photo Archive," in *Photo-Objects: On the Materiality of Photographs and Photo Archives in the Humanities and Sciences*, eds. Julia Bärnighausen, Costanza Caraffa, Stefanie Klamm, Franka Schneider, and Petra Wodtke (Berlin: Max Planck Research Library for the History and Development of Knowledge, 2019): 11–32.

Costanza Caraffa, "Photographic Itineraries in Time and Space: Photographs as Material Objects," in *The Handbook of Photography Studies*, ed. Gil Pasternak (London: Bloomsbury, 2020): 79–96.

Gilles Deleuze and Félix Guattari. *A Thousand Plateaus: Capitalism and Schizophrenia*, trans. Brian Massumi (Minneapolis: University of Minnesota Press, 1987).

Georges Didi-Huberman, *Confronting Images: Questioning the Ends of a Certain History of Art*, trans. John Goodman (University Park, PA: Pennsylvania State University Press, 2005).

Elizabeth Edwards, "Material Beings: Objecthood and Ethnographic Photographs," *Visual Studies*, 17, 1 (2002): 67–75.

Elizabeth Edwards, "Objects of Affect: Photography Beyond the Image," *Annual Review of Anthropology*, 41 (2012): 221–234.

Elizabeth Edwards and Christopher Morton, "Between Art and Information: Towards a Collecting History of Photographs," in *Photographs, Museums, Collections: Between Art and Information*, eds. Edwards and Morton (London: Bloomsbury Academic, 2015): 3–23.

Steve Edwards, *The Making of English Photography: Allegories* (University Park, PA: The Pennsylvania State University Press, 2006).

Francis Galton, "Composite Portraits, Made by Combining Those of Many Different Persons Into a Single Resultant Figure," *The Journal of the Anthropological Institute of Great Britain and Ireland*, 8 (1879): 132–144.

Peter Geimer, *Inadvertent Images: A History of Photographic Apparitions*, trans. Gerrit Jackson (Chicago: The University of Chicago Press, 2018).

Paul Graves-Brown, ed., *Matter, Materiality and Modern Culture* (London: Routledge, 2012).

Laurie E. Gries, *Still Life with Rhetoric: A New Materialist Approach for Visual Rhetorics* (Logan: Utah State UP, 2015).

Richard Grusin, ed., *The Nonhuman Turn* (Minneapolis: University of Minnesota Press, 2015).

Tom Gunning, "Invisible Worlds, Visible Media," in *Brought to Light: Photography and the Invisible, 1840–1900*, ed. Corey Keller (San Francisco: San Francisco Museum of Modern Art; New Haven: Yale University Press, 2008): 51–63.

Hans Peter Hahn and Hadas Weiss, "Introduction: Biographies, Travels, and Itineraries of Things," in *Mobility, Meaning and Transformations of Things: Shifting Contexts of Material Culture through Time and Space*, eds. Hahn and Weiss (Oxford, UK: Oxbow Books, 2013): 1–14.

Graham Harman, *Immaterialism: Objects and Social Theory* (Cambridge, UK: Polity Press, 2016).

Michelle Henning, *Photography: The Unfettered Image* (Abington, UK: Routledge, 2018).

James L. Hevia, "The Photography Complex: Exposing Boxer-Era China (1900–1901), Making Civilization," in *Photographies East: The Camera and its Histories in East and Southeast Asia*, ed. Rosalind C. Morris (Duke University Press, 2009): 79–99.

Peter G. Johansen and Andrew M. Bauer, eds., *The Archaeology of Politics: The Materiality of Political Practice and Action in the Past* (Newcastle upon Tyne: Cambridge Scholars, 2011).

Rosalind E. Krauss, "Reinventing the Medium," *Critical Inquiry*, 25, 2 (1999): 289–305.

Petra Lange-Berndt, ed., *Materiality: Documents of Contemporary Art* (Cambridge, MA: The MIT Press, 2015).

Bruno Latour, *Pandora's Hope: Essays on the Reality of Science Studies* (Cambridge, MA: Harvard University Press, 1999).

Bruno Latour, *Reassembling the Social: An Introduction to Actor-Network Theory* (New York: Oxford University Press, 2005).

Bertrand Lavédrine and Jean-Paul Gandolfo, *The Lumière Autochrome: History, Technology, and Preservation*, trans. John McElhone (Los Angeles: The Getty Conservation Institute, 2013).

Esther Leslie, *Synthetic Worlds: Nature, Art and the Chemical Industry* (London: Reaktion Books, 2005).

Patrick Maynard, *The Engine of Visualization: Thinking Through Photography* (Ithaca: Cornell University Press, 1997).

Elizabeth Anne McCauley, *Industrial Madness: Commercial Photography in Paris, 1848–1871* (New Haven: Yale University Press, 1994).

Daniel Miller, ed., *Materiality* (Durham, NC: Duke University Press, 2005). W. J. T. Mitchel, *Picture Theory* (Chicago: The University of Chicago Press, 1994).

Timothy Morton, *Hyperobjects: Philosophy and Ecology after the End of the World* (Minneapolis: University of Minnesota Press, 2013).

Christopher Pinney, "Introduction: 'How the Other Half...,'" in *Photography's Other Histories*, eds. Christopher Pinney and Nicholas Peterson (Durham: Duke University Press, 2003): 1–16.

Raphaël Pirenne and Alexander Streitberger, eds., *Heterogeneous Objects: Intermedia and Photography after Modernism* (Leuven: Leuven University Press, 2013).

John Carlos Rowe, *Literary Culture and U. S. Imperialism: From the Revolution to World War II* (Oxford, UK: Oxford University Press, 2000).

Daniel Rubinstein and Katrina Sluis, "The Digital Image in Photographic Culture," *The Photographic Image in Digital Culture*, ed. Martin Lister (Abington, UK: Routledge, 1995/2013): 22–40.

Kyla Wazana Tompkins, "On the Limits and Promise of New Materialist Philosophy," *Lateral: Journal of the Cultural Studies Association*, 5, 1 (2016), http://csalateral.org/issue/5-1/forum-alt-humanities-new-materialist-philosophy-tompkins.

Eyal Weizman, "Forensic Architecture: Only the Criminal Can Solve the Crime," *Radical Philosophy*, 164 (2010): 9–24.

Section I

# The Materialities of Process and Product

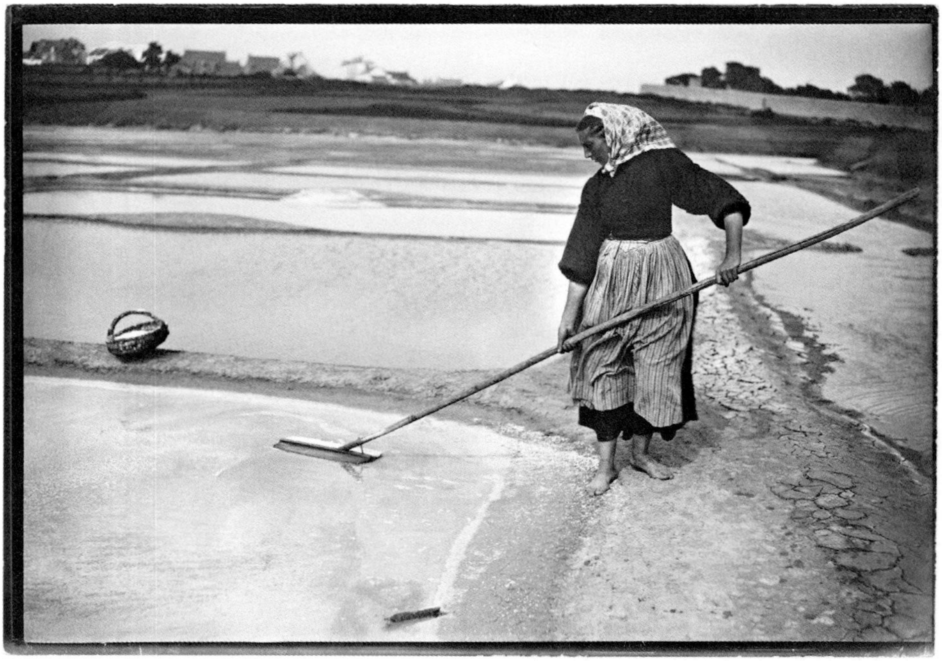

Fig. 1.1. Paul Géniaux, *Marais Salants de Billiers,* c. 1900. Gelatin silver print, 12.8 × 18 cm (5 × 7 in). Musée de Bretagne, Rennes. Public Domain. http://www.collections.musee-bretagne.fr/ark:/83011/FLMjo215321.

# Silver Salts: Realism and Materiality in a French photograph c.1900[1]

Maura Coughlin

> *Imagine a Carthage sown with salt, and all the sowers gone, and the seeds lain however long in the earth, till there rose finally in vegetable profusion leaves and trees of rime and brine. What flowering would there be in such a garden? Light would force each salt calyx to open in prisms, and to fruit heavily with bright globes of water – peaches and grapes are little more than that, and where the world was salt there would be greater need of slaking.*
> **– Marilyn Robinson (1980: 152)**

When Paul Géniaux took this photograph in 1900, there must have been something oddly satisfying about the image of a young woman harvesting salt from the surface of a shallow pool in Billiers, France, on the south coast of Brittany (fig. 1.1). It belongs to a larger series of images (by Paul and his brother Charles Géniaux) that archives traditional trades or *métiers* in their native Brittany such as the splitting of slate, the carving of wooden clogs, the processing of sardines and the making and selling of salt (fig. 1.2) (Boulouch, 2019: 41–46; Coughlin, 2021). Despite the documentary qualities of this image, its form and narrative are rooted in (and conversant with) French realist and regional imagery at the turn of the century. The young woman's pose, costume and the site of her labor mark her as a Breton *paludiere*, or salt-worker. A breeze ripples the surface of the pools behind her but hers appears frozen, as she shaves white salt from its glassy surface. A material transformation, occurring at this moment, was registered by light-sensitive silver salts. This image, in turn, unleashes a series of associations: like the crystals of *fleur de sel* that she draws from the water, Géniaux's photographic practice gathered up the world around him.

Géniaux's photograph (fig. 1.1) is a gelatin silver print that was shot in brilliant sunlight with a substantial depth of field. This photographic medium offered a reproducible grayscale, velvet blacks, crisp whites and suggestive blurs; it produced an image of a figure working within a carefully described landscape (Simmons,

2008: 33). In 1900, amateur photographers ventured into the rural world, making images that used newly available consumer cameras, sensitized glass plates, and cotton rag-based printing papers. The entire world was seemingly being archived by the disinterested, documentary or promiscuous gaze of the camera as the Géniaux brothers translated their photographic images into book and journal illustrations and later issued them as postcards. Yet despite this proliferation, some photographs, like this remarkable one (fig. 1.1), remain traces of momentary encounters: they still promise real presence, bodies that once stood before witnessing lenses. John Berger put it so well: "a photograph arrests the flow of time in which the event photographed once existed" (Berger and Mohr, 1981: 86). She was there, salt was drawn from water, a light-sensitive, silver gelatin emulsion registered this and was it was fixed to glass and later paper: prosaic facts were registered in material terms.

In this chapter, Géniaux's photograph is a central node in a network of ideas that include the picturing of skilled human labor, the social and environmental history

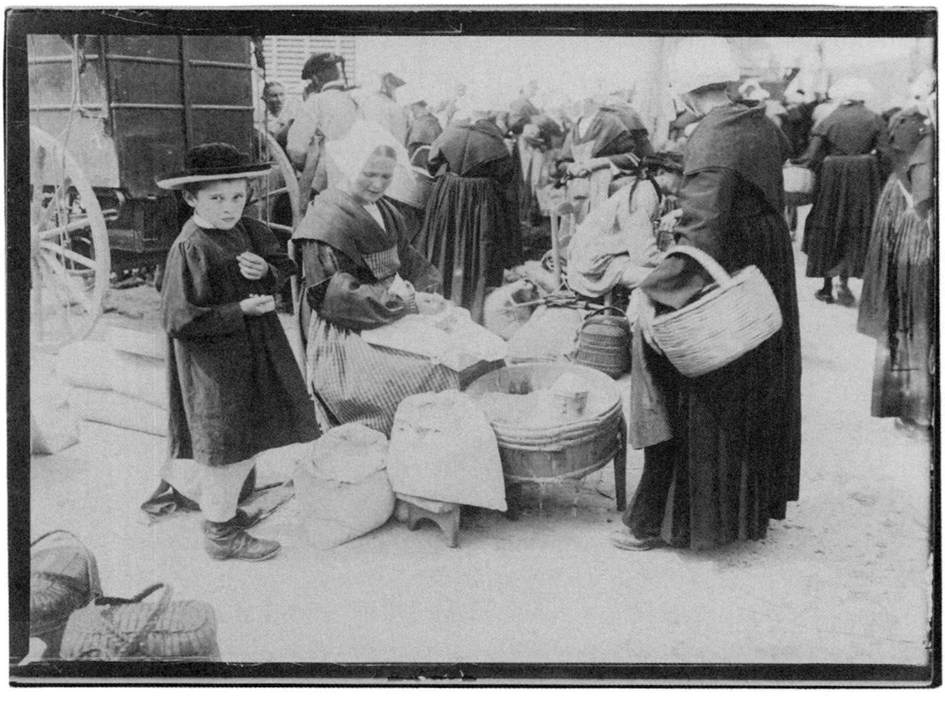

Fig. 1.2. Paul Géniaux, *Salt Merchant*, c. 1900. Gelatin Silver print, 9×12 cm (3.5×4.7 in). Musée de Bretagne. Public Domain. http://www.collections.musee-bretagne.fr/ark:/83011/FLMjo215323.

of this coastal encounter and the making of salt on the French Atlantic coast. My methodology draws from ecomaterialist criticism to read salt's ecologies alongside the materiality of photography in 1900. As an interdisciplinary perspective, ecomaterialism draws from the work of Bruno Latour (2005), Alfred Gell (1998), and Jane Bennett (2010) (among many others) to encourage thinking about relational networks of the human and more-than-human worlds and the ways that objects can afford action. As Stacy Alaimo notes, the widespread social constructivist critique of "nature" that pervaded visual culture studies in the 1990s, today seems coldly disengaged with "lived, biological bodies and the actions and significations of the nonhuman world" (2016: 542).

When images of landscape or rural life are treated as spectacles purely manufactured for a metropolitan gaze (Solomon Godeau, 2017: 114) they become divorced from both their indexicality and materiality (Batchen, 1999: 8–12). Alaimo's influential concept of "trans-corporeality" is an ecomaterialist response to social constructivism that productively works to "recast nature and the environment in ways that stress them as agential, emergent, and intertwined with whatever it is we have been demarcating as exceptionally human or cultural" (2016: 544). Ecomaterialists Serenella Iovino and Serpil Oppermann deftly outline that "new materialist" thought like Alaimo's embraces

> a pronounced reaction against some radical trends of postmodern and post-structuralist thinking that allegedly 'dematerialized' the world into linguistic and social constructions. The new attention paid to matter has...emphasized the need for recalling the concreteness of existential fields, with regard to both the bodily dimension and to non-binary object-subject relations. (2012: 76)

In addition to thinking through Alaimo's trans-corporeality, I am using several other ecological terms to counter this binary framing of the rural world as purely a metropolitan social construction. Briefly, anthropologist Tim Ingold's term "dwelling perspective" reads interconnectedness as "meshworks" in the lived landscape, allowing one to move past the "sterile opposition between the naturalistic view of the landscape as a neutral, external backdrop to human activities, and the culturalistic view that every landscape is a particular cognitive or symbolic ordering of space" (Ingold, 1993: 152). Like Ingold, philosopher Timothy Morton employs the metaphor of a "mesh" to consider "ecology without nature" in reference to the interconnectedness of all living and non-living things (2009, 2010). Archeologist Andrew Jones uses the term "encultured landscapes," (1998: 302) to also counter binary thinking and to acknowledge interdependence. In the context of Atlantic coastal communities that work on and with the ecology of the shore, historian Jeffrey Bolster similarly collapses previous nature/culture distinctions by describing the way that "human maritime communities" interact with "marine biological communities" (2014: 6). Ecomaterialism (and these aligned concepts) provides an interdisciplinary lens for viewing transformations and exchanges between human maritime communities and the materiality of the interstitial world of the coastline. Thus, rather than dismissing Géniaux's representation of past rural life as a nostalgic or primitivist artefact, I treat the material, photographic picturing of salt-making as part of an ecological and embodied entanglement of shoreline communities. Géniaux's images of salt-making both prosaically document regionally specific work and more poetically meditate on the firm edges between things in the process of material transformations.

## Working Women in Rural Images

The labor of rural women was a constant theme of 19th-century art and visual culture. By 1900, French naturalist artists long had been following the lead of Camille Corot, Jean-François Millet and Jules Breton in depicting peasant women at work in the rural world. Like Millet's painting *Woman with a Rake* (pl. 1), countless academic, popular and avantgarde images repeated the confident and practiced gestures of harvesters, milkmaids, herders, washerwomen, gleaners, sowers, and wood gatherers performing their seasonal labors out of doors. An even earlier generation of Romantic-era artists (like illustrator Hippolyte Lalaisse in Guérande, pl. 2) had produced similar images to accompany travel writing about the French provinces. Verbal and visual descriptions of peasants' appearance, clothing, speech, and labors marked these cultural traits as timeless features of the unchanging landscape – as markers of the local (Coughlin, 2003).

Throughout the French Second Empire and Third Republic, itinerant artists had sought "authentic" peasant subject matter, whether observed or posed, in rural landscapes, urban studios, or in artist colonies such as Barbizon, Grez-sur-Loing, Giverny, and Pont Aven. Working on the North-Atlantic coast, later 19th-century artists such as Jules Breton, Francis Tattegrain, Antoine Vollon, Alfred Guillou, and brothers Eugène Feyen and Auguste Feyen-Perrin repeatedly depicted muscular fishwives, laundresses, seaweed harvesters, shell-fishers, and salt harvesters. These women's monumental bodies bent, stooped, strained, and bore burdens in paintings, prints, photographs, and popular imagery. Géniaux's image is compositionally and thematically rooted in this tradition; it asks to be read as a timeless rural image of women's labor, both observed from life and yet drawn from a rustic archive of images that represent an unbroken relationship of peasant to the soil.

As Griselda Pollock notes, as the visual language of photography emerged, it was "heavily indebted to existing visual conventions and practices" but it also "offered a new kind of visuality when it restaged those poses and gestures in its own, emergent semiosis" (Pollock, 1994: 365). Pollock and fellow feminist art historian Linda Nochlin have noted that the nurturing or seemingly natural body of the working class rural woman became a long-standing "woman as nature" trope of 19th-century visual culture. In her 1988 essay "Women, Art and Power," Nochlin describes the "assimilation of the peasant woman to the realm of nature" in Millet's painting *The Gleaners:*

> this particularly unrewarding labor must be read as ordained by nature itself rather than brought about by specific conditions of historical injustice...as women they slide more easily into a position of identity with the natural order. Millet emphasizes this woman-nature connection in a specific aspect of his composition: the bodies of the bending women are quite literally encompassed and limited by the boundaries of the earth itself. It is as though the earth imprisons them, not feudalism or capitalism. (1988: 22)

In a critique of the working-peasant-woman imagery of Jules Breton, Pollock notes that "over these selective bodies a range of stylistic possibilities were played out, probing the dense freight of meaning the feminized countryside could carry within both a bourgeois political and a sexual economy" (1999: 53). Working women's bodies were scrutinized and fetishized for their visible differences from ideal bourgeois feminine forms: illustrators, photographers, and painters repeated details of their exposed and tanned skin, strong arms and solid, muscular physiques. In academic naturalist painting, the female rural worker is ubiquitous, but her implied industrial counterpart – the waged factory worker – is less common a subject.

Annales School historian Lucienne Roubin, in her essay "Savoir et Art de Vivre Campagnard," argues that enculturation in peasant know-how included "familial" knowledge (secrets shared only among family members) and technical skills that were *corporatif* (shared by those who practiced a *métier*) (1977: 97).[2] Some rustic imagery demonstrates closely observed, encultured peasant skills; John Berger, for example, reads Millet's imagery as very accurately recounting peasant bodily experiences of "scything, sheep shearing, splitting wood, potato lifting, digging, shepherding, manuring [and] pruning" (1980: 77). Describing a photograph by August Sander of German peasant men, Berger continues this line of thought, noting that the "characteristic physical rhythm which most peasants, both men and women acquire...[is] related to the energy demanded by the amount of work which has to be done in a day, and is reflected in typical movements and stance" (1980: 37). Roubin and Berger encourage a reading of working peasant bodies that are just as enculturated by their daily realities, by the specificity of their corporeal demands and practices, as any other carefully trained bodies.

When we look at an image of a working rural woman across time and geographic distance, the mere fact of our unfamiliarity (or lack of visual literacy) with a skilled task should not lead to assigning these cultural practices to the "realm of nature." In "The Image of the Working Woman," Linda Nochlin identifies a winnowing machine in Gustave Courbet's painting *The Grain Sifters* (1854) that she reads as "an image of progress in the realm of agricultural operation" (1999: 98). As a nod to agricultural modernization, this detail, she argues, rescues the image from being nostalgic. However, one cannot assume that other represented types of unmechanized labor are instinctive or were unaffected by social change. As very few artists or photographers represent types of physical labor that they themselves have performed, there is often a gap in comprehension between the observed subject (whether posed or not) and the resulting image that enters "the spaces of bourgeois representation in the 19th century" (Pollock, 1993–94: 3). And yet, I would like to suggest that some images of rural work are more informed and locally specific than others and that Géniaux's image depicts the specific, cultural knowledge of a rural *métier*, despite its conformity to 19th-century tropes of gender, provinciality, and class.

Although a Breton by birth and a summer resident of Billiers, Paul Géniaux did not have special authority to speak for salt workers, but he may have understood aspects of their labor. As a well-educated, bourgeois Breton he lived differently, yet in proximity with his peasant subjects; as John Berger writes (in another context): "we do not live apart and we share many practices with those around us.... We remain strangers who have chosen to live here. We are exempt from those necessities which have determined most lives in the village. To be able to choose or select was already a privilege" (1979: 7). His photograph is, in part, a representation of both familiarity and distance. Salt workers did not represent themselves, and, as photographic subjects, they most often stood for regional types. When she stood before his camera, she may have tacitly agreed to perform her labor as locally specific *corporatif* knowledge, aware of being watched.

Géniaux's image shows us an embodied skill that was learned through shared collective knowledge and repetitive local practice. Despite being formally "contained" by the horizon, her figure seems monumental. She stands in a confident, but not casual pose, with firmly planted, bare feet that are tough, cracked, and used to walking on salt. Her stance takes a very matter-of-fact relationship to the terrain: her hips face forward, her right shoulder sinks as her left elbow rises to guide the tool across the pool's surface. This careful bodily array clearly demonstrates the use of the long-handled *lousse* that she displays to the viewer in a pose that Géniaux might have encouraged or asked her to hold. By showing the learned technique of her *métier* to the lens, she invites us to think about the trans-corporeal, material consequences and productivity of her actions that result in crystals being drawn from water and deposited in the basket that tips precariously with the weight of the salt already inside. We see her profile as she concentrates on her task: her darkly tanned face and her hair are framed by a bright white *coiffe* that is mostly covered by a patterned cotton kerchief. Over a dark dress is a striped apron, long since new or clean. As Iovino writes,

> "materiality" is the condition through which bodies act with and relate with each other, shaping other bodies [...]. Reflecting on matter means reflecting on the modes of production and consumption of nature(s) as reservoirs of usable elements; it means reflecting on the way the matter of the world is embodied in human experience, as well as in human "mind." (2012: 76)

The materially evocative details of Géniaux's photograph ask viewers to further consider and find affinity between the sensitivity of salts in the silver gelatin dry plate (that only needed a short exposure on this blazingly sunny day) and how they registered the dark skin of her face, long-exposed to the same summer sun and wind that had crystalized the salt she skimmed from the surface. It is no great associative leap from the making of salt from seawater to the magical optics and chemistry of photography.

## Local Histories and Images of Salt Making

Salt has been made in this region of France for millennia and, despite its large-scale production, harvesting techniques had changed very little in 1900 (Kurlansky, 2002: 117). Gildas Buron, curator of the Musée des Marais Salants (Batz-sur-Mer), the foremost historian of salt in the Guérande region, describes the first discovery of salt extraction in the area: crystals formed naturally in tidal pools and on rocks and were doubtlessly noticed by Neolithic people in the Bay of Morbihan who gradually worked with this natural process to intentionally produce salt (2001: 11). The sheltered bays and inlets along the coastline from Noirmoutier to the Gulf of Morbihan and the Bay of Quiberon occupy the most northern Atlantic zone where salt can be made from seawater, using only sun and wind for evaporation. Brittany's economy had long been entwined with its south-coast salt production: in the 16th century, an exemption for Brittany's salt from the *gabelle*, the salt tax, was an important condition of the duchy's union with the French kingdom (Buron, 2001: 143–168). Breton salt works were enormously profitable as they answered both French and global demands for sea salt, especially in the North Atlantic cod fisheries (with home ports were on Brittany's north coast) that boomed from the 16th century onward.

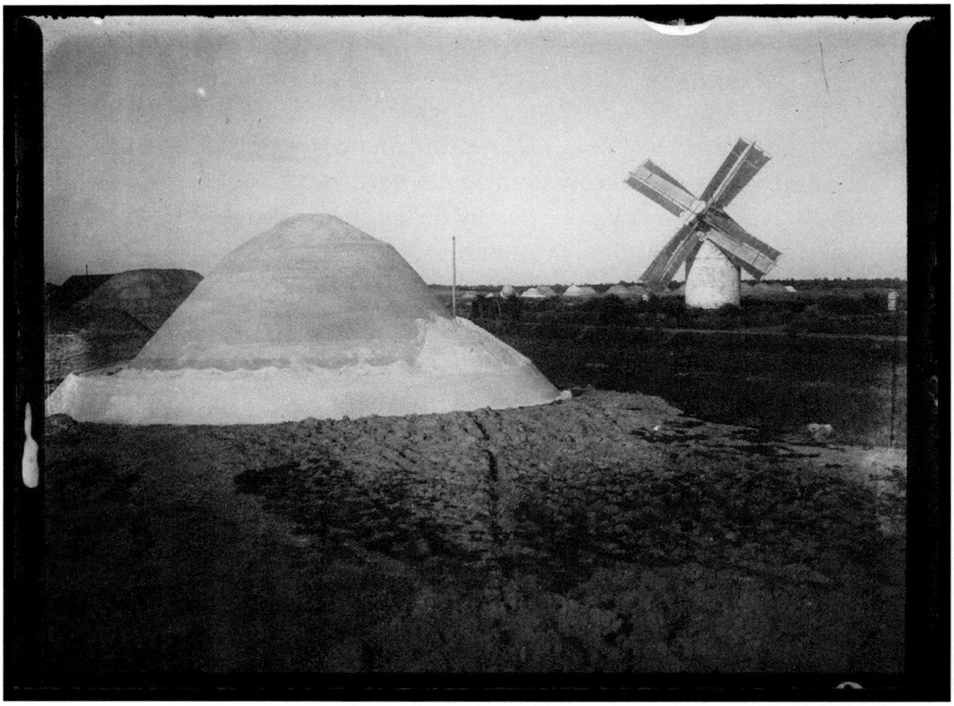

Fig. 1.3. Charles-Hippolyte-Jean Géniaux, *Marais Salants, Batz-sur-Mer*. 11.9×8.9 cm (4.7×3.5 in). Musée de Bretagne. Public Domain. http://www.collections.musee-bretagne.fr/ark:/83011/FLMjo303619.

However, after the French Revolution, the *gabelle* was reformed and the economics of salt making no longer favored Brittany.

The Cistercian monastery in Billiers began producing salt in the 13th century, and it maintained the saltworks until the Revolution (Piéderrière, 1863: 72). By 1900, Billiers had about 1000 residents, most of whom were involved in fishing; its salt production was in decline from environmental degradation, rural depopulation, and the retirement of *paludiers* with no young replacements to carry on. By 1930, the saltworks were defunct, as were many others in the Bay of Morbihan (Buron, 2001: 72–75). Most of Géniaux's other salt-trade photographs depict piles of salt (fig. 1.3), workers, sellers (fig. 1.2) storehouses and customs agents in the Guérande region, 40 kilometers south of Billiers, where salt is still taken from the *marais salants* on a large scale, as an artisanal practice of the *terroir*.

Ecologically speaking, *marais salants* are encultured and controlled landscapes, marsh realms carved, directed, and maintained explicitly for the extraction of salt. With carefully tended, clay-lined pools and channels, saliculture resembles the intertidal work of aquaculture (farming shellfish), but in its emphasis on extraction of salt (from seawater), the only rock that we eat, it also operates a bit like quarrying. Water is channeled through canals and basins to concentrate the salinity but also to lose its organic matter. To purify the water, the potential ecologies of the salt marsh (fish, eels, algae) are removed or blocked from the reservoirs that precede the final pans. Weather conditions must be worked with: only the heat and wind of mid-summer can accelerate evaporation. *Paludiers* maintained their marshes in the winter months when salt could not be made; weeds were pulled, the clay pans were re-lined, and accumulated algae was cleared out. Although salt marsh zones are typically biologically diverse intertidal habitats of shellfish, birds, fish, and other wildlife, marshes worked for salt have had this vitality cancelled. Honoré de Balzac melodramatically described the Guérande area as "the most gloomy and melancholy scenery" with "soil that seemed sick and unwholesome...divided into unequal squares, each encased in a deep cutting of grey earth, and each full of brackish water...a gloomy chess-board, where the abundance of salt chokes all vegetation" and "the grey earth [is] shunned by every Breton flower" (1895: 282).

For many 19th-century writers and artists, the paludiers seemed radically different from the agricultural peasants who lived nearby. Romantic-era writer Eusèbe Girault de Saint-Fargeau (1829: 9) drew very stark comparisons: salt workers are white in costume, complexion and cleanliness, while the nearby peasants of the earth are tan and filthy. As Buron explains, some writers went as far as claiming racial origins for this group that ranged from Anglo-Saxon, Celtic, Spanish to Flemish ancestors (2000: 152–153). In two works of fiction (published in 1834 and 1839), Balzac echoed the observation of earlier travel writers in provincial France – that peasant insularity, suspicion and impenetrability to outsiders is universal. *Paludiers* serve as a case study in this trope: to maintain the trade secrets of their *corporatif* labor, they were clannish, they did not marry outsiders, they lived in their own villages like Saillé that were built on clusters of rocks in the marshes, only slightly above sea level. At the heart of a completely French landscape, they spoke Breton. They were uninterested in cultivating the soil, and, although born by the edge of the sea, they were neither fishermen nor sailors (Balzac, 1895: 282; Saint-Fargeau, 1829: 9–10; Grandpré, 1836: 221). They had a higher standard of living than peasant laborers, and observers found their homes and furnishings aesthetically pleasing (especially in Marie Pichon's museum, below) (Buron, 2000: 146–17).

Balzac (and many later writers and artists) orientalized the practical white clothing that *paludiers* adopted to work in the summer sun. He furthermore described the marsh landscape as "an African desert banked by the ocean, – a desert without a tree, an herb, a bird; where, on sunny days, the laboring *paludiers*, clothed in white and scattered among those melancholy swamps where the salt is made, remind us of Arabs" (Balzac, 1896: 7; Williams, 2007: 55). Most early images and textural descriptions of salt-making focus on the seemingly exotic spectacle of women balancing salt on their heads like living caryatids (Buron, 2000: 167). In 1851, an article in the *Magasin pittoresque* explained both the specialized vocabulary of salt-making and the constructed landscape of its extraction on the Atlantic coast: "when the salt is taken from the *ladures*, it is left to drain for two days, then the women come early in the morning, and running barefoot on the slippery walls of the saline; they carry the salt in *yèdes* or wooden jars balanced on their heads to the reserve called *trémé*" (Anon, 1851: 358). Women's work here is only mentioned in terms of this one role: "the *oeillet* is a kind of box higher in the middle than on the edges.... This is where crystallization takes place. The cream that condenses on the surface and especially in the corners, forms a white and extremely fine salt; it is given in payment to women who bear the loads of salt" (Anon, 1851: 358). However, female salt harvesters as in Géniaux's photograph also worked the surface of the pans to remove the precious crystalized *fleur de sel*, whereas the heavy, coarse *gross sel* was raked up from the bottom by male workers.

In 1887, Adèle Pichon, a nun who was the daughter of a *paludier* founded the Musée des Anciens Costumes (Museum of Ancient Costumes) in Batz; this was one of the first folklore museums in France, several years ahead of Fréderic Mistral's Museon Arlaten (Arles Museum). By the time that Géniaux took his photograph, the specific cultural identity of the *paludier*, both male and female, was elaborate and folkloric in the French popular imagination due to festive displays and parades, festivals, images of costumed weddings, dolls sold to tourists, and children dressed in *paludier* costumes. Pichon's collection of this specialized and formerly exotic material culture is the foundational core of the Musée des Marais Salants in Batz-Sur-Mer (Buron, 2000: 147–151, 162).

Throughout the 20th century and up to the present, the ubiquitous image of the paludier has been used to advertise sea salt and French products flavored with it (e.g. butter, biscuits and caramel) (pl. 3). As a brand, this image offers a sense of material certainty about things in the world: pure salt can be removed from brine.

Salt's crystallization, pictured in Géniaux's photograph, points to a moment of appearance, of seemingly firm transformation. And yet this sense of finite separation of one thing from another is complicated by the kind of ecological thinking that Morton has articulated so well: "things are partial, yet 'organic.' There are things, but they don't come with a handy little dotted line that says *Cut Here* to separate the essence from the appearance" (2015, 4). To think about making salt in enmeshed, material, ecocritical terms: at what moment did this salty water stop being the sea? As it was guided through the channels, leaving its soupy, biological vitality behind? As it was domesticated, condensed, refined, and de-natured in this clay-lined maze? As the water drained from the crystals on the edge of the pan? Extraction reinforces the fiction of the cut: the salt taken from the sea – the salt refined, stored, hoarded, then sold. But once it is consumed, it returns to undifferentiated, abject matter. Firmly apart from other things, they might seem, yet salt crystals are neither purged from the sea nor the land: Sel de Guérande is specifically valued in France because of its *impurity*. Marked by the environmental specificity of *terroir*, traces of brine-born minerals, clay, and micro algae tint its color and inflect its flavor.

## Photography in Brittany

Photography historian Gérard Berthelom has documented the many mid- to late-19th-century studios in Brittany – such as Villard in Quimper – that produced *carte de visite* images of costumed Breton peasants (sold at the 1867 Universal Exhibition) (Jeaneau and Berthelom, 2006: 20). There are many known late-19th and early-20th-century studio portraits of *paludiers* in traditional holiday costumes. Likely these images first took the form of albumen prints in *carte de visite* format, and they were wedding portraits. Many of these were later reproduced in sets of souvenir photographs intended for tourists and were later mass reproduced as picture postcards. Outside of France, earlier precedents for the archiving of coastal labors include the large-format salted paper prints depicting Scottish fisherfolk, made in the 1840s by the Scottish partners David Octavius Hill and Robert Adamson. In these early images of rural workers, the subjects are photographed to define or represent a type (rather than an individual), one defined by labor and costume. They are often calmly posed for the camera, as if about to, but not quite working. In another well-known example, Arthur Munby gathered his obsessive archive of images of working women, especially Welsh miners in the mid-19th century (McClintock, 1995: 100–103).

By 1900, photographing a peasant performing a traditional task or *métier* was a commonplace in France, as demonstrated in the exhibition *100 Métiers Vus Par Les Artistes en Bretagne* (Bellec et al, 2017). Although the Géniaux brothers' photographs were allied with a realist approach to photography rather than the more technically manipulated aesthetics of nascent French Pictorialism in the 1890s and early 1900s, they echoed established realist and naturalist images of rural work from travel writing to Salon painting (Croix, 2012: 99–331). The journal *Bretagne Revue*, launched by the Géniaux in 1893 and renamed *Revue Pittoresque de Bretagne,* worked to claim an artistic status for photography by promoting clubs, exhibitions, and competitions. Their response to the newly widespread access to photography (and the explosion of amateur photographic practices) was to create artful images in the spirit, if not formally in the camp, of Pictorialism (Prod'homme, 2012: 40; Prod'homme, 2019: 15). But unlike the materially "authentic" Pictorialist print, with its suggestive blurs or retouched surfaces, the Géniaux's "artful" images were destined for photomechanical mass production and consumption. Their evident promotion of this aesthetic is spelled out in an advertisement titled "*Nos Concours*" (Our Competition) in the March 1893 issue of *Bretagne Revue,* which called for photographic submissions (proofs on paper) to a contest with the following themes:

1. A photographed instant, preferably artistic;
2. A marine scene (boats, waves, coastline, etc.)
3. A genre scene of one of these subjects:
a. There's none so small who might not help*
b. After the Day's Work.
c. Evening in Springtime
(* from Aesop's fable of the Mouse and the Lion)

Paul Géniaux's image was perhaps a bit posed, but most certainly chosen, plucked from the endless stream of possible moments afforded by his encounter with the salt worker. The ambiguity of its artfulness on the one hand, and its evocation of documentary materiality on the other hand makes it an ideal image through which to consider the nature of photography in 1900, a time at which it is difficult, if not impossible, to draw a definitive line between documentary photographs and more picturesque images "taken from life" (Poivert, 2009). French photography historian Lucie Goujard argues that as faster film speeds enabled more spontaneous (and less staged) images, photographs became increasingly ambivalent in their meanings and destinations (2009). Susan Sontag referred to this ambivalence as "a promiscuous form of seeing" at the heart of photography's nature, that became "in talented hands, an infallible medium of creation" (1973: 129). But as Berger comments, "*an instant photographed* can only acquire meaning insofar as the viewer can read into it a duration extending beyond itself. When we find a photograph meaningful, we are lending it a past and a future" (Berger and Mohr, 1981: 89). This given ambiguity of photography, Berger tells us, can be embraced as "another form of telling" (1981: 89). Many variants of realism (and naturalism) proliferated in French painting from the 1880s to the Great War, and photographers often emulated or quoted compositions from well-known realist paintings. Thus, by 1900, French photographs of rural work both emulated the figure groupings and settings of paintings – Charles Lhermitte and Adolphe Piriou are very good examples – and they were also made as picturesque resources to inform or inspire new paintings. Before 1900, photographers often made image sets to sell to painters (especially in artist colonies), and eventually painters like André Dauchez became adept at producing their own working views (Berthelom, 2017).

The Géniaux brothers capitalized on photography's expanding potential, finding many other formats to market their images such as photo postcards, and collographic book journal illustrations. Like peasant wedding portraits that became postcard images, their photographs served many purposes (functioning as early "stock" images). They were first sold as prints in sets: evidence of this can be seen on the reverse of one print of the Billiers image (in the collection of Batz museum). The stamp of Paul Géniaux's Paris studio is above the stamp of the distributor Charles Trampus. Between these, two handwritten lines describe the subject and location. Below all this, a different hand, perhaps that of the purchaser, notes that it showed the work of women in the region that had been visited one summer.

The theme of the paludier working on a gridded marsh was one of the traditional trades featured in many works of mid-20th-century modernist artists such as René

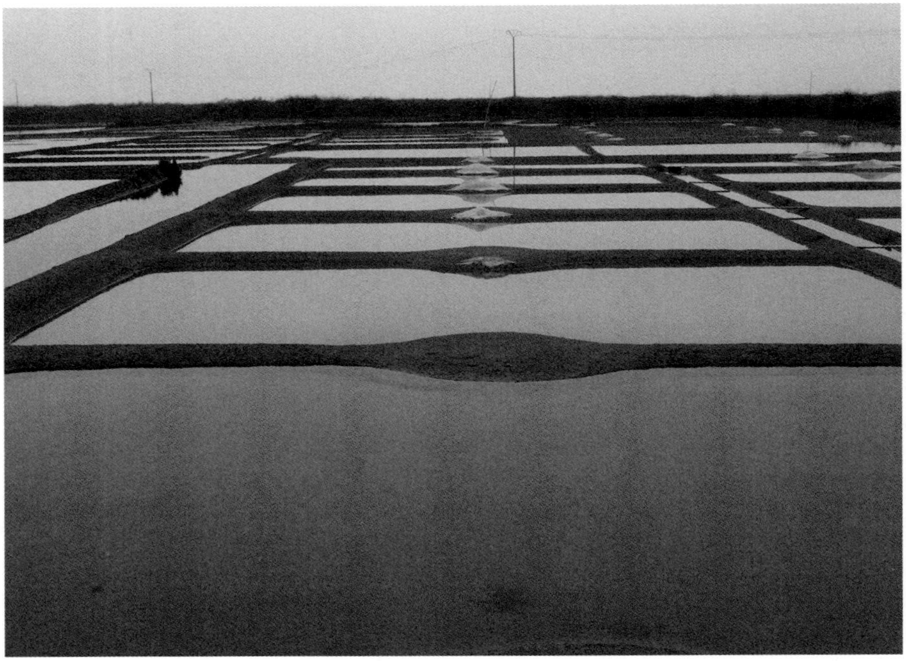

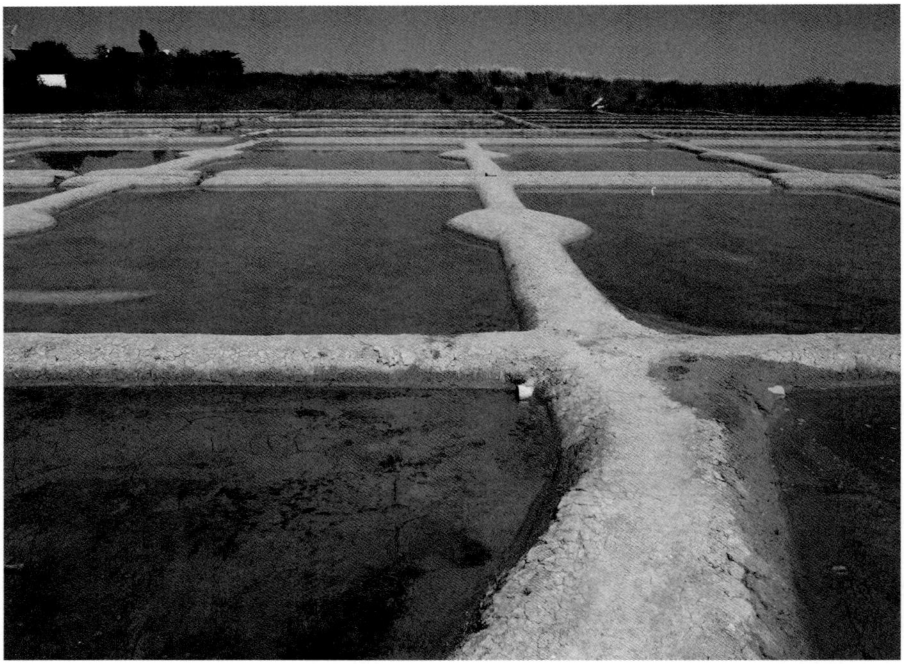

Figs. 1.4 & 1.5. Marais Salants in different light conditions. Overcast (above) and sunny (below). Digital photos by author, near Guérande, May 2017.

Creston and Mathurin Méheut in the "100 *Métiers*" exhibition at le Faouët, mentioned above (Bellec et al, 2017: 43–52). While walking and driving through the *marais salants* between Guérande and Batz-sur-mer in May, 2017, I understood the enduring formal appeal of this gridded landscape: it offers readymade grayscale compositions, just as black and white checkerboard floors had appealed to so many Renaissance and Baroque painters eager to demonstrate their command of perspective. At any point of view in a salt pan, the formal arrangement conveys an immediate geometric effect of objectivity, as the optical effects of almost endless edges of rectangles seemingly diverge from the photographic eye (figs. 1.4, 1.5). Similarly, the reflection of moonlight across a body of water always seems to point its tip to the viewer, offering a Cartesian perspectival certainty about being in and regarding things in the world. Artistic conventions of one-point perspective convey a sense of mastery of all one surveys. As Morton muses,

> The vanishing points in the painting dictate where to place your gaze in order to make a two-dimensional surface appear three-dimensional. Your gaze is encoded into the picture surface. In the same way, perhaps, a flower's subject position is that of a bee, if it's painted with ultraviolet landing stripes. It tells the bee where to put her proboscis. (2012: 123)

In the graphic salt-making landscape, Géniaux responded to the geometrical challenges that it offered his lens, focusing on the crystallization of salt and its removal from the brine. The clay-covered axis upon which his subject stands also locates our unseen photographer, and we, instinctively, are there, too.

I began this essay with Marilyn Robinson's poetic evocative passage on the blooming of salt and the slaking of craving. It seems fitting that Géniaux's photo spoke a satisfying language of material longing: clear geometry produced a rural world "made whole" that was seemingly legible, inhabited, and traditional. It articulated a known and already classified place, where salt could still be drawn from water. Although the notion of "timelessness" in the rural world holds persistent appeal, critical approaches to 19th-century images of working women (like Géniaux's) in the rural world, should not be limited to critiques of paternalistic primitivism. The technical knowledge of peasant work, the extractive logic of the littoral and the global demand for salt all complicate this seemingly straightforward documentary photograph. The compound effect of thinking about images like Géniaux's photograph through an ecologically informed perspective, that sees all human activity entangled in its landscape, rather than selectively divided from it, is that relationships between places and people (whether residents or visitors) emerge as complex, bodily, and temporal engagements. Salt works are case studies of hybrid or enmeshed landscapes: as open-air factories, they merge specific ecologies of coastlines and large-scale extraction for a global market. Somewhat like the industrial workplaces of sardine packers on the docks and in the canneries of Brittany that Géniaux photographed at about the same time, these are simultaneously provincial yet modern photographic subjects. Ecological thought, despite or perhaps because of its messy and enmeshed complexity, gives us so much to talk about as we gaze upon images across distances of time and space and then look down to the material ground upon which we stand as all the waters rise.

## Notes

1 The majority of this essay was written before the 2019 exhibition of the Géniaux brothers photography at the Musée de Bretagnes, Rennes and the publication of the accompanying catalog (Prod'homme et al, 2019), although several notes from the catalog are included in this text to signal the most recent and thorough discussions available. A few of the observations from this essay are included in my one-page entry on this photograph that was translated to French. I could not have researched this essay without the generous collegiality of scholars in Brittany including Laurence Prod'homme, Gildas Buron, Hubert Chermereau, Gérard Berthelom and Caroline Boyle-Turner. Bryant University librarian Sam Simas was an invaluable ally as was my dear colleague, Emily Gephart, and photo historians Joanne Lukitsch and Elizabeth Hutchinson. Many thanks to the participants of the Ubiquity: Photography's Multitudes Symposium in Rochester, New York, especially organizers Jacob Lewis and Kyle Parry, where an earlier version of this paper was presented. Funding for this project was generously provided by a research stipend from Bryant University.

2 All translations from French are mine unless otherwise noted.

## Bibliography

Anon., "*Marais Salants et Sauniers,*" *Le Magasin Pittoresque*, 19 (1851): 356–360.

Stacy Alaimo, "Nature," in the *Oxford Handbook of Feminist Theory*. (New York: Oxford University Press, 2016): 533–550.

Honoré de Balzac, "A Tragedy by the Sea" (translation of "*Un drame au bord de la mer,*" 1834) in Balzac, Honoré, *Shorter Stories* (Philadelphia: H. Altemus, 1895).

Honoré de Balzac, "Béatrix," in *The Works of Honoré de Balzac* (United States: Athenaeum Club, 1896): vol. 2, 1–437.

Geoffrey Batchen, *Burning with Desire: The Conception of Photography* (Cambridge, MA: MIT Press 1999).

Christian Bellec, Denise Delouche, and Anne le Roux-Le Pimpec, *100 métiers vus par les artistes en Bretagne: [exposition, Musée du Faouët, 1er avril-8 octobre 2017]* (Le Faouet: Liv'éditions, 2017).

Jane Bennett, *Vibrant Matter: A Political Ecology of Things* (Durham: Duke University Press, 2010).

John Berger, "Millet and the Peasant," in John Berger, *About Looking* (London: Bloomsbury, 1980/2009): 69–78.

John Berger, "The Suit and the Photograph" in John Berger, *About Looking* (London: Bloomsbury, 1980/2009): 31–36.

John Berger, *Pig Earth* (London: Hogarth, 1979).

John Berger and Jean Mohr. *Another Way of Telling: A Possible Theory of Photography* (New York, Pantheon Books, 1981).

Gérard Berthelom, email correspondence, August 28, 2017.

W. Jeffrey Bolster, *The Mortal Sea: Fishing the Atlantic in the Age of Sail* (Cambridge, MA: Belknap Press/Harvard University Press, 2014).

Nathalie Boulouch, "Photographier la Bretagne qui s'en va," in *Charles et Paul Géniaux: la photographie, un destin*, ed. Laurence Prod'homme (Châteaulin: Locus Solus, 2019): 41–46.

Gildas Buron, *Hommes Du Sel* (Morlaix: Skol Vreizh, 2000).

Gildas Buron, *Bretagne des marais salants: 2000 ans d'histoire* (Morlaix: Skol Vreizh, 2001).

Maura Coughlin, "Millet's Milkmaids," Nineteenth Century Art Worldwide / Association of Historians of Nineteenth Century Art (AHNCA) (2003). http://www.19thc-artworldwide.org/winter03/247-millets-milkmaids 2/1.

Maura Coughlin, "Material Ecologies in the Géniaux Brothers' Picture Archive of Brittany, c. 1900," in *Ubiquity: Photography's Multitudes*, eds. Kyle Parry and Jacob W. Lewis (Leuven: Leuven University Press, expected 2021).

Alain Croix, *La Bretagne Des Photographes. La Construction D'une Image De 1841 À Nos Jours* (Rennes: PUR, Presses Universitaires de Rennes, 2012).

Alfred Gell, *Art and Agency: An Anthropological Theory* (Oxford: Clarendon, 1998).

Lucie Goujard, "Photographie pittoresque. L'influence des modèles esthétiques traditionnels sur les photographies de la pauvreté," *Apparence(s)*, 3 (2009). https://apparences.revues.org/1052 (accessed September 12, 2017).

Gustave Grandpré, *Le Nouvel Anacharsis Français Ou Promenades Dans Diverses Contrées De La France: Suivi D'une Histoire De L'abbaye De La Trappe* (Paris, 1836).

Timothy Ingold, "The Temporality of the Landscape," *World Archaeology*, 25, 2 (1993): 152–174.

Serenella Iovino, "Material Ecocriticism: Matter, Text, and Posthuman Ethics" in *Literature, Ecology, Ethics*, eds. Timo Müller and Michael Sauter (Heidelberg: Winter Verlag, 2012): 51–52.

Serenella Iovino and Serpil Oppermann, "Material Ecocriticism: Materiality, Agency, and Models of Narrativity," *Ecozon@: European Journal of Literature, Culture and Environment*, 3, 1 (2012): 75–91.

Corinne Jeaneau and Gérard Berthelom, *Photographes Au Xixe Siècle: Les Nouveaux Imagiers De La Bretagne* (Spézet: Coop Breizh, 2006).

Andrew Jones, "Where Eagles Dare: Landscape, Animals and the Neolithic of Orkney," *Journal of Material Culture*, 3, 3 (1998): 301–324.

Mark Kurlansky, *Salt: A World History* (New York: Penguin, 2002).

Bruno Latour, *Reassembling the Social: An Introduction to Actor-Network-Theory* (Oxford: Oxford University Press, 2005).

Anne McClintock, *Imperial Leather: Race, Gender, and Sex in the Colonial Contest* (New York: Routledge, 1995).

Timothy Morton, *The Ecological Thought* (Cambridge, MA: Harvard University Press, 2010).

Timothy Morton, *Ecology without Nature: Rethinking Environmental Aesthetics* (Cambridge, MA: Harvard Univ. Press, 2009).

Timothy Morton, "Art in the Age of Asymmetry: Hegel, Ecology, Aesthetics," *Evental Aesthetics*, 1, 1 (2012): 121–142.

Timothy Morton, "This Biosphere Which Is Not One: Towards Weird Essentialism," *The Journal of the British Society for Phenomenology*, 46, 2 (2015): 141–155.

Linda Nochlin, *Women, Art, and Power: And Other Essays* (New York: Harper & Row, 1988).

Linda Nochlin, "The Image of the Working Woman" in *Representing Women* (London: Thames and Hudson, 1999): 81–105.

Abbé Piéderrière, "Histoire de Prières," *Bulletin de la Société Polymathique du Morbihan* (1863): 57–78.

Griselda Pollock, "*Differencing the Canon: Feminism and the Writing of Art's Histories* (London: Routledge, 1999).

Griselda Pollock, "'With my own eyes': Fetishism, the Labouring Body and the Colour of its Sex," *Art History*, 17, 3 (1994): 342–382.

Griselda Pollock, "The Dangers of Proximity: The Spaces of Sexuality and Surveillance in Word and Image," *Discourse*, 16, 2 (Winter 1993–94): 3–50.

Laurence Prod'homme, et al, *Charles et Paul Géniaux: la photographie, un destin* (Châteaulin: Locus Solus, 2019).

Laurence Prod'homme, *Charles Et Paul Géniaux: Deux Frères En Photographie* (Lyon: Fage Editions, 2014).

Laurence Prod'homme, *Reflets De Bretagne: Les Collections Photographiques Du Musée De Bretagne* (Lyon: Fage, 2012).

Michel Poivert, "Degenerate Photography? French Pictorialism and the Aesthetics of Optical Aberration," trans. Hillary Goidell, *Etudes Photographiques*, 23 (2009). http://etudesphotographiques.revues.org/3429.

Marilynne Robinson, *Housekeeping* (New York: Picador, 1980).

Lucienne Roubin "Savoir et Art de Vivre Campagnard," in *The Wolf and the Lamb: Popular Culture in France: From the Old Regime to the Twentieth Century*, eds. Jacques Beauroy, Marc Bertrand, and Edward T. Gargan (Saratoga, CA: Anma Libri, 1977): 93–100.

E. Girault de Saint-Fargeau, *Histoire Nationale Et Dictionnaire Géographique De Toutes Les Communes De La France: Formant Pour Chaque Département Un Ouvrage Complet* (Paris: Beaudouin, 1829): 9–10.

Becky Simmons, "Amateur Photographers, Camera Clubs and Societies," in *Encyclopedia of Nineteenth Century Photography: Vol 2*, ed. John Hannavy (London: Routledge, 2008): 31–35.

Abigail Solomon Godeau, "Framing Landscape Photography" (first published in 2010), in *Photography after Photography*, ed. Sarah Parsons (Durham, Duke University Press 2017)

Susan Sontag, *On Photography* (London: Penguin Books, 1973).

Heather Williams, *Postcolonial Brittany: Literature between Languages* (Bern: Peter Lang 2007).

# Early Photogravure & the Material Unconscious

Jacob W. Lewis

Upon encountering the new daguerreotype process in 1840, Edgar Allan Poe described how the viewer's experience of this novel kind of image allowed for a collapse between the real and its representation. The plate and its image, he argued, disclose "a more absolute truth, a more perfect identity of aspect with the thing represented" (Poe, 1980: 38). The daguerreotype, being a thing in the world as well as an image of that very world, hinted at a breakdown in the codes of representation and by extension the accepted relations between material images and viewers, not seen since Byzantine theological debates on icon painting in the previous millennium (Mondzain, 2005). Not long after the daguerreotype was introduced, however, its status as an unique, non-reproducible object was tested when artists, printers, and publishers sought to translate the unique plate and its delicate image traced in silver, into a functional intaglio printing matrix that could reproduce hundreds of copies of the same image as ink on paper. In short, this was an attempt to transform photography from a metal curio into an object of mass visual culture. While these early photo-prints failed to approximate the level of detail recorded in the camera images traced onto polished metal (and then subsequently on waxed paper, glass, and celluloid), commentators from the 1840s onward still shared Poe's level of astonishment at the proximity of representation and the real in early examples of not only photography but of its related printing methods like photogravure. In effect, the daguerreotype's mirrorlike facture was not simply singular and unique; rather, early photography and its hybrid applications shared the same oscillations between material support and immaterial image, as well as between unconscious substances and their attentive viewers.

Conceived alongside permanent camera images first successfully made by the inventor Nicéphore Niépce (1765–1833), photogravure was the subject of improvement by many, including physicist Hippolyte Fizeau (1819–1896), inventor Abel Niépce de Saint-Victor (1805–1870), archaeologist and patron Honoré d'Albert Luynes (1802–1867), as well as artist Charles Nègre (1820–1880). The story of photomechanical printing has been the domain of social and technical accounts of photography as well as of the history of the printed image (Jussim, 1974; Beegan, 2007; Benson, 2008). While these practitioners yielded positive improvements to the process and aimed to capitalize on their findings, they did so alongside a perverse fascination with Romantic aesthetics, Orientalist cosmologies, and organic materiality. In early photographic practice, the substances of silver, gold, asphalt, gelatin, and ink and the support materials of paper, glass, metal, and stone all carried tacit histories that informed both the photographer's approach to the material and the spectator's response to the visual. An account of photography's expansive spate of constituents, and their use in processing and production of waste, calls for an episodic and cumulative approach whose inestimable totality remains beyond my intentions here (Maynard, 1997). Rather, a materialist approach to a certain group of photographic works can produce a better sense of how ideas and images are at times inextricable from the substances and materials that make them.

This chapter charts the flux of a few materials and processes in a period of innovation for photogravure, stretching from the 1820s and into the 1870s. In their use of the material named bitumen of Judea, Niépce and later Nègre pursued a reproducibility that was inseparable from bitumen's mysterious composition and its geological and geographic associations; it was a photo-polymer and petroleum product that was mined from pits in the mountains of France and Switzerland, lakes in Trinidad and Venezuela, tar-sands in Canada, as well as the titular site of seepage from the Dead Sea, located in what was ancient Judea. Likewise, the revolutionary process of electrotyping or galvanoplasty – used to adhere metals like gold and copper to steel for the production of hardy, acid-resistant plates – was primarily understood by patrons and critics through associations with fine metalwork traditions that characterized ancient and medieval art and armor from Persia and the Middle East, particularly in markets forged in encounters between Islamic makers and Christian patrons during the Crusades (Hoffman, 2004).[1] What is at issue is that photography, in the age of its invention and innovation, gave rise to an unstable experience of the printed image's material reality as ahistorical and globally displaced, whose meanings shifted between a mythic golden age and an anticipated technocratic future. In the subsequent era of photography's industrialization in the 1860s onward, this approach to materiality ceded its place to what Walter Benjamin called the "optical unconscious," wherein the ubiquity of film and photographic illustration afforded access to new perceptual truths that were intimately linked with an accelerated and serialized temporality alongside the proliferation of photographic images in culture (Benjamin, 2008; Smith and Sliwinski, 2017). What remains to be explored is how a "material unconscious" in early photographic applications envisioned the promise of an indivisibly networked world, all the while signaling a very different register of time, action, and presence that bring its constituent elements conspicuously into view.

## Bituminous Terrain

In Bruno Latour's *We Have Never Been Modern* – a work of critical skepticism that forms a basis for many object-oriented projects in the humanities – the author laments the modernist myopia of his own scholarly discipline. "Why would we no longer be capable of following the thousand paths," he writes, "with their strange topology, that lead from the local to the global and return to the local? Is anthropology forever condemned to be reduced to territories, unable to follow networks (Latour, 1993: 116)?" This oft-cited line not only hints at ideas bandied about in the popular consciousness – from eco-clichés like "think globally, act locally" to popular general histories of material networks in the world, like Mark Kurlansky's *Salt: A World History* (Kurlansky, 2002) – it also puts self-critical thought at the forefront of studies that take the limits of continuity, autonomy, and geographic specificity for granted.

While Latour identifies his discipline as necessitating an alternate perspective, his method and the claim that follows remains relevant beyond anthropology and the "science studies" that preoccupied Latour. Shifting our sights from territory to network can also serve an object-based approach to a history of the materials that make up photography, whose public introduction in 1839 was already wholly embedded in the era that saw the novel invention as a confusion not only between art and science, but more importantly between nature and culture (Batchen, 1997). Any number of substances adapted to the technical practice of photography – wood, glass, silver, salt, paper, wax, celluloid, to name only a few – serve as a launching point for object-based histories that can further trace these networks rather than map their territories. In photography's incunabula, inventors conceived of the material components of the medium as well as its virtual identity as *always already* ubiquitous and universally practicable. Writing in England in 1842, the polymath John Herschel recognized how photography in the abstract "is no longer an insulated and anomalous affection of certain salts of silver and gold, but one which, doubtless, in a greater or less degree pervades all nature," which led him equally to experiments with organic "vegetable photography" alongside refined inorganic processes like the cyanotype (Herschel, 1842: 201). Thus, the fleeting images of the camera obscura that photography made material weren't simply the consequence of one reactive substance; rather, all facets of nature offered up an expansive materiality *in potentia* for photography's transformations (Maimon, 2015: 149–165).

Yet this pervasive sense of photography in its early years stands in contrast to the actual representations made by its inventors: William Henry Fox Talbot in England, Niépce, Louis Daguerre, and also Hippolyte Bayard in France. To these practitioners, their novel project was understood as a hyperlocal thing in the world, one that produced a radically contingent image forever attached to its own specificity of time and place. Photographic representation first realized its decidedly local dimensions in early images by Niépce and his subsequent partner Daguerre, both of whom oriented the first photographic cameras out of their attic studios to record landscapes already framed by the window. An example of what Niépce termed "*points de vue*" is the famous view taken from the attic interior of his manor near Châlone sur Saône; this work is rightly understood as the first permanent photograph made with a camera (pl. 4). It recorded the roofline and trees visible outside onto the knobby surface of the pewter plate in an eight-hour exposure.

The sensitive surface that Niépce used to capture his *point de vue* was not a compound of silver, but a photopolymer substance employed in various representative processes by printmakers, painters, and early photographers in the 19th century. Identified as Bitumen of Judea, it is a form of petroleum that holds a long and storied history from antiquity to the modern age. Since the third millennium BCE, bitumen harvested from natural lakes and seepage sites had been used for sealing roads and as both a binder and waterproofing agent for various manufactures. The most storied natural springs and seepage of bitumen occurred in sites around the Dead Sea, the *lac asphaltite* of ancient Judea, whose water "casts up black clods of bitumen in many parts.... [Th]ese swim at the top of the water, and resemble both in shape and bigness headless bulls," according to the Romano-Jewish historian Josephus. Bitumen was harvested by ship in the Dead Sea, and used for sealing the hulls of vessels, embalming the dead, and healing the living (Whiston, 1870, Vol. 2: 132).

Bitumen also found itself as a key node in early modern petro-cultures, where the harvesting described by Josephus centuries later transformed into mining, refining, and processing in the modern energy discourse (Bellamy & Diamanti, 2018).[2] In the late 16th century, the Portuguese and subsequently the Englishman Sir Walter Raleigh wrote accounts of the pitch lake at La Brea, Trinidad; the latter even used the viscous bitumen to re-caulk and waterproof his ships off shore. Around 1710, miners discovered natural asphalt in and around limestone and sandstone in the

Jura Mountains near Neuchâtel, Switzerland, facilitating one of the first scientific monographs on the substance by a doctor named Eirini d'Eyrinys (d'Eyrinys, 1721). With the help of the latter's son (and with the financial support of King Louis XV) the diplomat Louis Pierre Ancillon de Sablonnière founded the Pechelbronn bitumen mine in Alsace, exploiting the seepage at a natural site that would later be classified as *tar sands*, akin to current controversial sites of extraction located in Alberta, Canada (Vassiliou, 2009: 352).

Bitumen, and the relative kinds of synonymous *asphaltum* that include *naphtha*, *pitch*, and *tar*, came to the attention of early modern scientists in the midst of a general shift in scientific analysis and the field of chemistry. Historian of science Robert Jacobus Forbes identifies this shift as moving from "qualitative alchemy to quantitative chemistry" that precipitated the origins of an "organic chemistry," the modern domain investigating hydrocarbons and their various applications (Forbes, 1959: 54–55). Chemistry then formed a crucial supplement to infrastructure and its own stories of innovation; by the 1830s, bitumen from sites around France (in particular from Seyssel on the Rhône) were being used as mortar for the mosaic of paving stones installed throughout the Place de la Concorde, as well as for sealants on top of new sidewalks in Paris (*Journal des Débats*, 1838). Later in the century, real estate developer Amzi Barber, new to the asphalt business, secured a lucrative 42-year monopoly on the natural pitch available in Trinidad, which he used to pave city streets across the United States (Holley, 2003).

Bitumen thus carried a historic legacy long before Niépce harnessed it for photography, but it was in the arts where he understood the material properties of such a resin, and bitumen's reaction to light in particular, that enabled the inventor to capture the first permanent photographic images. First employed by etchers as an acid-resistant ground for their plates, bitumen found its way into 18th-century painting practice as a pigment. Dutch painters began to employ bitumen, known as Antwerp brown, and painters like Sir Joshua Reynolds, as well as those in the school of Jacques-Louis David combined, pulverized bitumen with oil and wax to apply on canvases, either as a pigment or a varnish (White, 1986: 62–63; Hunter, 2015). The cool, dark tonalities that dominate certain works by later Romantic artists, including the Barbizon landscape painter Théodore Rousseau, informed how later critics blamed an "abuse" of the pigment for some irreversible color degradation that paintings displayed not long after their completion (Sensier, 1872: 78–79).

When the daguerreotype process was disclosed to the world in 1839, its spokesperson François Arago made sure to accord as little importance to Niépce's heliographic method using bitumen, despite it forming the basis for Daguerre's

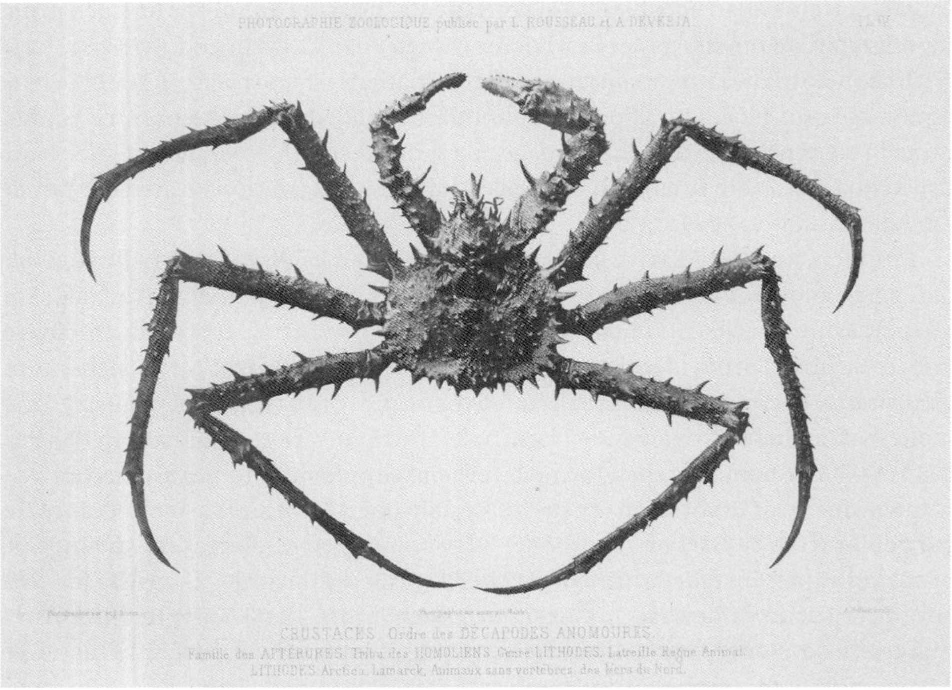


Fig. 2.1. Mante & A. Riffaut, after Bisson frères, *Crustaces*, from *Photographie zoologique Ou Représentation des Animaux Rares des Collections du Musée D'histoire Naturelle*, 1853. Photogravure. Private Collection. Courtesy of Mark Kratzman.

advancements with camera images recorded using silver (Marignier, 1998: 135). It was not until the 1850s that bitumen once again became an essential element of photo-reproduction. In 1852, a team of scientists and publishers working together patented their process of photolithography, which used the mineral resin of bitumen dissolved in ether, and then spread across the litho-stone as a grain, as opposed to the glaze used in Niépce's process. The following year, a family member, Félix Abel Niépce de Saint-Victor, returned to the photopolymer basis of his uncle Niépce's method, fashioning a photogravure process that again utilized bitumen, although this time suspended in benzene (a related hydrocarbon) that was then used to coat steel plates as opposed to pewter. Cleaned after exposure, the hardened bitumen on steel was then bitten in an acid bath, just as in etching, to hold ink for the plate to transfer onto paper in a press (Marignier, 1998: 135–136). Working to demonstrate a printing process that distanced itself from silver compounds and again regarded photography's more organic beginnings, Niépce de Saint-Victor hired the duo of engraver A. Riffaut and photographer Pauline Riffaut to help him manufacture and then, by hand, enhance the speckled mid-tones on the plates prior to printing. Despite the need for intervention by the skilled hand of the engraver, Niépce de Saint-Victor's process gave rise to the first planned photo-illustration series in 1854. Inscribed with the title *Photographie Zoologique*, the resulting prints helped viewers, such as visitors to their display in the Exposition Universelle of 1855, imagine massive image-banks of knowledge, and in this particular case natural specimens photographed at the Musée d'Histoire Naturelle and funded by the Académie des Sciences (fig. 2.1) (Rosen, 1997).

Niépce de Saint-Victor's research and his process, when paired with his decision to share it without patent, fueled an immediate explosion of interest in photogravure and related processes throughout the 1850s and 1860s. From industrialists and amateurs to chemists and artists, a long list of experimentalists in photomechanical process jumped into the ring for a variety of reasons: to generate the interest of the State or to court investors, to pave the way to industrialize photographic production or to help remedy the issue of fading in silver-based photographs like Daguerre's silvered plate and Talbot's salted paper print. Those who followed in the wake of Niépce de Saint-Victor's method rehearsed many of the same procedures, and some even relied on the use of bitumen, like the artist Charles Nègre and architectural photographer Édouard Baldus, both of whom refined their own distinct approaches to photogravure. Counter to the viscous materiality and slow reactivity of bitumen, photogravure's next phase of innovation with makers like Nègre included another element – more of a technical practice than a specified material – that, like photography, was celebrated for its speed, efficiency, and repeatability: here I refer to electrotyping, or *galvanoplastie*.

## Damascus Steel

In early accounts, photography often found a place among the electric telegraph and the steam locomotive as one of the triumvirate of wonders produced by modern science. Indeed, the collapse of former regimes of time and displacement – through instantaneous communication, rapid networks of travel, spontaneous visual reproduction – are succinctly emblematized by those inventions (Marien, 1997: 62). Yet what this trope fails to grasp is that these were part of an even larger list of novel technologies that also encompassed technical practices and energy processes that didn't share the same spectacular iconography as steam, current, or photon. As poet, writer, and critic Théophile Gautier began in his account of the second Société Française de Photographie exhibition held in 1857, "While we may claim to disdain it, the first half of this century in art and science will count among the climactic epochs of humanity, realizing astonishing marvels: steam-power over land and sea, gas, telegraphy and electric light, *galvanoplasty*, the daguerreotype" (Gautier, 1857: 193). What can fall from discussions of the litany of modern marvels was photography's frequent comparison to electrotyping, a process that produces metallic layers of gold or copper upon a model (or in this case, an engraved plate) through the action of a solution excited by a galvanic battery. Like the photograph, the electrotype was understood as a reproduction, only the latter was the result of harnessing electricity rather than light for the purpose of making automatic visual forms.

While priority for the invention goes to the Russian chemist Moritz Hermann von Jacobi, like photography in its phase of invention, the practice of electrotyping can be credited to various experimenters working independently of each other (Heinrich, 1938: 565). The process was quickly adopted by the publishing industry to create separate printing plates from moveable type and wood engraving blocks, freeing up the reuse of those materials in print production. This was an invention whose immediate effects were relative to industrial efficiency, in direct contrast to the medium of photography, with its initial resistance to growth by capital investment, as well as factors like prohibitive cost, unpredictable sensitivity, and limited reproducibility (Edwards, 2006: 23–116).

Following Daguerre's announcement, several scientific experimenters attempted to convert the daguerreotype's delicate silver surface (mounted on copper) into printable intaglio plates, and turned to galvanoplasty as part of their work. This included the young physicist Hippolyte Fizeau, and the physicians Alfred François Donné and Christian Joseph Berres – the former two in Paris, and the latter in Vienna (Eder, 1945: 577). In 1840, an incentive-based competition held in connection with the Société d'Encouragement pour l'Industrie Nationale led to the demonstration of photogravure processes by Donné, Fizeau, and others to Académie audiences as well as through various scientific journals (Séguier, 1839; Séguier, 1844). The most successful was Fizeau, who combined Niépce's and Daguerre's photo-processes with Jacobi's galvanoplasty. Taking an exposed daguerreotype plate, Fizeau submerged it into a galvanic bath to deposit an acid-resistant layer of copper or gold on to exposed areas of the image, making recesses in the plate to hold ink in preparation for pressing (Lecuyer, 1945: 246–248). An example of a plate produced by Fizeau survives in the Getty Museum, showing the baroque dome of the Hôtel des Invalides in polished copper (pl. 5). Here, the copper layer is deposited onto the silver of the daguerreotype image, cloaking the new surface with the older look of an engraving plate. The result is at once a work of experimental metallurgy, an ornamental object made from thin layers of copper and silver, as well as a functional printing matrix from which one can generate exact copies in ink on paper.

Further refining the process of electrotyping daguerreotypes, Fizeau produced three images to be included in the 1842 supplement to Noël Lerebours's *Excursions Daguerriennes*, an early photo-book *qua* armchair travelogue that featured hand-engraved or copied graphic images after daguerreotypes in Lerebours's collection. Fizeau's non-manual photogravures shared space alongside the book's other graphic translations. Uncharacteristic of the many views of world architecture in *Excursions,* Fizeau's photogravure of a bas-relief on Notre-Dame de Paris reads as if it were made in direct contact with the soot-stained stones of Paris's signature monument. Fizeau's gravure, according to the accompanying text by illustrator Pierre-Joseph Challamel, "renders perfectly all the details and into the smallest traces of dilapidation *impressed* by the centuries on to the stone of the old monument" (Challamel, 1840–43; emphasis mine). Challamel calls attention to the graphic traditions and techniques behind Fizeau's process, as well as how the results are able to suggest a correlation between the sculptural relief represented in the image and the etched recesses of the plate that produced the image, relaying a series of positive-negative correspondences that came to dominate both photographic and galvanic discourses.

In reproducing a work of sculpture, Fizeau grasped at manufacturing an image of materialism that also doubled as an image of art and of national culture. But the only issue was that these galvanized, illuminated forms connected to much larger, broader empires of translation – of various frameworks of originals and copies – that went beyond the reach of France and its claims to universality. How can such a machine that elides the difference between nature and culture be considered nationally as French in an age of materialism? This was a particularly 19th-century problem that animated the early decades of photography; and it would seem that photography marks one of the last pangs of revolutionary universality that the previous century's Revolution set into motion (Tresch, 2012: 89–122).

A figure taken with galvanoplasty and the parallels between this modern innovation and its historical precedents was Honoré Théodoric d'Albert de Luynes. The 19th-century Duc de Luynes was a formidable figure in French culture; in art history, he is primarily associated with his oversight of the lavish restoration of the

17th-century Château de Dampierre, choosing the architect Félix Duban for restorations and the painter J. A. D. Ingres for a new decorative cycle (Shedd, 1988). His other lasting contributions are in the field of archaeology, publishing various studies of ancient art as well as founding the *Annales de l'institut archéologique* with the art theorist Quatremère de Quincy. What distinguished d'Albert de Luynes from the field was his privileged access to his vast art collection, and from this his expertise on the physical and chemical composition of historic decoration and manufacturing. For instance, in *Description de quelques Vases Peints Étrusques, Italiotes, Siciliens et Grecs* from 1840, he not only identifies the mythological scenes portrayed in black-figure vases, but also shares his observations on the pots' material manufacture, including the frequent use of liquified bitumen, or *naphtum* for waterproofing (Luynes, 1840).

Pushed to study the metallurgy behind damascened blades (*lames damassées*) by the painter and chemist Léonor Mérimée, the Duc de Luynes examined the composition of works in his collection hailing from medieval Syria, Iran, and India, whose surfaces displayed a wavy, watery pattern (*moiré*) that differed from known processes by French metallurgists (Mille & Mérimée, 1836: 348–352). In 1844, the Duc then published his account of the technical and chemical makeup of his own specimens of *acier damassé* (Luynes, 1844). For his research in unveiling (according to his biographer) the "secrets of the Oriental armorers," the Duc garnered a silver medal at the 1844 Exposition de l'Industrie, whose jury duly recognized the research's applicability for the modern manufacture of surgical instruments (Huillard-Bréholles, 1868: 33).

In the subsequent decade, the Duc pursued research in the field of photography, and took to his own experiments "with the vivacity of an amateur and the well-reasoned zeal of a chemist" (1868: 39). Just like the elemental makeup of Islamic metalwork that was the subject of his research, the Duc approached photography's materials and its chemical solutions like a metallurgist, and in 1859 he submitted proofs made with gold and platinum salts to the Société Française de Photographie, constituting his effort to explore alternatives to the ubiquitous silver compounds that were prone to fading over time ("Procès-verbal," 1859: 302–304). At this same time, the Duc put up the funding for a large international competition – the first of its kind organized by the Société – to reward the inventor of a practicable non-silver forms of photography and photomechanical printing. This included examples of photogravure processes built on the research of Niépce and his nephew, Niépce de Saint-Victor, as well as demonstrations of non-silver photographic processes that were the topic of the Duc's own dabbling.

The Société Française de Photographie announced in 1855 the Concours du Duc de Luynes, a competition whose grand prize of 8000 francs was reserved for the founder of the most improved process of photomechanical printing: ink-based prints on paper, whether produced by photo-relief, photogravure, or photolithography. According to the competition's sponsor, the aim was to foster a "spirit of emulation" among actors in the international photographic community (Foliot, 1990: 235–236). In all likelihood, the presumption that emulation would fuel technological progress came from the Duc's position as an amateur; from this position, competitors were to find the progress of photography in overcoming its perceived limitations to be their governing motivation. In actuality, the competition's submission process sent many participants scrambling to patent their work and to police its use, improvement, or alteration by claiming themselves as authors and owners of their respective technical practices and processes (Lewis, 2017).

Working with Niépce de Saint-Victor's bitumen-based process, the artist Charles Nègre took to photogravure initially to reproduce and publicize his own photographs of the south of France. Patenting his own photogravure technique in 1856, he then entered into the Concours du Duc de Luynes to compete amongst various artists, entrepreneurs, chemists, and publishers. Trained in painting and printmaking, Nègre had moderate success at the Paris Salon des Beaux-Arts. Taking up the paper photo-process around 1850, he began to produce views of the city of Paris, studies of workers and street types, as well as a large series devoted to his home region of Provence. To publicize and print his work, he turned to photogravure and Niépce de Saint-Victor to learn the process, as well as to modify the latter's bitumen process by the addition of galvanoplasty to make printing plates as well as decorative metalwork that he termed "*damasquinure héliographique*": heliographic damascening.[3] With the announcement of the Concours du Duc de Luynes, Nègre submitted examples of his process and drummed up support for his work in spite of an unknown chronic illness slowing him down in the 1860s. Nevertheless, his photogravures ably demonstrate his level of skill in physical, material manufacture; as art critic Philippe Burty noted in 1861, Nègre was "as familiar with the brush as he is with the burin, with the chemist's retort as with the camera lens" (Burty, 1861: 179).

While Nègre's work garnered recognition from his fellow members in the Société Française de Photographie, his claim to the invention of a photo-based *damasquinure* was by no means secure. Upon outlining his process to a regular meeting of the Société at the end of 1856 (Nègre II, 1856), Nègre encountered a dispute over the priority of his invention from Henry Dufresne, an artist and illustrator who, just like Nègre, came from the atelier system and began his career in the studio of painter Paul Delaroche. Dufresne claimed his own invention of a combination of photography and electrotyping, which he touted as the modern reproduction of the ancient metalwork process ("Procès-verbal," 1857: 3). Winning over some in the press, it was Dufresne's "damascening" process, and not Nègre's, that the March 1857 issue of *L'Illustration* profiled as part of the history of metalwork harking back to the ancient Near East (Falampin, 1857). Upon identifying the distinctions between each process, the issue of priority and patent infringement went unresolved; later, Dufresne dropped out of the competition but not before lending his full support to Nègre's direct competitor Alphonse Poitevin, whose photolithographic process had already proven itself industrially viable in operation at Lemercier's art publishing firm (Davanne, 1867: 101).

With the oversight of the Société Française de Photographie, it was eventually announced in 1867 that the chemist Alphonse Poitevin deserved the competition's grand prize. However, the competition's sponsor Duc de Luynes had two years prior already commissioned the once favored contestant, Nègre, to reproduce a spate of photographs documenting the Duc's 1864 travels in Syria and Palestine for a multivolume study titled *Voyage d'Exploration à la Mer Morte, à Petra, et sur la rive gauche du Jourdain*, which achieved publication posthumously in 1874. For the expedition, the Duc traveled with a team of experts in geology and cartography, including the expedition's navigator and Naval Officer Louis Vignes (1831–1896), who had experience with a camera earlier in Sicily and Lebanon, at the time using the paper photographic method (Aubenas & Roubert, 2010: 312). To combat the harsh sun and dust of the environment, Vignes employed the new process of prepared dry collodion-on-glass to record the historic cities, ancient olive groves, archeological sites, desert landscapes, and vital waterways that travel brought them, stretching from Damascus south to the Dead Sea and finally to Petra, Jordan. In 1865, Nègre signed a contract with the Duc to produce plates and first proofs from Vignes's negatives for a total sum of 23,250 francs – almost three times the amount of the competition's grand prize.[4] In total, Nègre manufactured 64 of Vignes's negatives into photogravure plates made between the beginning of 1866 and the fall of 1867 (Heilbrun, 1980: 343). After both the conclusion of the competition and the Duc's death in Rome in late 1867, these photogravures were eventually incorporated into the atlas volume of *Voyage d'Exploration* (Luynes et al, 1874). It is in the atlas's pages, illustrated by Nègre's photogravures after Vignes's photographs, in connection with the Duc's research, wherein the networked paths of photopolymer resins, galvanoplasty, gilded Damascus steel, and the bituminous Dead Sea converge, anticipating a new kind of attention and analysis in the age of technical images.

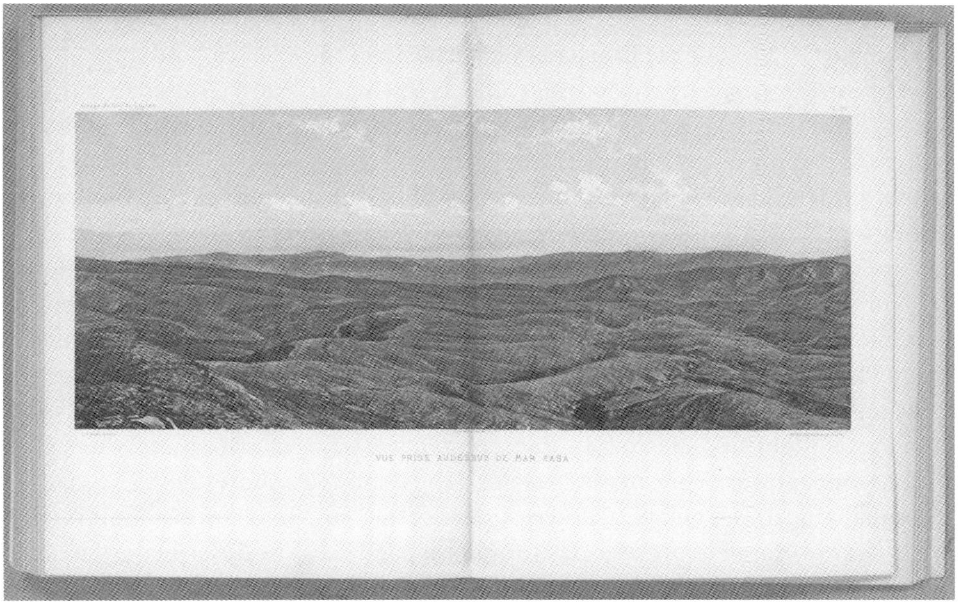


Fig. 2.2. Charles Nègre, after Louis Vignes, *Vue prise audessus de Mar Saba*, 1874. Photogravure, from *Voyage d'exploration a la mer Morte, a Petra, et sur la rive gauche du Jourdain*, vol. 4 (Paris: A Bertrand, 1874). Dorot Jewish Division, New York Public Library. Public Domain.

## From Optical Unconscious to Liquid Intelligence

The sole fold-out photographic illustration included in the atlas volume of *Voyage d'exploration à la Mer Morte* is a panoramic *point de vue* taken above the hillside monastery of Mar Saba (fig. 2.2). The image was made using two exposed negatives made by Vignes, and then translated into a photogravure by Nègre, who augmented the photographs' blank skies with a series of aquatint clouds designed and added by the artist in the process of etching the plate. The image represents a nearly barren landscape, bereft of signs of civilization apart from two stone towers at center right; what remains are the Judean Hills and slivers of the dry water-channels and valleys, or *wadis*, that in times of rain feed the Dead Sea. These same hills and *wadis*, identified in previous expeditions but not photographed in detail until the Duc's expedition, here take on a new force of meaning not of archaeology or the storied place of the Holy Land that saturate the output of previous photographic travelers like Francis Bedford and Auguste Salzmann (Solomon-Godeau, 1981; Gordon, 2013; Behdad, 2017). West of the monastery is Jerusalem; the eastern landscape that is present in *View Taken from Above Mar Saba* is the mass of earth, salted liquid, and viscous bitumen that governs both the features of the landscape and the production process that reproduces it in the atlas.

Just as in the above image, bitumen acts as both fact and metaphor in the various accounts included in the *Voyage d'exploration à la Mer Morte*. With regard to the former approach, the Duc recounts how the party's geologist, Louis Lartet, explored sites on the southern shores of the Dead Sea near the famed Jebel Usdum (Mount Sodom), where he found between its slopes and the water "banks or escarpments of alluvium impregnated with a bitumen which, in places, arises in stalactites" in addition to the tar pits made up of liquid bitumen (de Luynes, 1874, Vol. 1: 243–245). Lartet identified these sites of interest in the voyages map, indicating "bituminous emanations" concentrated around the Dead Sea's shores (Vol. 3: 300–317). Accompanying these geological descriptions are the Duc's notes on encounters with locals near Al-Karak in present-day Jordan. In particular, he describes a "Moabite woman" (named for the ancient kingdom east of the Dead Sea) "drawing water and giving a drink to one of our riders" whose physiognomic traits, according to the Duc, were more African while her skin held a "tint of bitumen" (Vol. 1: 108). The Duc here correlates the natural resources, the antiquity of the site, and the racialized appearance of its current inhabitants into a syrupy discourse that, like photography, confounds distinctions between nature and culture.

In his account of their visit to Mar Saba, the Duc betrays a weariness of and distaste for certain elements of the voyage, and has nothing to say about the arid land recorded in Vignes's panoramic view. Instead, he notes the character of the built landscape at Mar Saba, providing a sliver of its recent history:

> We saw the cave where Saint John of Damascus [*Saint Jean Damascène*] retired and wrote his works, as far as one can tell; then several chapels under various invocations, decorated with poor paintings in the Byzantine style. The church, repaired at cost by Russia after the Tiberias earthquake (in 1835 [*sic*]),[5] is of the most mediocre interior architecture, pitifully decorated like the other small shrines in the same place. Only its buttresses make for quite a nice effect. (Vol. 1: 186)

What he disregards in his description of Mar Saba is what Vignes takes as his *point de vue*, just as Niépce accomplishes in his own first camera image, pointed out and away from the interior and into the world. The combination print made by Vignes and then modified and printed by Nègre shows us none of the disappointments recorded by the elder Duc – of Byzantine mediocrities and of recent renovations, funded by the Eastern Church, that do no favors to what was already there for centuries. In this context, Nègre's photogravures overlay dimensions of the material, the historical, and the symbolic, by reproducing sites along one of the largest natural reserves of bitumen, a material used in everything from road construction in ancient times to painting to photography in the modern era. The resulting photogravures were printed from plates made with the slow substance of bitumen – likely mined from the same area represented in the gravures. In the fullest sense, space and time collapse in the most unlikely of ways, surfacing in photogravures by a man not known to have ever taken a photograph outside of the territory of France.

Various elements important to the Dead Sea commission – Vignes's dry collodion glass negatives, the photopolymer bitumen, the electrotyped photogravure plates composed of gold and steel that modernize *damasquinure* for the age of mass production – reveal more agency than often attributed to liquids, materials, and processes, rendering them far from neutral vessels for social or cultural meaning. Rather, these photogravures, their process of production, and the chemicals used in that process merit consideration as "actants," Bruno Latour's term for those things presumed to be inactive in social exchange, that instead overwhelmingly orient the relation between nonhuman and human elements, or more generally between culture and nature (Latour, 1999: 180). One can press Latour's idea to suggest that photography at this stage, in the hands and minds of a close-knit network of inventors, amateurs, and artists, reveals a "material unconscious" of otherwise unacknowledged connections between elements and producers. Here, I embrace an analogy with Walter Benjamin's own analogical concept of the "optical unconscious," an "Other" like that of the instinctual unconscious discovered by Freud: "another nature which speaks to the camera as compared to the eye" (Benjamin, 2008: 37). The signs of this other nature are only analyzable by the kinds of visualizations that arise from technical practices like instantaneous photography and cinematography. Instantaneity and its attendant optical disruptions were not simply byproducts of faster shutter speeds; one must also credit a wide array of materials brought to the fore in late 19th-century industrial refinements, from gelatin (a material refined from the marrow of cow carcasses) to coal tar (an industrial waste byproduct from gas refineries), both of which were utilized to manufacture more stable and higher sensitivity photo-emulsions by the photography industry (Henning, 2018: 96–99).

The optical unconscious appears to be at its most pervasive in the era of mass-culture, when photography, as Vilém Flusser argues, moved toward a "black box" technology whose labor and processes become less and less comprehensible while its input and output become more and more programmatic (Flusser, 2000: 16). An early example of its power may be perceived in Eugène Atget's photograph of *Asphalters* on the streets of Paris from 1899–1900, produced by the stock photographer's own hybrid technical practice that paired then anachronistic wet collodion-on-glass negatives and view-cameras with more modern gelatin silver printing-out-papers (pl. 6). What results is a demonstration of the camera's optical unconscious, in its ability to capture indiscriminately the blurred gestures of the workers in the midst of their labor, the stolid silhouette of their overseer, as well as the vaporous steam and glossy sheen of the hot asphalt poured and then smoothed out in the dappled sunlight of the Parisian sidewalk. Yet what remains only tacit in a surface reading of unconscious gesture in the catholic forms of photography's perceptual field is the assembly of semifluid materials responsible for the image's production and its recorded effects. Accompanying the bitumen of the street, depicted in its sublimation into heat and vapor, are the binding gelatin that holds the image and the tacky emulsion that preserved Atget's fingerprints all over the glass negative.

In Canadian artist Jeff Wall's 1989 text "Liquid Intelligence," he notes how variable, natural forms, not unlike the silvery bitumen and hot steam recorded in Atget's image, "are compelling when seen in a photograph because the relation between them and the whole construct, the whole apparatus and institution of photography, is of course emblematic of the technological and ecological dilemma in relation to nature" (Wall, 1996: 90). Liquid, vapor, solution, and suspension all appear to supplement Benjamin's "optical unconscious" with an object-oriented "liquid intelligence" that Wall describes, in which the "echo of water in photography evokes its prehistory," in contrast to how photography's dry elements of optics and mechanics and subsequent electronic hardware of the digital turn signal technological modernity minus its material composition. "In photography," Wall concludes, "the liquids study us, even from a great distance" (90–93).

In adjoining these concepts of Benjamin and Wall in relation to the photogravure panorama taken from Mar Saba, I cannot help but perceive the inadequacy of both concepts in the description of these nascent electro- and petro-cultures that form around early photogravure and its metallic forms, viscous resins, and electric baths. Perhaps, we can return to Poe's account of the first public form of photography to view how the mirrored surface of the daguerreotype is not marked by either its solidity or its identity with the thing represented, but by its "viscosity" – a modality of form theorized by Timothy Morton. To slide between a material unconscious and a liquid intelligence, then, might lead us to see our photographic world as interpenetrating our social and material existence in viscous ways like the mirror tropes analyzed by Morton. "In its sincerity," he writes, "reality envelops us like a film of oil. The mirror becomes a *substance*, an object" (Morton, 2013: 35). Representation and the real are forever fused, not simply as a consequence of an action – of an ostensible sliver of light exposed to a sensitive ground – but in the perpetual binding of observer and the material world. Thus, photography's objects, in all their manifestations on metal, glass, and paper, present as viscous a substance as the bitumen bubbling up on the shores of the Dead Sea.

## Notes

1 I thank Zirwat Chowdhury for her insight here on metalwork and her many expert comments and suggestions offered in reading an early draft of this essay.

2 I am thankful for Daniel Worden's input on energy discourse and several critical sources.

3 Charles Nègre, "Méthode pour transformer les images photographiques plaquées en planches gravées," patent no. 28802 (Bureau des brevets: Paris, 1856).

4 Contract between Duc de Luynes and Nègre, ODO 2002 2.10.02.1–2, Fonds Charles Nègre, Département des Arts Graphiques, Musée d'Orsay, Paris.

5 The earthquake took place in 1837, not 1835.

## Bibliography

Sylvie Aubenas and Paul-Louis Roubert, eds., *Primitifs de la Photographie: Le Calotype en France, 1843–1860*, exh. cat. (Paris: Gallimard; BNF, 2010).

Geoffrey Batchen, *Burning with Desire: The Conception of Photography* (Cambridge, MA: MIT Press, 1997).

Gerry Beegan, *The Mass Image: A Social History of Photomechanical Reproduction in Victorian London* (Basingstoke: Palgrave Macmillan, 2007).

Ali Behdad, "Mediated Visions: Early Photography of the Middle East and Orientalist Network," *History of Photography* 41, 4 (2017): 362–375.

Brent Ryan Bellamy and Jeff Diamanti, eds., *Materialism and the Critique of Energy* (Chicago: MCM, 2018).

Walter Benjamin, "The Work of Art in the Age of Its Technological Reproducibility (1936)," in *The Work of Art in the Age of Its Technological Reproducibility, and Other Writings on Media*, eds. Michael Jennings, et al. (Cambridge, MA: Belknap Press of Harvard University Press, 2008): 19–55.

Richard Benson, *The Printed Picture* (New York: MoMA, 2008).

Philippe Burty, "La gravure et la lithographie à l'exposition de 1861," *Gazette des Beaux-Arts* (August 1861): 172–179.

M. Challamel, "Un des bas-reliefs de Notre-Dame de Paris," *Excursions Daguerriennes* (Paris: 1840–1843): n.p.

E. Eirini d'Eyrinys, *Dissertation sur l'asphalte ou ciment naturel, découvert depuis quelques années au* Val Travers dans la Comté de Neufchatel (Paris: n.p., 1721).

Alphonse Davanne, "Rapport de la commission chargée de décerner le prix de 8000 francs, fondé par M. le duc de Luynes pour l'impression à l'encre grasse des épreuves photographiques," *Bulletin de la Société française de photographie* (April 1867): 89–112.

Josef Maria Eder, *History of Photography*, trans., Edward Epstean (New York: Columbia University Press, 1945).

Steve Edwards, *The Making of English Photography: Allegories* (University Park, PA: Pennsylvania State University, 2006).

G. Falampin, "Damasquinures anciennes et modernes. La damasquinure héliographique de M. Dufresne," *L'Illustration* (March 7, 1857): 148–149.

Vilém Flusser, *Towards a Philosophy of Photography*, trans. Anthony Mathews (London: Reaktion Books, 2000).

Philip Foliot, "Louis Vignes and Henry Sauvaire: Photographers of the Expedition of the Duc de Luynes," *History of Photography*, 14, 3 (1990): 233–250.

R. J. Forbes, *More Studies in Early Petroleum History* (Leiden: E. J. Brill, 1959).

Théophile Gautier, "Exposition photographique," *L'Artiste* (March 8, 1857): 193–195.

Sophie Gordon, et al., *Cairo to Constantinople: Francis Bedford's Photographs of the Middle East*, exh. cat. (London: Royal Collection Trust, 2013).

Françoise Heilbrun, ed., *Charles Nègre: Photographe, 1820–1880* (Paris: Éditions des Musées Nationaux, 1980).

Herbert Heinrich, "The Discovery of Galvanoplasty and Electrotyping," *Journal of Chemical Education* 15, no. 12 (1938): 565.

Michelle Henning, *Photography: The Unfettered Image* (London: Routledge, 2018).

John Herschel, "On the Action of the Rays of the Solar Spectrum on Vegetable Colours, and on Some New Photographic Processes," Philosophical Transactions of the Royal Society of London, 132 (1842): 181–214.

Eva R. Hoffman, "Christian-Islamic Encounters on Thirteenth-Century Ayyubid Metalwork: Local Culture, Authenticity, and Memory," *Gesta*, 43, 2 (2004): 129–142.

I. B. Holley, Jr., "Blacktop: How Asphalt Paving Came to the Urban United States," *Technology & Culture* 44, 4 (2003): 703–733.

Jean-Louis-Alphonse Huillard-Bréholles, *Notice sur M. le duc de Luynes, membre de l'Institut* (Paris: Henri Plon, 1868).

Matthew C. Hunter, "Joshua Reynolds's 'Nice Chymistry': Action & Accident in the 1770s," *Art Bulletin*, 97, 1 (2015): 58–76.

*Journal des Débats* (March 16, 1838): 2.

Estelle Jussim, *Visual Communication and the Graphic Arts: Photographic Technologies in the Nineteenth Century* (New York: R.R. Bowker Co., 1974).

Mark Kurlansky, *Salt: A World History* (New York: Walker & Co., 2002).

Bruno Latour, *We Have Never Been Modern*, trans. Catherine Porter (Cambridge, MA: Harvard University Press, 1993).

Bruno Latour, *Pandora's Hope: Essays on the Reality of Science Studies* (Cambridge, MA: Harvard University Press, 1999).

Raymond Lecuyer, *Histoire de la photographie* (Paris: Baschet, 1945).

Jacob W. Lewis, "Copies & Clouds: Charles Nègre and the Death of Emulation," in *Photography & Failure: One Medium's Entanglement with Flops, Underdogs, and Disappointments*, ed. Kris Belden-Adams (London: Bloomsbury, 2017): 163–179.

Honoré d'Albert de Luynes, *Description de quelques vases peints étrusques, italiotes, siciliens et grecs* (Paris: Firmin Didot, 1840).

Honoré d'Albert de Luynes, *Mémoire sur la fabrication de l'acier fondu et damassé* (Paris: Firmin Didot, 1844).

Honoré d'Albert de Luynes, et al., *Voyage d'exploration à la mer morte, à Petra, et sur la rive gauche du Jourdain. Oeuvre posthume*, 4 vols. (Paris: A. Bertrand, 1874).

Vered Maimon, *Singular Images, Failed Copies: William Henry Fox Talbot and the Early Photograph* (Minneapolis: University of Minnesota Press, 2015).

Mary Warner Marien, *Photography and Its Critics: A Cultural History, 1839–1900* (Cambridge: Cambridge University Press, 1997).

Jean-Louis Marignier, "Le procédé de Nicéphore Niépce dans les procédés photomécaniques après 1850," in *Nicéphore Niépce: Une Nouvelle Image = A New Image* (Chalon-sur-Saône: Société des amis du musée Nicéphore Niépce, 1998): 134–140.

Patrick Maynard, *The Engine of Visualization: Thinking through Photography* (Ithaca: Cornell University Press, 1997).

M. Mille and Léonor Mérimée, "Procédé pour fabrique l'acier damassé. Rapport sur les lames damassées présentées par M. le duc de Luynes," *Bulletin de la Société d'encouragement pour l'industrie nationale* (September 1836): 348–352.

Marie José Mondzain, *Image, Icon, Economy: The Byzantine Origins of the Contemporary Imaginary* (Stanford: Stanford University Press, 2005).

Timothy Morton, *Hyperobjects: Philosophy & Ecology after the End of the World* (Minneapolis: University of Minnesota Press, 2013).

Charles Nègre, "Mémoire sur la damasquinure et la gravure héliographique," *Bulletin de la Société française de photographie* (December 1856): 334–339.

Edgar Allan Poe, "The Daguerreotype (1840)," in *Classic Essays on Photography*, ed. Alan Trachtenberg (New Haven: Leete's Island Press, 1980): 37–38.

"Procès-verbal de la séance du 19 décembre 1857 [*sic*]," *Bulletin de la Société Française de Photographie* (January 1857): 1–15.

"Procès-verbal de la séance du 21 octobre 1859," *Bulletin de la Société Française de Photographie* (November 1859): 293–307.

Jeff Rosen, "Naming and Framing 'Nature' in 'Photographie Zoologique'," *Word & Image*, 13, 4 (1997): 377–391.

Baron Séguier, "Rapport sur la proposition de divers prix pour le perfectionnement de la photographie," *Bulletin de la Société d'encouragement pour l'industrie nationale* (December 1839): 477–483.

Baron Séguier, "Rapport sur les resultants du concours pour le perfectionnement de la photographie," *Bulletin de la Société d'encouragement pour l'industrie nationale* (July 1844): 297–301.

Alfred Sensier, *Souvenirs sur Th. Rousseau* (Paris: Léon Techener, 1872).

Meredith Shedd, "Ingres as Archaeologist: The Image of Saturn in 'L'Age d'or' at Dampierre," *Zeitschrift Für Kunstgeschichte*, 51, 2 (1988): 269–279.

Shawn Michelle Smith and Sharon Sliwinski, eds., *Photography and the Optical Unconscious* (Durham, NC: Duke University Press, 2017).

Abigail Solomon-Godeau, "A Photographer in Jerusalem, 1855: Auguste Salzmann and His Times," *October* 18 (1981): 90–107.

John Tresch, *The Romantic Machine: Utopian Science & Technology after Napoleon* (Chicago: University of Chicago Press, 2012): 89–122.

Marius S. Vassiliou, *Historical Dictionary of the Petroleum Industry* (Lanham, MD: Rowman & Littlefield, 2009).

Jeff Wall, "Liquid Intelligence (1989)," in *Jeff Wall*, eds. Thierry de Duve, et al. (London: Phaidon, 1996): 90–93.

William Whiston, ed., *The Works of Josephus, with A Life Written by Himself*, 2 vols. (New York: Oakley, Mason, 1870).

Raymond White, "Brown and Black Organic Glazes, Pigments, and Paints," *National Gallery Technical Bulletin*, 10 (1986): 58–71.

Section II

# Material Remediations

# Every Contact Leaves a Trace: Edith Wharton and the Forensic Imagination

Mary Marchand

*The gloves are off, and there's blood on the wall.*
**–Terence Davies**[1]

The equipment for photographing crime scenes was available by mid-nineteenth century, and photography was widely used by the police in other contexts as early as the 1840s, but photographs of crime scenes were not taken until the 1890s. Why? Because prior to that time, officials did not conceive of the place a crime occurred *as* a scene. This chapter examines how the scene was invented by a new science, which revealed that objects contain records of past activities and developed an array of technologies and protocols for harvesting these records. It also explores how Edith Wharton's 1905 novel *The House of Mirth* took up this forensic imagination, which is, above all else, attuned to the communicative capacity of objects. In revisiting this history, we see into the origins of our own "object-oriented juridical culture" (Weizman, 2010: 14), which has replaced people with physical evidence as the most reliable witnesses to an event.

The invention of the crime scene is uniquely connected to the fluctuating fortunes of the French criminologist Alphonse Bertillon (1853–1914). Bertillon was internationally famous for two innovations, both of which changed the course of criminology. His method for measuring parts of the body in order to document the identity of criminals was adopted throughout Europe and the United States, and he was also one of a small group of pioneers credited with establishing a scientific approach to solving crimes. His most important contribution to the new science of forensics was in the subfield of "legal photography," where his protocol for photographing crime scenes became the standard in the field. It was on the strength of his reputation for unlocking the testimony of objects that Bertillon was called as an expert witness at the military and civil proceedings that constitute the Dreyfus Affair. His outlandish testimony at these proceedings provoked widespread skepticism about the fledgling science, especially, as we will see in Wharton's novel, about the limitations of objects' human translators.

Both the contours and the limits of the forensic imagination come into play in Wharton's novel. As we know from her autobiography, *A Backward Glance* (1934), where she refers to the revolution in thought inaugurated by his methods, Wharton was familiar with Bertillon's work.[2] Her novel reveals a preoccupation with the reciprocal relation between events and objects. This relation is enacted in one of the most arresting scenes in her fiction, the final chapter of *House of Mirth*, where the downward spiral of society beauty Lily Bart ends with her lover, Lawrence Selden, rushing to her bedside only to discover she has died from an overdose of a sleeping draught. Selden's attitude toward Lily's dead body and his systematic survey and interrogation of the objects in her room suggest that the literary influence of forensic science was felt far beyond the genre of detective fiction. Wharton represents objects as providing more voluble, candid, and persuasive testimony than humans, even as she underscores the disturbing lessons about the elusiveness of evidence and forensic detachment that emerged from the Dreyfus Affair.

## Locard's Exchange Principle

In his book *Symmetry, Causality, Mind* (1992), Michael Leyton asks his reader to imagine standing on an empty subway station observing the surrounding detritus. We see the dent in a trash can and imagine an angry kick; we attribute the coffee stain on the platform to an accidental spill, and a crumpled newspaper recalls the compacting motion of a pair of hands. Leyton argues that the subway station is analogous to the human condition. We are locked in the "silent chamber" of the present, and our most common access to a past that we were not witnesses to is through the shape of objects (1992: 1). We can retrieve history through objects because certain features (e.g., a dent) reveal the object's history. While Leyton argues that memory-via-objects characterizes all human cognition, it surely finds its apotheosis in the forensic imagination. A crime transforms a place into a scene of aftermath, and the question that organizes our perception of aftermath is, "What happened here?" The belief that material clues can help us reconstruct past events is as old as hunter's lore, but when did science promise that it could reconstruct our unseen deeds?

To those of us schooled by countless crime dramas, it is surprising to learn that for most of the 19th century neither the police nor the public viewed the site of a murder as a field of evidence. In one of the earliest allusions to a crime scene, an 1874 newspaper piece on "Crime and Its Detection," the author attributes the greater success of French police to the new procedure of cordoning off the crime scene to await "secret detective officers" (1874: 4). These officers have been specially trained to look for "those evanescent indications which may be pregnant with suggestion for him, although they might have no meaning for the ordinary police officer" (1874: 4). While it is not altogether impossible that a criminal has obliterated his trail, the author concedes, it must all the same be remembered that absolute obliteration is the rarest thing in the world. Whether in approaching his victim and the scene of the crime, or in withdrawing from them, the murderer must thread his way through a number of chances and contingencies, any one of which may turn into evidence against him. This assertion, that the human body, like all bodies, invariably leaves and acquires physical evidence of its passage through the world, represents a novel claim that goes to the very heart of the forensic endeavor. It is the forerunner of what came to be called Locard's Exchange Principle or Locard's Theory, after Edmond Locard (1877–1966), the French forensic investigator. Locard is credited with formulating the dictum "every contact leaves a trace," which asserts that objects that come into contact with one another transfer or exchange materials.[3] Here is what Locard actually said: "On the one hand[,] the criminal leaves marks at the crime scene of his passage; on the other hand, by inverse action, he takes with him, on his body or his clothing, evidence of his stay or his deed" (1920: 139). This principle remains the basis of modern forensic science. As rendered in more colorful terms by the criminologist Paul Kirk, the Exchange Principle serves as the epigraph for virtually every forensic textbook:

> Wherever he steps, whatever he touches, whatever he leaves, even unconsciously, will serve as silent evidence against him. Not only his fingerprints or his footprints, but his hair, the fibers from his clothes, the glass he breaks, the tool mark he leaves, the paint scratches, the blood or semen he deposits or collects – all these and more bear mute witness against him. (1953: 4)

In the stark materiality that underlies the Exchange Principle, every object, not just the body and murder weapon, presents a surface for recording the event. This evidence is envisioned as easily overlooked or, in the case of trace evidence, imperceptible to the unaided eye, easily destroyed (by clumsy police work) and yet stubbornly remanent. By the turn of the century, the detection of these criminal vestiges had become a profession involving scientific methods and specialized tools. In

1915, when Raymond Fosdick conducted his comprehensive study of European and American police systems, he could confidently conclude that "crime detection" is now being approached as "medicine and biology have been approached – from the standpoint of facts. A burglary is a fact, the tools with which it is accomplished are facts, every incident surrounding its commission is a fact. The science of crime detections springs from the analysis and systemization of these facts" (1915: 361–62).

The crime scene protocols for ensuring the integrity of these facts were first standardized and disseminated by the Austrian jurist Hans Gross (1847–1915), whose *System der Kriminalistik* is widely considered the first handbook of criminalistics.[4] Gross repeatedly admonishes investigating officers to observe what are now accepted as the most basic rules for preserving the crime scene: never move or touch an object until it's been minutely described in the police report, no object is too small to have a bearing on the case, and avoid contaminating the scene. In recounting dozens of cases that hinged on seeming trifles – the disturbance of a spider web, the lint found in a pocket, figs in fecal matter – *Criminal Investigations* reveals how the forensic imagination changed our relationship to objects. Objects track our movements and allow us to be tracked in turn. Indeed, legal, scientific, and popular accounts of criminal investigations from the end of the 19th century envision things testifying against people and even (when the crime involves personal effects) betraying their owners. For example, an article touting the work of the forensic chemist Paul Jeserich describes how the human blood discovered on a suspect's axe, which he had claimed was goat's blood, "witnessed with terrible effect" against him ("Detection," 1893: 2).

The increased reliance on material evidence emerged in the context of growing skepticism about the reliability of human witnesses. Gross opens *Criminal Investigations* with the observation that "at the present day the value of the testimony of even a truthful witness is much overrated" (1906: xxv). He goes on to draw the sharpest possible contrast between human testimony and physical evidence: "material things are all examples of incorruptible, disinterested, and enduring testimony from which mistaken, inaccurate, and biased perceptions, as well as evil intention, perjury, and unlawful cooperation, are excluded" (1906: xxv).[5] This conviction about the untrustworthiness of human testimony continues to animate modern forensics as well. In Kirk's words,

> [Physical evidence] is evidence that does not forget. It is not confused by the excitement of the moment. It is not absent because human witnesses are. It is factual evidence. Physical evidence cannot be wrong; it cannot perjure itself;

> it cannot be wholly absent. Only its interpretation can err. Only human failure to find it, study and understand it can diminish its value. (1953: 4)

Material evidence cannot dissemble but it also cannot speak. The end of the nineteenth century witnessed the emergence of a battery of experts who could be called on to interpret and supply their testimony.[6] Thus, alas, the problem of unreliability persists.

## Objects at the Scene

To read through the early treatises on forensics, with their goal of training investigators into scientific protocols, is to confront how objects are transformed by virtue of appearing in this scene. The most trifling or banal objects are bestowed with an extravagant attention that stands in stark contrast to the carelessness that marks both our daily interaction with these objects and their traditional legal significance. As Gross observes, forensic science reverses the "old axiom" of the Civil Law, *De minimis non curat lex*, or "The law doesn't bother with trivial things." Instead, "only too often he must seek the strongest proof in the smallest details" (1906: 136). Here Gross indicates how an item at the scene should be described in the police report:

> Quite near the corpse, an inch from the left hand, a red cloth rolled up in a ball, apparently of cotton and about the size of a pocket-handkerchief, one corner sticking out, lying on the ground in the direction of the head of the body. On picking up this piece of cloth it is found not to be cotton but half silk. It is a three-cornered scarf with hemmed borders and each side 17 inches (43 cms) in length. It is unmarked and has a hole in the middle about the size of a pie piece[,] probably due to use. Under the scarf is no trace of blood or anything remarkable. It is not identified by anyone present (naming those present, A, B, C, etc.); it probably therefore did not belong to the murdered person. (1906: 133)

As part of the scrupulous objectivity that presumes nothing, what is clearly a red handkerchief can only be gradually confirmed as such. This report includes all phases of the encounter with the object, from its misleading initial appearance, to what is revealed by closer visual inspection and, finally, by handling it. The investigator's gaze removes all of the object's everydayness even as it remains, stubbornly, an unremarkable handkerchief. In an essay for the catalogue of the 1997 exhibition *Scene of the Crime*, which brought together artists under the concept curator Ralph Rugoff calls "the forensic aesthetic," contributor Peter Wollen describes how the objects at the scene oscillate between their more familiar and portentous aspects. In his words, they are "full of resonances of inexplicable dread and destruction. At the same time they can appear stupidly banal and vacuous" (1997: 25).

The crime scene has the additional effect on objects of forging a temporary affinity among them. The body, or more precisely the harm or destruction to the body, magnetizes them, creating a force field that proves too weak past the tape, and that establishes the boundaries of the scene. This feature of the scene is registered in one of the shared features of contemporary reflections on early crime-scene photographs, including Luc Sante's classic *Evidence*, Eugenia Parry's *Crime Album Stories, Paris 1886–1902,* and Sandra Phillips' *Police Pictures*. Confronted with the quandary represented by an array of unrelated objects that are nonetheless constituents of a well-formed scene, these writers frequently fall back on making lists of these objects, connected at best with *and*, the weakest of relations. In *Evidence,* for example, Sante gives us "petticoats and button shoes and calendars and cuspidors and beer bottles and wallpaper" (Sante, 1992: ix). Wollen, in his essay for *Scene of the Crime*, describes the scene in terms of "matchboxes, bismuth tablets, eggcups, railway ticket, letter, contents of pocket" (1997: 26). In the forensic imagination, a heterogeneous collection of objects suddenly coheres by virtue of their association with the crime.

So, one answer to the question of how the locality of an incident became a "scene" is that objects, including human bodies, were newly envisioned as possible clues by virtue of their capacity to exchange trace material when they collide – and collision is treated as inevitable. But the forensic imagination assigned objects a much larger role in criminal investigations. They were pieces of a puzzle that properly interpreted allows for the reconstruction of complex events. As the organizers of a 2009 seminar on forensic architecture argue, "The principle of forensics assumes that events, as complex and multivalented as they might be, are registered within the material properties of objects/bodies/spaces" (Mara-Stream, 2009). Among the early advocates of crime-scene reconstruction, no one manifested greater confidence about retrieving records of past activities from the scene than Bertillon. His confidence on this score becomes the impetus for photographing the scene.

I have found indirect evidence that British police took photographs at the scene of murders as early as 1887. A British tabloid, the *Illustrated Police News*, published illustrations of a triple murder, including the "death chamber" of one of the victims and the suspenders presumably left behind by the perpetrator. A caption indicates that the illustrations were drawn from photographs. But like the famous photographs of the body of Mary Kelly (the fifth victim of Jack the Ripper), taken in 1888, it is not at all clear what evidentiary role, if any role, these photographs played in the police investigations, although at least one photograph of Kelly's body *in situ* was shown to the jury ("Horrible," 1887: 3).[7]

It is not until 1890 that Bertillon, most notably, will offer a detailed rationale and lay down a protocol for photographing crime scenes. Most of *La Photographie Judiciare*, published in France 1890 and translated into English in 1897, is devoted to the procedures for taking the profile and frontal views of suspects that we know as the mug shot. However, in a chapter on "Other Applications of Photography to Jurisprudence," Bertillon offers several arguments for the value of crime scene photographs, including preservation of ephemeral clues (footprints in the snow, contusions that would fade, etc.) and details (a stopped clock) that may eventually prove important. More intriguingly, Bertillon imagines the camera as performing its own detective work, uncovering clues that are either overlooked or undetectable by the human eye.[8] This category includes trace evidence revealed through photographic enlargement, as well as evidence that emerges as a result of the distinctive features of the photographic process. In his chapter on forensic photography, Gross offers two dramatic examples of cases that were solved in just this way. In both cases, photographic evidence overturned initial verdicts of suicide.

In one case, a crime scene photograph, which deepened the red pigments, revealed signs of violence on the body; in the second case, a photograph of a woman's body on a park bench captured disturbances in the dew that revealed someone had been sitting next to her (Gross, 1906: 257). Like Bertillon, Gross values the photographic image both for its absolute accuracy – "the sensitized plate is the new retina of the man of science" – and its distinctive point of view. As an inverted image that is differently sensitive to certain colors and details, the photographic image furnishes "another point of view," and "the new colour, the new situation, and the new aspect enable us to see [the crime scene] from another point of view" (Gross, 1906: 252).[9]

As he had done with photographing suspects and criminals, Bertillon provided very precise specifications for photographing the scene and for the specially made equipment designed to produce these images. He directs the police to photograph the scene from two angles: a wide angle taken from the fixed height of 1 meter 50 ("which corresponds about to the height of the eyes of a man of ordinary stature") (fig. 3.1), with the goal of encompassing as much of the area around the corpse as possible; and a second, taken from above, using a specially

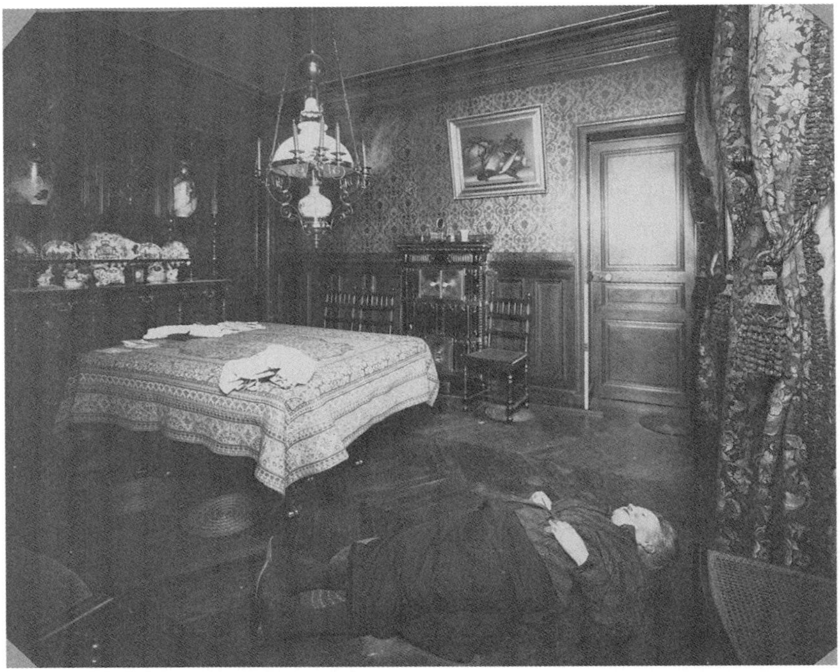

Fig. 3.1. Alphonse Bertillon, Crime Scene at 32 Rue de Turenne, Paris, March 25, 1904. Metropolitan Museum of Art, Online Database: Entry 284718. Public Domain.

made tripod, an angle Bertillon referred to as the "god's eye view" (in Tomellini, 1908: 15) (fig. 3.2). He also pioneered the use of metric photographs – photographs taken with measuring scales that allowed police officials and lawyers to recreate the size of objects as well as their relative position at the scene (fig. 3.3). Bertillon's method was sufficiently novel to be demonstrated at numerous world fairs and exhibitions, including the 1893 World's Fair, where several of the Chicago papers remarked on the unsettling crime scene photographs on display as well as the "realistic wax corpse" positioned below "a peculiar looking camera mounted on a tripod" (fig. 3.4) ("Anthropometry," 1893: 455).

Bertillon's specifications, which were subsequently adopted throughout Europe and the United States, produced immediately recognizable images. Ironically, in his quest "to make photography a purely mechanical operation" (Bertillon in Tomellini, 1908: 6), he gave birth to what Bret Wood has described as the crime scene aesthetic (2002: 1). What is the visual vernacular of these images? Certainly their special status as scientific-legal documents whose sole goal is to see and record as much

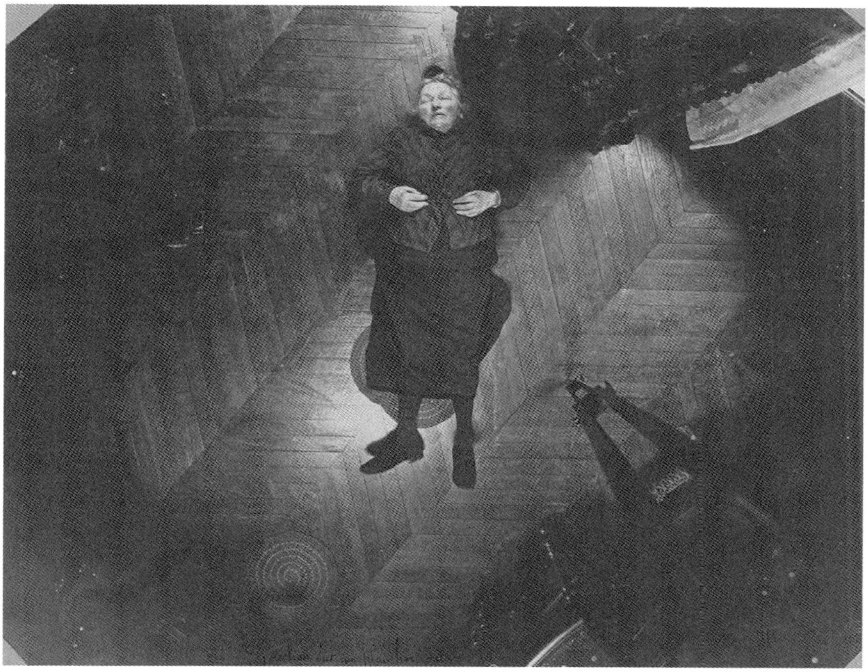

Fig. 3.2. Alphonse Bertillon, Crime Scene at 32 Rue de Turenne, Paris, March 25, 1904. Metropolitan Museum of Art, Online Database: Entry 284718. Public Domain.

as possible results in a distinctive gaze – detached, unemotional, and unflinching. As Sante observes in *Evidence*, "these photographs lack the functions that are usually attached to images of death. They do not memorialize, or ennoble, or declare triumph, or cry for vengeance. As evidence, they are mere affectless records, concerned with details.... They are bookkeeping entries" (1992: 60). It is hard to know which is more unsettling, the unnatural overhead view or the wide angle that in the effort to be all-encompassing hollows out the space of even over-stuffed interiors. Wood notes the uncanny silence and emptiness that reign in these images (2002: 20). Here is death untransfigured by any larger moral meaning.[10]

Bertillon's photographs point to another feature of the forensic imagination. As a function of the wide angle, which bespeaks the overriding imperative to encompass as much potential evidence as possible, the image relegates the body to the status of one among other objects in the room. This demotion of the body is re-enacted by how we look at photographs of crime scenes, and by extension the scenes themselves, which require a different kind of scrutiny than other depictions of death. We

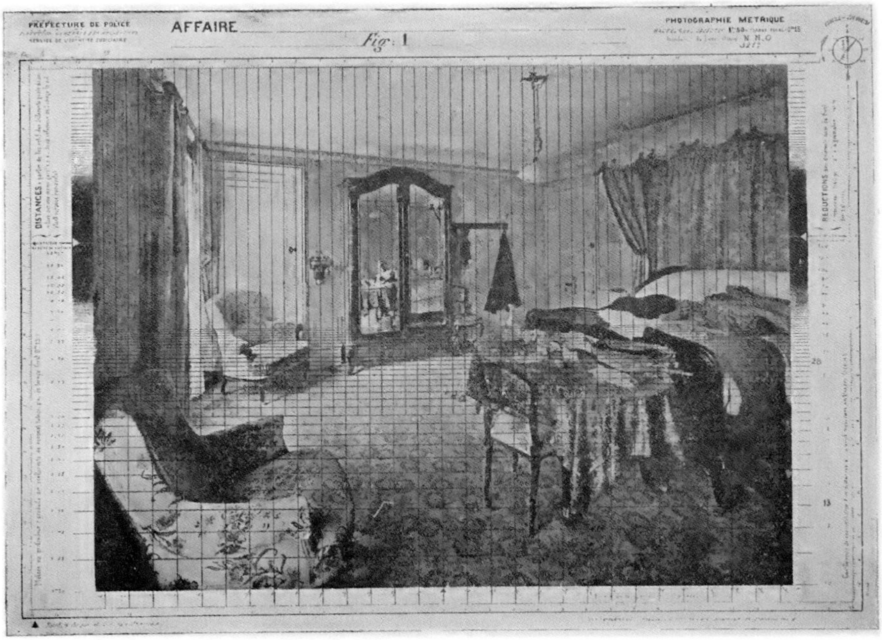


Fig. 3.3. A crime scene photograph with the measured grids used to indicate the scale and exact position of object. In Tomellini (1908: 104b). Public Domain.

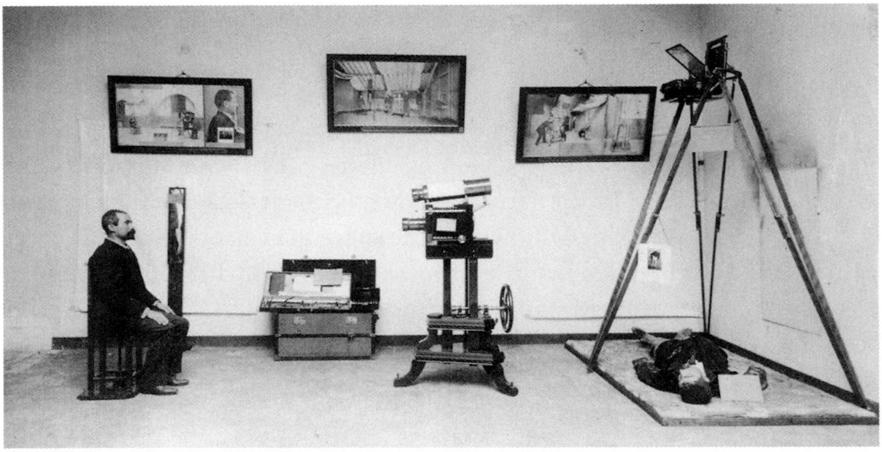

Fig. 3.4. Photograph from Bertillon's exhibition at the 1893 World Columbian Exhibition in Chicago. National Gallery of Ottawa, Canada. Public Domain.

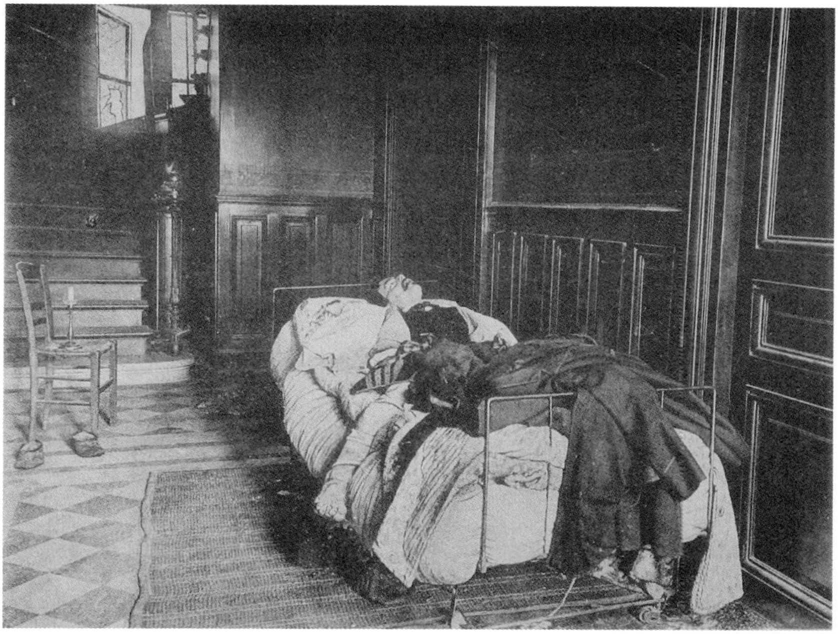

Fig. 3.5. Alphonse Bertillon, Photograph of "l'infortuné R--" in Bertillon, *La Photographie Judiciaire, avec un Appendice. Sur la Classification et l'Identification Anthrométrique.* (Paris: Gauthier-Villars et Fils, 1890): 49. Public Domain.

look for the body and then we start scanning the scene. As Mark Haworth-Booth observes, we recognize crime-scene photographs as "something to be scanned, surveyed, and examined all over, for any scrap of evidence" (1997: 38).[11]

Only one demonstration of how Bertillon used photographs to reconstruct a crime from evidence at the scene remains (fig. 3.5). The case involved the murder of a night watchman by a band of tramps in a villa in the suburbs of Paris:

> The broken pane of glass, the half-open window and the abandoned list slippers, which we perceive on the floor to the left, enable us to imagine the path followed by the assassins, in order to penetrate surreptitiously into the dark room. You see them lighting the candle, which was found upon the chair; you divine the rage which they feel when perceiving their progress barred by the unfortunate R---, stretched out like a faithful watchdog, but less watchful, across the doors of the rooms to which he forbade entrance. We mentally take part in the terrible drama which follows: the victim, surprised in sound sleep, made no resistance

> (the position of his body upon the bed proves this); the murderers could not even invoke the excuse of a sudden fright – seeing the obstacle, they could have withdrawn by the same road they came without fear of being surprised, recognized and denounced. We do not believe that we are exaggerating in asserting that this picture placed before a jury would render the task of the defense much more difficult. There is not a man who, brought face to face with such a crime would not feel aroused in himself that sentiment of reprisals, which our code calls *la vindicate publique* and which we find in all countries under the name of lynch law, law of retaliation, etc. (Bertillon, 1897: 37–38)

Bertillon does not in fact draw attention to any pioneering scientific techniques that might have been deployed to solve this case. Instead, we see how the crime is told by and through commonplace objects. Their translator uses them to confidently reconstruct not simply a sequence of events but a full-blown story, replete with motives, emotions, and dispositions. In both the framing of the image and the story reconstructed from it, the body of the watchman is moved off center in order to accommodate the equally important evidence of the broken window, chair, candle, and list slippers. In capturing these objects, the crime scene photograph brings not just the crime scene but the crime itself before an imagined jury, whose outraged verdict reveals that the amorality of the protocol is a temporary strategy devised for the sake of reaching a moral resolution, namely punishment and accountability for the crime.

Scientific reconstructions of crimes like the murder of the watchman – crimes unseen, crimes committed under the cover of night – captured the public's imagination. An article that appeared in the *Baltimore American* in 1905 describes the wonder invoked among his colleagues by a police sergeant's application of scientific methods at the scene of a murder. Sargent Casey, attached to the city's "Bertillon Bureau," arrives at the scene with his camera and realizes the papers scattered around the victim represent his first opportunity to test his fingerprinting technique. The sergeant dusts the paper with black powder and the reporter describes the "uncanny feeling" that accompanies the appearance of the prints: "for everyone thought there could be no doubt about them being the prints for the same fingers which had circled the horrible instrument that killed the old watchman" (watchmen, apparently, were especially vulnerable) ("Finger," 1905: 15). This new form of evidence does not simply help identify the perpetrator but also, properly interrogated, activates and revives the past event.[12] As we see in Wharton's novel, fascination with the literary possibilities represented by this uncanny science was not confined to the writers of detective fiction.

## Wharton and The House of Mirth

Wharton certainly knew about Bertillon, who had become an international celebrity by the 1890s. In addition to the passing allusion to his method in her autobiography, there is the distinct possibility that she saw Bertillon demonstrate his crime scene protocol at the Paris Exposition of 1900, which her most recent biographer speculates she attended (Lee, 2007: 273). Leroy Panek notes that the detective fiction published between the turn of the last century and the 1920s frequently features the scientist-detective, as well as countless allusions to Bertillon in particular (2006: 79–81). Wharton's work, however, reveals a broader forensic impulse. What happens when we reread the last chapter of *The House of Mirth* as produced by the forensic imagination?

Wharton's novel follows the declining fortunes of a beautiful young woman, Lily Bart, who is born into a wealthy New York family but gradually loses her footing by leaving herself open to scandal. Over the course of the novel she slowly descends into poverty and finally dies in her room in a shabby boarding house from an overdose of a sleeping medication. The last chapter begins the next morning, with Lily's suitor, Lawrence Selden, rushing to her boarding house to propose marriage only to learn of her death. He is greeted at the door by their mutual friend, Gerty Farish. Behind Gerty he registers an "agitated blur" of activity, and a disembodied "voice in the background" intones, "the doctor might be back at any minute – and…nothing, upstairs, [is] to be disturbed" (1905/1985: 325). Lily's bedroom has already become an official scene, an institutional space subject to the "formalities," as Gerty calls them, of a forensic investigation. Indeed, the entire chapter is the product of this investigation. It unfolds in the half hour allotted by the coroner, who breaks with protocol to allow Selden this time alone with Lily's body. While the novel concludes with Selden kneeling at Lily's bedside, the coroner's imminent return, which is invoked no fewer than three times in as many pages, is the anticipated endpoint.

But what does Selden do with what he calls "this supreme half hour"? He briefly kneels, grieving, by her bedside. Then, reflecting that her death "left the gate unbarred" (Wharton, 1905/1985: 327), he uses the time to systematically inspect the contents of her bedroom. Despite characterizing his search as in keeping with Lily's wishes, presumably by removing any potentially embarrassing personal effects, Selden's investigation takes an entirely different course. He approaches the objects as evidence to resolve the question of her moral character. He is looking for clues that will allow him to "unravel her story" – a story described in this chapter as "the mystery" (Wharton, 1905/1985: 329). It follows from the logic of this protocol that the most important evidence for Lily's character emerges only after her suspected suicide, which transforms her room into a crime scene and allows Selden untrammeled access to her personal effects and her inert body. Indeed, Selden, a practicing lawyer, both anticipates and usurps the activities of the coroner.

After a mental shake that signals his transposition from grief-struck lover to self-composed detective, he begins his investigation with an inventory of the room, starting with a description of her body in its narrow bed along the wall and proceeding clockwise:

> He turned and looked about him, sternly compelling himself to regain his consciousness of outward things. There was very little furniture in the room. The shabby chest of drawers was spread with a lace cover, and set out with a few gold-topped boxes and bottles, a rose-coloured pin-cushion, a glass tray strewn with tortoise-shell hairpins – .... There was no other token of her personality about the room, unless it showed itself in the scrupulous neatness of the scant articles of furniture: a washing-stand, two chairs, a small writing-desk, and the little table near the bed. On this table stood the empty bottle and glass, and from these also he averted his eyes. (Wharton, 1905/1985: 327)

While Lily's body lies a few feet away, he moves into the space he has just inventoried, touches, and speculates about her personal effects, lifts the lid of her desk, opens and reads her letters, and examines her check book, all the while trying to get to the bottom of the gossip and innuendo that surrounded her during her lifetime. With each new piece of evidence, he enacts the wavering judgments that have characterized his assessments of Lily throughout the novel. One of the most damaging rumors linked Lily to Gus Trenor, the husband of her close friend. The discovery of a recent letter addressed to Trenor gives rise to "ugly uncertainties" (Wharton, 1905/1985: 327). Then he discovers a letter he had written Lily, and this poignant evidence of her feelings for him causes him to rethink and revise his bitter suspicions. Finally, careful examination of her checkbook entries and check stubs yields evidence that while she borrowed money from Trenor she also found this indebtedness so repugnant that she preferred to be penniless. Thus, the seemingly definitive clue allows him to "construct an explanation of the mystery" (Wharton, 1905/1985: 329) that expiates Lily. At this point, his investigative task completed, the lawyer reverts to the grieving lover, and he returns to her bedside to await the coroner.

It is worth quoting this last passage in full to see the extent to which Wharton emphasizes Selden's role as investigator while underscoring the clue-like status of the objects in her room:

> Did the cheque to Trenor explain the mystery or deepen it? At first his mind refused to act – he felt only the taint of such a transaction between a man like Trenor and a girl like Lily Bart. Then, gradually, his troubled vision cleared, old hints and rumours came back to him, and out of the very insinuations he had feared to probe, he constructed an explanation of the mystery. It was true, then, that she had taken money from Trenor; but true, also, as the contents of the little desk declared, that the obligation had been intolerable to her, and that at the first opportunity she had freed herself from it. (Wharton, 1905/1985: 329)

Wharton casts the seemingly voluble and direct fashion in which Lily's objects speak to Selden – the contents of the desk "declare" the truth; the envelope addressed to Trenor "asks" pointed questions – in stark contrast to the stubborn silence that emanates from Lily's body, whose "mute lips" "refuse" Selden answers. Lily and Selden's relationship is haunted by the specter of crucial failed conversations. Wharton has carefully prepared the way for the possibility that these objects have greater potential to reveal the truth about Lily than a colloquy with Lily herself. Even though much of the evidence at the scene is language-based, it is their non-textual features that signify. This is true even of the envelope addressed to Trenor. Selden does not read the letter inside, despite realizing the envelope is not sealed; instead, the mere fact of the letter testifies to some kind of tie with Trenor and raises the crucial question of whether it was written before or after Selden and Lily's last conversation. There are many striking features to this scene – the systematic survey and inventory of the room's contents; that Selden's "task" or "work," as he describes it, entitles him to open her letters, her desk, her cheque book – but the most unsettling is how his absorption with her effects while her body lies nearby approximates Bertillon's protocol for photographing crime scene interiors, where the task of recording as many details as possible relegates the body to the periphery of the frame.

So thorough is Selden's inventory that even attentive readers can forget that one of the most important pieces of evidence regarding the question of Lily's moral character is entirely missing from the scene: the love letters written by a married woman, Bertha Dorset, to Selden – material evidence of their long-standing affair. Early in the novel, Lily purchases these letters from Selden's cleaning woman, who retrieves them from his wastebasket with an eye to blackmailing Lily, whom she mistakenly believes is the author of the letters. Lily initially buys the letters to protect Selden and then is repeatedly tempted to use them against Bertha Dorset to regain her place in society. This temptation is sharpened by Bertha's unrelenting assaults on Lily's reputation. Lily overcomes this temptation hours before she kills herself, when she furtively burns the letters in Selden's fire grate during their final exchange. These missing letters, crucial evidence of Lily's moral victory as well as Selden's entanglement in the crime scene, form Wharton's critique of the forensic imagination.

## Bertillon and the Dreyfus Affair

Understanding the nature of her critique requires recognizing that even as Wharton was writing *The House of Mirth*, a similar constellation of key players and objects had resurfaced at the center of the most famous trial in the history of France. The events that comprise the Dreyfus Affair turned on an incriminating letter retrieved from a wastepaper basket by a cleaning woman who was paid for the information these letters contained. It was on the basis of the infamous letter, or bordereau, that Captain Alfred Dreyfus was convicted of high treason. The most celebrated expert called in to verify the authenticity of the letter was none other than Bertillon. Bertillon's testimony in the trial was, by almost all accounts, a stunning fiasco, one that severely damaged his reputation as well as the reputation of this fledgling science.

From the very beginning, Bertillon played a crucial and highly questionable role in the proceedings. The French military linked Dreyfus to the notorious bordereau, which had been retrieved in 1894 from the wastebasket of the German military attaché, on the slenderest of evidence. Bertillon was called in by the Prefect of Police to analyze the handwriting only after the first expert's findings were ambiguous.[13] Despite the growing chorus of experts weighing in on the defense's behalf, Bertillon appeared as a stalwart witness for the prosecution in Dreyfus's 1894 trial and again at his retrial in Rennes in 1899. In his testimony, Bertillon had to account for the obvious dissimilarities between Dreyfus' handwriting and the handwriting in the bordereau, as well as the obvious similarities between the actual traitor's handwriting and the bordereau. His explanation at the retrial, which required seven hours of convoluted testimony buttressed by photographs, bulging satchels of papers, and diagrams that resembled the battle plans for a medieval siege, was nothing short of cockeyed. His testimony was roundly ridiculed in the press for having "no scientific value." In a piece entitled "Science and Mystery," the *New York Times* denounced him as the "prince of quacks" (1899: 1).

The skepticism that greeted Bertillon's testimony encompassed much more than his credibility as a handwriting analyst. Press reports register the comparative novelty of a legal case constructed almost entirely around a disputed object and the battery of human scientists and experts who assert their power to make the object yield the indisputable truth. We can gauge the damage done to his reputation as well as forensic science from a series of fifteen caricatures of Bertillon that appeared in the French satirical journal *L'Assiette au Beurre* in July 1909. The caricatures are directed equally at his system of anthropometry, his testimony in the Dreyfus Affair, and his crime scene protocols. The first image in the series depicts Bertillon in a primitive public bathroom looking for clues with a magnifying glass and a tape measure (fig. 3.6). He overlooks the obvious clues (a bloody rag and broken window), focusing instead on the traces of his own fingerprints. The caption reads, "Every murderer leaves a trace – somewhere."[14] In another cartoon, the first frame depicts a naked man stabbing a woman in bed (fig. 3.7). The second frame depicts Bertillon at the scene of the crime examining the prints on the bedclothes left by the murderer's buttocks, while a policeman holds curious onlookers at bay. The caption reads, "This print doesn't agree with the right hand. What precautions the murderer has taken!"[15]

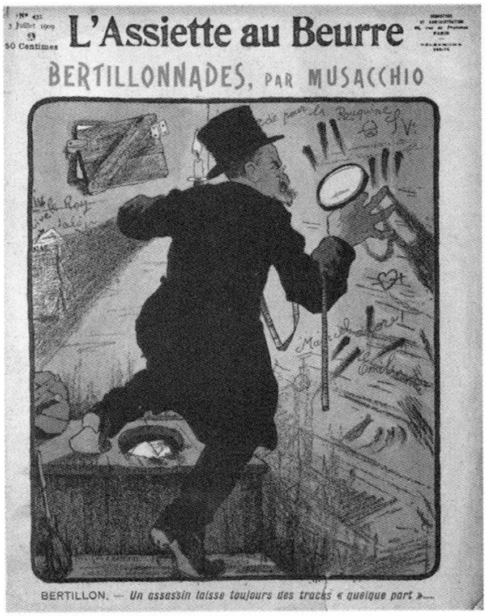


Fig. 3.6. Satirical Cartoon by Musacchio, *L'Assiette au Beurre* (July 3, 1909): cover.

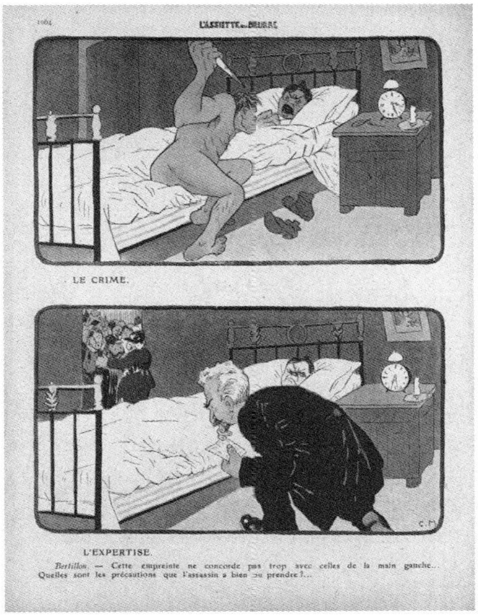


Fig. 3.7. Satirical Cartoon by Musacchio, *L'Assiette au Beurre* (July 3, 1909): 1064.

The questionable nature of the evidence against Dreyfus appalled many, including Wharton, who despite her anti-Semitism believed he was innocent.[16] Even as she was composing *The House of Mirth* in the summer of 1904, the Criminal Chamber was reexamining the evidence and recalling the witnesses against Dreyfus, including the bordereau and the testimony of the cleaning woman, Mme Bastian, who had retrieved it from the wastepaper basket. I do not want to get lost in the details of the problems with Bertillon's testimony, especially since I do not think Selden serves as a stand in for Bertillon. I do think that when Wharton wrote this final scene she saw an opportunity to underscore the twin dangers that had become apparent to almost everyone by this point: the extraordinary power of even fallacious material evidence and the seductive confidence of the imperious expert.

Her critique proceeds along several lines. First, it is directed against the very premise of the "scene," which maintains that the relevant history of a crime materializes in a bounded space. The letters are not simply absent from the room; they are present as ash in another location. For the reader, the niggling awareness of these ashes means Lily's room can never be a complete, self-contained scene. The ashes of the letters, trace residue of an extramarital affair, blackmail, and a hard-won moral victory, serve to confirm the dictum "every contact leaves a trace" even as they mock science's power to retrieve these strands of illicit, criminal, and moral history. In its appearances in the novel, Wharton highlights ash's dual nature as incontrovertible evidence of an irrecoverable event. On the one hand, burning the letters is characterized as the solution to the problem of "how [to] destroy them so effectually that there should be no second risk of their falling into such hands" (Wharton, 1905/1985: 107). At the same time, what twice stops Lily from burning the letters is that the residue is all too conspicuous, first against the "forbidding lustre" of Mrs. Peniston's clean fire grate and then in the "brilliantly polished" grate in her own room (Wharton, 1905/1985: 109). Derrida had these same qualities of ash in mind when in interviews he repeatedly stated his preference for ash "as the better paradigm for what I call trace – something that erases itself totally, radically, while presenting itself" (1987: 177). He further distinguishes the meaning of ash by contrast with other forensic traces: "the best paradigm for the trace is not...the trail of the hunt, the fraying, the furrow in the sand, the wake in the sea, the love of the step for its imprint, but the cinder." This is the very distinction Wharton exploits when she turns the missing evidence into a trace that cannot be traced.

But the full force of her critique is directed at all that is implied about the investigator by the overhead "god's eye view" and the confident judgments that derive from his detachment from and unparalleled access to the scene. Without the letters, Selden never realizes how thoroughly implicated he is in the aftermath he purports to investigate. The missing piece of evidence is not just *somewhere* outside this scene, but at the end of a straight line that runs from Lily's room back to Selden's own apartment and fire grate. Lily initially buys the letters because she realizes that "Selden was inextricably involved in their [the letters'] fate." As part of the double standard by which men's and women's infidelities are judged differently, she recognizes that should the affair come to light, society will judge Bertha far more harshly than Selden. However, she also realizes that "where a man of Dorset's ticklish balance was concerned," Selden ran "graver risks" (Wharton, 1905/1985: 105). When Lily purchases the letters, we're asked to imagine that she is protecting Selden from possible violence at the hands of George Dorset.

We only have to imagine the revelations that would have followed from Selden's discovery of this bundle of letters in her desk to see what is at stake in their absence: that despite his intermittent fantasies of rescuing and protecting Lily, she has been his protector all along; that she sacrificed both her social rehabilitation and, with it, her last chance at financial solvency rather than trade on his seedy secret; that even as he weighed the evidence for and against her affair with a married man, she had unambiguous evidence of his with a married woman. In the scene where Lily burns the letters, there is a wrinkle that suggests Wharton was trying to walk the finest of lines as to whether Selden fails to see or actually disregards this important piece of evidence: "When she rose he fancied that he saw her draw something from her dress and drop it into the fire; but he hardly noticed the gesture at the time" (Wharton, 1905/1985: 310). What does it mean that he sees it without understanding it? The "at the time" is especially curious, with its ultimately misleading implication that Selden will eventually correct this oversight and recover the missing clue. Instead, like the ashes they become, which are there but not there, the letters are seen but not *seen* – a crucial lapse in attention to objects with profound consequences for his capacity to understand the scene of aftermath and his place in it.

In trying to understand the subtleties of Wharton's critical stance, it is vital to recognize that Selden does not misinterpret the evidence at the scene. Using the objects in the room, he discerningly reconstructs Lily's actions, as well as her motives and struggles. The efficiency with which her personal effects speak to Selden stands in stark contrast to the misunderstandings that plague Lily and Selden's exchanges. For Wharton, as long as one doesn't succumb to the hubris of complete objectivity, attending to objects really does represent an improvement over pre-forensic reliance on human testimony. Selden's error originates in his confidence that the scene of aftermath is complete, that all her actions have left a recoverable trace and that he is sufficiently outside the mystery to see it whole.

In Selden's confidence, Wharton isolates the emerging influence of crime scene photography and forensic science, which had just begun to turn heads with compelling demonstrations of how they could recover the past from objects. Their influence is registered as well in Wharton's characterization of Lily's death as the unbarring of a door that affords Selden untrammeled access to material evidence whose probative value surpasses the living Lily's own words. If one of the novel's concerns is the shift of emphasis from human testimony towards objects in the investigations of crimes, this is closely related to the question of the fallibility of expert judgments about the evidence. The "father of scientific detection" was embroiled in a notorious trial that exposed his abuses of this evidence. Stirred by the promise of a purely empirical basis for legal judgments, the forensic imagination has always had to contend with evidence to the contrary.

## Notes

1 Terence Davies, director of *The House of Mirth* (2000), on the difference between Edith Wharton and Jane Austen.

2 Wharton singles out the contributions of the "Bertillon-Morelli methods" to the field of art connoisseurship (1934/1990: 890). Giovanni Morelli (1816–1891) was an Italian diplomat and art critic. I have written elsewhere about the surprising fact that Wharton and her contemporaries perceived a kinship between the methodologies in two such different fields (Marchand, 2011). In this essay I want to focus on one side of this equation – the Bertillon method – and explore what Wharton's familiarity with his work illuminates in her fiction.

3 See Horswell's detailed account of the origins and history of this phrase (2004: 46–50).

4 First published in 1893 under the full title *Handbuch fur Untersuchungsrichter als System der Kriminalistik*. Citations are from the English edition, which first appeared in 1906 as *Criminal Investigations: A Practical Handbook for Magistrates, Police, Officers, and Lawyers*.

5 See Claire Valier's (1998) account of how the adoption of scientific methods of investigation was tied to the perceived limitations of *mémoire visuelle*.

6 In a chapter on "The Expert and How to Make Use of Him," Gross offers examples of cases that were solved by consulting everyone from linguists to chemists (1906: 149–224).

7 The photograph of the aftermath of the Clerkenwell Prison explosion in 1867 is widely considered the first photograph of the scene of a crime. See Linda Steer's fascinating account of the photographs of Kelly's corpse, their use in the investigation of Jack the Ripper, and their subsequent appropriation by the surrealist playwright Maurice Heine (2008: 110–122).

8 It's in part the photograph's potential for creating rather than simply recording evidence that raised vexing question about its legal status. See Mnookin (1998) for the early history

of photographic evidence, which was alternately treated as demonstrative evidence – visual aids analogous to drawings – and as evidence in its own right – a witness supplying its own information.

9 Greg Siegel describes the scientific applications of photography as exploiting "a specular paradox intrinsic to the technical apparatus." The "reflection and inversion" of the mirror image "shows us more than the eye, even when it shows us no more than the eye can see" (2011: 99).

10 Compare this account of the crime scene aesthetic to Siegel's, which focuses on Bertillon's metric photographs: "grids and maps belong to a distinctly modern practice – namely, the use of technical media to turn ostensibly disorganized places into perfectly geometrical spaces, thereby rendering them available to inspection and amenable to rational understanding" (Siegel, 2011: 99–100). It's worth noting the differences between the angles and perspectives Bertillon advocates and those currently used by investigators. According to Tim Thompson, "appropriate lenses are used to ensure a natural view of the scene (therefore wide-angled lenses are not used and the photographs are taken from eye-level)" (2008: 171).

11 See Zoe Crossland's discussion of the multiple ways in which the body is used as evidence, including using bodily symptoms to diagnose interior states; using bodily features to establish identity; using the body as evidence of the past; and using the body as evidence of crime. Crossland, "Of Clues and Signs: The Dead Body and Its Evidential Trace," *American Anthropologist* 111.1 (2009): 69–80.

12 Interestingly, William James compares the feats of a clairvoyant woman to this new science. In "A Case of Clairvoyance," James observes that one woman's ability to describe the complex chain of events that culminated in a woman drowning, including the specific location of the rubber boot that allowed a diver to retrieve the body, would be "almost as great a mental miracle" had she reconstructed the events on the basis of her observations of physical clues – but this is exactly what forensic scientists were promising (James, 1907/1986: 241).

13 For a full account of the Dreyfus Affair as well as Bertillon's role in it, see Read (2012).

14 *Un assassin laisse toujours des traces "quelque part"....*

15 *Cette empreinte ne concorde pas trop avec celles de la main gauche.... Quelles sont les precautions que l'assassin a bien pu prendre?*

16 See Lee's account of how Wharton's position on the Dreyfus Affair put her at odds with close friend Paul Bourget (2007: 271–72).

## Bibliography

"Anthropometry," *The Law Times*, Chicago (September 23, 1893): 455.

Alphonse Bertillon, *La Photographie Judiciaire, avec un Appendice. Sur la Classification et l'Identification Anthrométrique.* (Paris: Gauthier-Villars et Fils, 1890).

Alphonse Bertillon, *Legal Photography*, trans. Paul R. Brown (New York, 1897).

"Crime and Its Detection," *Daily Inter Ocean*, (March 31, 1874): 4.

Terence Davies, "Production Notes for *The House of Mirth*" (New York: Sony Pictures Classics, 2000).

Jacques Derrida, "On Reading Heidegger: An Outline of Remarks to the Essex Colloquium," *Research in Phenomenology*, 17 (1987): 171–188.

"Detection of Crime by Photography," *Albany Law Journal* (December 30, 1893): 2.

"Finger Prints [sic] in Police Work," *Baltimore American* (July 10, 1905): 15.

Raymond B. Fosdick, *European Police Systems* (New York: Century Company, 1915).

Hans Gross, *Criminal Investigations: A Practical Handbook for Magistrates, Police, Officers, and Lawyers*, trans. John Adam and J. Collyer Adam (Madras: A. Krishnamachari, 1906).

Mark Haworth-Booth, "A Camera Eye as Rare as a Pink Zebra," *Police Pictures: The Photograph as Evidence* (San Francisco: San Francisco Museum of Modern Art, 1997): 33–39.

"Horrible Triple Murder in Paris: Portraits of the Three Women (from Photographs)." *Illustrated Police News*, 23 (Apr 1887): 3.

John Horswell, *Practice of Crime Scene Investigation* (New York: Taylor and Francis, 2004).

William James, "A Case of Clairvoyance," *Essays in Psychical Research* (Cambridge: Harvard University Press, 1907/1986): 231–245.

Paul Kirk, *Crime Investigation: Physical Evidence and the Police* (New York: Interscience Publishers, 1953).

Hermione Lee, *Edith Wharton* (New York: Knopf, 2007).

Michael Leyton, *Symmetry, Causality, Mind* (Cambridge: MIT Press, 1992).

Edmond Locard, *L'Enquete Criminelle et les Methods Scientifiques* (Paris: Ernest Flammarion, 1920).

Mara-Stream, "Forensic Architecture 2009–2010." http://www.marastream.org/research/forensicarchitecture (accessed January 2014).

Mary Marchand, "Object Lessons: Wharton's *The Custom of the Country* and the New Connoisseurship," *Edith Wharton* Review, 27, 1 (2011): 1–10.

Jennifer Mnookin, "The Image of Truth: Photograph Evidence and the Power of Analogy," *Yale Journal of Law and the Humanities*, 10, 1 (1998): 1–74.

Leroy Panek, *The Origins of the American Detective Story* (New York: McFarland, 2006).

Piers Paul Read, *The Dreyfus Affair: The Scandal that Tore France in Two* (New York: Bloomsbury Press, 2012).

Luc Sante, *Evidence* (New York: Farrar, Strauss and Giroux, 1992).

"Science and Mystery," *New York Times* (August 26, 1899): 1.

Greg Siegel, "The Similitude of the Wound," *Cabinet*, 43 (Fall 2011): 95–100.

Linda Steer, "Surreal Encounters: Science, Surrealism and the Re-Circulation of a Crime-scene Photograph," *History of Photography*, 32, 2 (2008): 110–122.

Louis Tomellini, *Metric Photography: Bertillon System* (Lyon: A. Rey, 1908).

Claire Valier, "True Crime Stories: Scientific Methods of Investigation, Criminology, and Historiography," *British Journal of Criminology*, 38, 1 (1998): 88–105.

Tim Thompson, "The Role of the Photograph in the Application of Forensic Anthropology and the Interpretation of Clandestine Scenes of Crime," *Photography and Culture*, 1, 2 (2008): 165–184.

Eyal Weizman, "Forensic Architecture: Only the Criminal Can Solve the Crime," *Radical Philosophy*, 164 (2010): 9–24.

Edith Wharton, *The House of Mirth* (New York: Penguin, 1905/1985).

Edith Wharton, *A Backward Glance* (New York: Library of America, 1934/1990).

Peter Wollen, "Vectors of Melancholy," in *Scene of the Crime*, ed. Ralph Rugoff (Cambridge: MIT Press, 1997): 23–36.

Bret Wood, "Photo Mortis: Resurrecting Photographs of Crime and Death," *Art Papers*, 24, 2 (2002): 18–23.

# Structuring Desire in Thomas Eakins's Painting and Photography

Rasmus R. Simonsen

For most of the 19th century, male nudes were frequently and without impropriety used as models in the French art world. Up until 1863, Susan Waller points out, "for reasons of propriety and ideology, only male models posed nude in the École des Beaux-Arts" (2002: 41). Different kinds of models, with different kinds of bodies, were used to fit the artist's particular purpose. Thomas Eakins, a dedicated anatomist, and influenced by the French scene, swore by the practice of using nude male models, even though it didn't translate well to the moral context of 19th-century America.

Eakins spent three-and-a-half years in Paris, from 1866 to 1870, studying with some of the foremost French artists of the century. In fact, the main inspiration for his most famous painting, *The Swimming Hole* (1885), or simply *Swimming* (pl. 7), can be traced to Frederic Bazille's *Summer Scene* (1869), which Eakins most likely saw in 1870 (Brettell, 1996: 83). During his time in France, Eakins studied with another famous artist, Léon Bonnat, who became known as the "'official' painter of republican France" after having in 1877 painted a portrait of Adolphe Thiers, the first president of the Third Republic (Milroy, 1987: 94, 93). Eakins's admiration for Bonnat stemmed from the French artist's masterful grasp of anatomical forms. Bonnat's drawing from 1876, *Jacob Wrestling with the Angel* (fig. 4.1), resonates in Eakins's *Wrestlers* (fig. 4.2), his last study of the male nude form, completed in 1899.

*Wrestlers* came into existence on the cusp of a new, confusing century and concurrent with, or just after, the "invention" of the twin categories of homosexuality and heterosexuality. This new system of classification attempted to solidify former merely obscure or "odd" acts and behaviors into distinct and quantifiable categories.[1] The fact that Eakins completed his last painting of this kind at this time is therefore significant. Peter Coviello has identified in the literature of the late-19th century a sense of "rupture" from the "presexological past" and the emergence of a

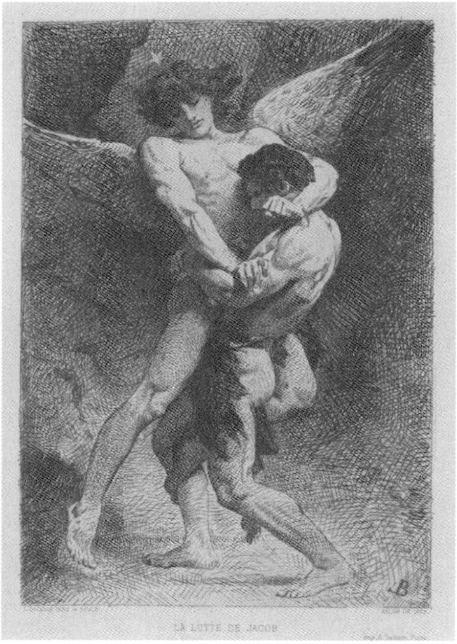

Fig. 4.1. Léon Bonnat, *La Lutte de Jacob* [*Jacob Wrestling with the Angel*], 1876. Drypoint in black on laid paper, 26.3 × 16.9 cm (10 3/8 × 6 5/8 in). National Gallery of Art. Courtesy of the René Huyghe Collection. 1994.42.3. Open Access.

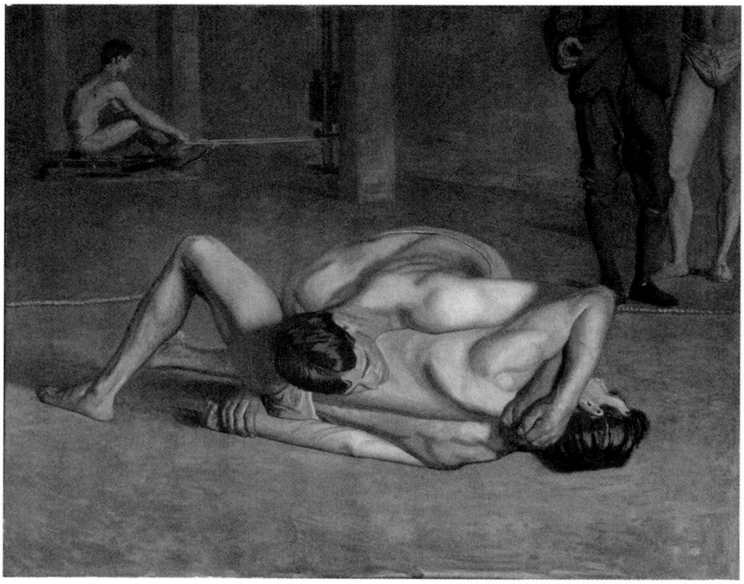

Fig. 4.2. Thomas Eakins, *Wrestlers*, 1899. Oil on canvas, 122.87 × 152.4 cm (48 3/8 × 60 in). Los Angeles County Museum of Art, Gift of Cecile C. Bartman and The Cecile and Fred Bartman Foundation. M.2007.1.

new perspective on male intimacy (2013: 3) – one that would spread to all art forms. Bonnat's drawing of Jacob and the angel can be read, in a sense, as the representation of this epistemological rift. The drawing depicts a muscular, bearded Jacob tightly embracing the male form of the angel, whose face and locks are otherwise clearly feminine. The angel is barely resisting Jacob, and he appears almost listless. His downcast eyes signal erotic passivity. The homoeroticism, if not the *homosexuality*, of the drawing is unmistakable.

Inspired by his European mentors, Eakins would insist on using nude models in his American work and teaching, which would become a major source of controversy. In 1886, Eakins removed the loincloth of a male model in front of a mixed-gender class of art students, and his disregard for American sensibilities was finally what led to his dismissal from the Academy of Fine Arts in Philadelphia. Those familiar with Eakins's paintings can attest to his intense and uncompromising interest in the naked human form. Prior to his dismissal, Eakins explored and extensively documented nude subjects. His interest was scientific as well as cultural – and extended to his photographic work. In fact, about 800 nude photographs have been attributed to him (Rosenheim, 1994: 45). In his discussion of Eakins's photo nudes, Jeff Rosenheim cites eight enlarged platinum prints that were donated to the Metropolitan Museum of Art in 1943. Two of these depict females; six, males. As Rosenheim notes, the male nudes are warmer in tone and about four times the size of his female subjects (1994: 47). Of central significance in this series is the portrait of Eakins and his student, J. Laurie Wallace (fig. 4.3), for what it reveals to us about the aesthetics of interaction between male nudes, visual rhetoric, and desire, both in Eakins's painting and photography.

In the introduction to this book, Geoff Bender and I point out that a photograph, or indeed any other visual kind of work, is considered intermedial when it "translates other media into its own terms and transitions visual content from one context to another." The question is not, thus, how "a photograph is composed, but instead [... what] work it performs once [it's] manifest in the world." In relation to Eakins, precisely, intermediality, as I will show, comes into play, first and foremost, as he translates the anatomical forms of his European precursors into a particularly American context. Subsequently, I will demonstrate how what Bruno Latour has called "a network of attachments" (1999: 27) is established through how male bodies "travel" between Eakins's photographic work and his paintings, the primary example of which is *Swimming*.

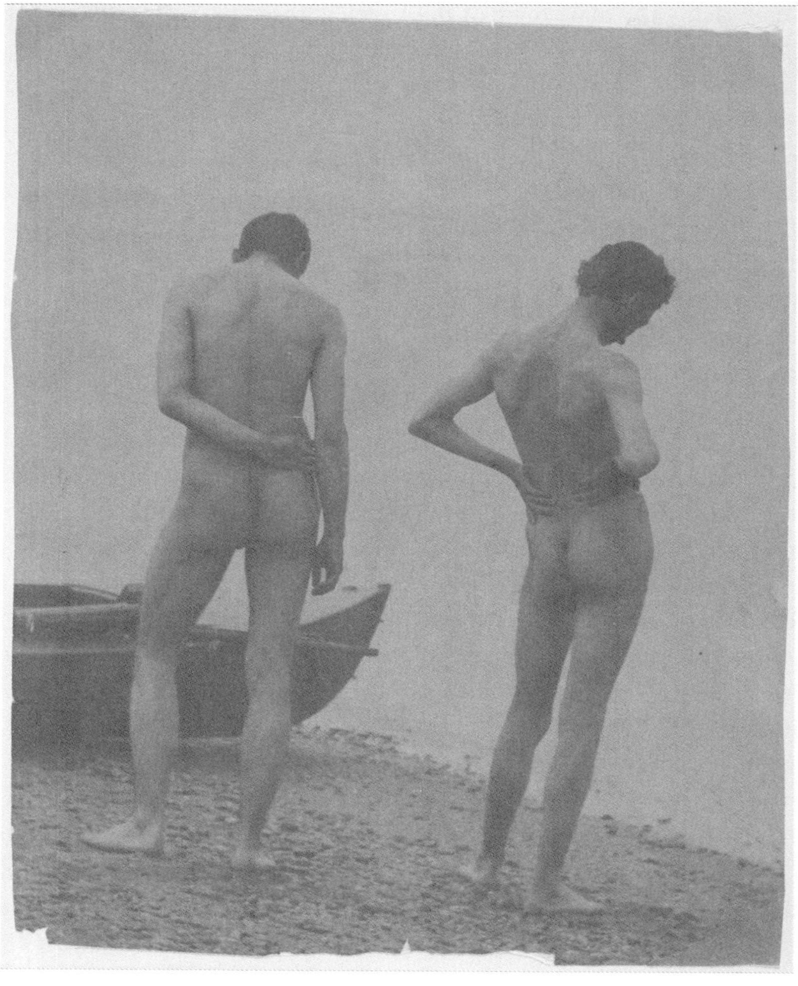

Fig 4.3. Unknown Photographer, *Thomas Eakins and John Laurie Wallace on a Beach*, c. 1883. Platinum print, 25.5 × 20.4 cm (10 1/16 × 8 1/16 in). The Metropolitan Museum of Art. Courtesy of the David Hunter McAlpin Fund, 1943. 43.87.23. Public Domain.

## Mediating Eakins's Desire

Despite his apparent disregard for institutional morality, Eakins wasn't blind to national anxieties regarding gender and sexuality. In the final composition of his *Swimming* painting (pl. 7) he was careful to position his figures to conceal all hints of genitalia and pubic hair. In a sense, he needn't have bothered, though, as it seems to have made everyone at the unveiling in October of 1885 uncomfortable enough as it was. The nude males in *Swimming* fall between the so-called "physical-culture movement" – which sought to turn young men into athleticized figures, emphasizing broad shoulders and chests but also round firm behinds (Davis, 1994: 315)[2] – and "academic classicism" (314), rooted in his French anatomical training. He also included unambiguous photographs alongside the painting (Lehne, 2007: 88). The silence surrounding the unveiling is significant, as Eakins was the director of the academy at the time; add to this that it had been commissioned by a trustee of the academy, Edward Coates (Kirkpatrick, 2006: 281), and the absence of commentary becomes the more conspicuous still. The most contemporary critics could muster in print was that it exhibited an "interesting subject matter," or that it was 'not agreeable." One critic disliked the background rendering but said nothing about the foreground subjects (Kirkpatrick, 2006: 292).

Since the 1885 unveiling, the painting has of course become central to speculations about Eakins's sexual leanings. In his essay, "The Question of the Homoerotic in Thomas Eakins' *The Swimming Hole*," Josh Lehne uses Eakins's well-known friendship with Walt Whitman and Whitney Davis's psychoanalytic interpretation of Eakins's visual structures to make a case for Eakins's evident but unacknowledged homosexuality (2007: 88–89). Davis's analysis, since it is steadfastly Freudian in scope, constructs a "psychoanalytic 'history'" of *Swimming*, in which he "personalizes" the photographic "events" that came to serve as studies for the composition of the painting (Davis, 1994: 322). Lehne concludes that the question of desire in *Swimming* remains vexing to scholars since "there is something unexplainable beneath the surface of the artist's work" (2007: 93). Towards the end of this chapter, I will return to Davis's reading of *Swimming* to show how a too-narrow psychoanalytic approach misses some of the nuances of desire in Eakins's representation.

The unexplainable quality of *Swimming* that Lehne calls attention to would suggest that the question of Eakins's sexuality should not be reduced to one of biography. Jennifer Doyle has shown how difficult, and, not to say, unproductive, it is to view Eakins's work according to his own sexual preferences. She notes that most of the sex scandals that dogged him revolved around women (1999: 7). Even if attempts to read Eakins, the man and the artist, through a contemporary gay lens would fail – due either to the fact that "the diacritical axis homo/hetero was neither a compelling nor a reliable means for describing [the] community or [the] emotional and libidinal affiliations" of 19th-century American queer figures, or to the fact that "Eakins's life is by no means legible as a gay one by today's definition" – his oeuvre is "shot through with a queerness that is immediately relevant to gay audiences" (Doyle, 1999: 7). Although it is not clear that the audience's own sexual identity is essential to recognizing Eakins's queerness, I would like to affirm Doyle's claim that "it is entirely possible to place Eakins and *Swimming*, for instance, near the beginning of a homoerotic (and even homosexual) visual tradition in American art" (1999: 7). Interestingly, Doyle goes on to link Eakins with later American queer artists such as Robert Mapplethorpe and Andy Warhol, explicitly connecting the latter's "spirit of play," as evinced in his film and photography, to Eakins's habit of photographing his students, nude and at play (1999: 8). Like Doyle, I am not going to worry about the "gayness" of Eakins' work; instead, I follow her, and other scholars – particularly Michael Hatt – in paying particular attention to what it meant to have a (masculine) body at the end of the 19th century, particularly as it was mediated by a photographic technology that constructed it, formally, for remediation in painting.

To arrive at my reading of masculine eroticism in Eakins's painting and photography, I will focus on how his intermedial practice can be understood according to what Latour has called a 'network of attachments" (1999: 27). In the context of media studies, the notion of attachments should be understood in relation to the fact that all media in a sense remediate "the techniques, forms, and social significance of other media." There is thus no such thing as an isolated medium "because it must enter into relationships of respect and rivalry with other media" (Bolter and Grusin, 1999: 65). These relationships, consequently, make up the intermedial network that ties different works and media forms together. We have already seen how Eakins's choice to depict nude males disrupted audience expectations of what American art should work towards in terms of "social significance" and proper aesthetic references. Although it is important to trace the intermedial relationships between Eakins and European artists such as Bazille and Bonnat (but also Caravaggio, as will become clear later), the main intermedial attachment I uncover in relation to Eakins appears on a more intimate level than what Bolter and Grusin have in mind, considering the context of their sweeping analysis of new digital media in the late 20th century. Primarily, I analyze the relationship between the Eakins/Wallace photograph and *Swimming* and the intermediality that the two works activate, initially, by the material connection between the bodies and locales they depict. The posture of Wallace in the photograph and that of the central nude in *Swimming* are near identical. As will become clear, it is this doubling effect, the ghostly reappearance of one form in another medium that brings about the intermedial spark of desire in Eakins's work.

The network of attachments that I will identify and analyze in this chapter is made up of distinct aesthetic forms and media phenomena, then, the connections of which are contingent on the lines of desire that emanate from Eakins's work. Although Latour's domain is (primarily) sociology, Rita Felski has made a persuasive claim for applying Latourian theory to the world of art. Latour can thus help us examine how "[w]orks of art invite and incite us, in ways that we do not always expect and may not be able to predict," with the stated aim of understanding "what spurs us to pick up a book or to become engrossed in a film" (Felski, 2015: 739) – or, indeed, to feel connected to a photograph or a painting. In a 1999 essay titled "Factures/Fractures: From the Concept of Network to the Concept of Attachment," Latour expands his concept of network to explicitly include a discussion of the role of aesthetics. The very root of Latour's understanding of network, in fact, is aesthetic, since, as he puts it elsewhere, "modern societies cannot be described without recognizing them as having a fibrous, thread-like, wiry, stringy, ropy, capillary character that is never captured by the notions of levels, layers, territories, spheres, categories, structure, systems" (Latour, 1996: 370).

Following this understanding of the social – which, etymologically, means "'someone following someone else,' a 'follower,' an 'associate'" (Latour, 2005: 108) – it becomes a matter of discovering what or whom we become attached to and how: "all setting-in-motion depends on the nature of attachments and their recognized capacity to render existent or nonexistent those subjects to which they are attached" (Latour, 1999: 4). Attachments can be defined by what we become "sensitive" to over time (Latour, 1999: 24). For instance, our sensitivity to a sonata by Bach or a painting by Eakins will compel us towards certain actions. Actions, in turn, are motivated by aesthetics: the smoothness of the marble sculpture invites my touch; the sfumato effect of the painting captures my gaze in the soft region between light and dark. For an attachment to become productive, the subject's sensitivity to a work of art should not be reduced to a passive state of pure absorption. The aesthetic force involved in what the artwork makes us do, we subsequently relay, in a "transfer of efficacy" (Latour, 1999: 26), to another point in the network of attachments that has preceded and may also supersede our moment of appreciation. Any network, then, is only "worth" as much as its relations.

In relation to Eakins, the network that I am striving to develop borrows from the concept of "chronography," coined by Etienne-Jules Marey – a French physiologist who was responsible for several innovations in shutter photography (Hillier, 2007: 28) – to indicate how desire is written, or "exposed," over time. Marey was concerned with inventing a single-lens camera with the ability to capture a sequence of images on one plate, a feat he achieved by 1882 (Hillier, 2007: 29), which would inspire Eakins's experiments with motion photography later in the decade. In contrast with Marey's techno-scientific approach, I am not interested in strict sequentiality. Networks are not sequential in nature, after all, which is not to say that temporality is not of importance; attachments take time to develop, but they may also become weaker or stronger according to different factors. In his scientific motion studies, Eakins used markers and measurements to record the precise mathematical intervals of how bodies move through time (Hillier, 2007: 32), but whereas his photographic research projects were ostensibly objectivist and linear, the lines of desire that can be traced in his work are not. I hope, therefore, to show how different attractions in Eakins's work come into focus at different points, and in different media, over the course of his career with the aim, finally, to establish a queer network of attachments that equally implicates artist, subject, media, context, and (not least of all) viewer. The importance of considering Eakins's work according to the concept of intermediality will thus become clear, as it refers to photographs, and other visual forms, as "heterogenous object[s] that acquire[] [their] meaning through various interactions and encounters with other media within a particular spatial, social, and institutional context" (Pirenne and Streiberger, 2013: ix).

## Latour with Lacan: Desire and Network Thinking

Beyond the synchronicity involved in strictly chronographic single compositions, I argue that it is the metonymic spark of desire between compositions that reveals the sexual drive of Eakins's work – that which allows for what Latour calls "*traceable associations*" (2005: 108; emphasis original) to come into view, whereby the viewer becomes embroiled in a potential attachment or eroticism out of time. In his contribution to this book, David LaRocca asks, "*When* is a photograph?" I would answer this by saying it begins when a line of desire is created between photographic object and viewer. In psychoanalysis, desire is understood as the dynamic between the verb *eingeschoben* (in the present perfect), when something has slid into view, and the noun *Verschiebung*, which means "shift" or "postponement," but which is commonly translated as displacement (Lacan, 2015: 102). Desire always takes an object, which must remain out of reach for the subject, however. As Jacques Lacan puts it, "The object [of desire] as something that, in its essential function, steals away at the level of our grasp is being pointed out there as such" (2015: 102). Lacan builds on Freud's theory of displacement [*Verschiebung*], which seeks to explain the link between unconscious impulses and conscious objects of attention. Freud explicates this link in *Totem and Taboo*:

> An unconscious impulse need not have arisen at the point where it makes its appearance; it may arise from some quite other region and have applied originally to quite other persons and connections; it may have reached the place at which it attracts our attention through the mechanism of "displacement." (2001: 82)

Importantly, the translation an object undergoes as a result of displacement renders it inherently strange. The revealed object is linked to a whole (unconscious) network of objects, which is organized by the desire of the viewer. Commenting on the Lacanian theory of objectivity, Clayton Crockett points out that there is an unconscious "trait that connects us to the object, and this trait goes from the object to us and distorts our perception and understanding in powerful ways" (2018: 88).[3] Every object we form an attachment to thus mediates a greater point of desire located elsewhere (in Freudian psychoanalysis, the mother's breast is the original object of desire), and this is what makes objects strange; they are secondary mediators that can never fulfill us as such, even as they hint at something more beneath the surface.

At first glance, connecting psychoanalysis with Latourian network theory might seem odd at best and incongruous at worst. A commonsense division would categorize psychoanalysis as a science of the *inside* – the formation of the ego, the unconscious, the drives – whereas network theory concerns the *outside* – relations forming between human and nonhuman actors. Latour and Geoff Bowker, in the essay, "A Booming Discipline Short of Discipline" – the aim of which is to define the field of "social studies science" in France in the late 1980s – have written somewhat contemptuously that Lacan marks "the origin of the trend in France to see all life as swimming in a sea of textuality" (1987: 729). Nevertheless, even though they seem to disregard that, for Lacan, not "all was discourse" (1987: 729),[4] Latour and Bowker, in what they allow might be a "caricature" of Lacan, are savvy not to reduce discourse to the interiority of "the individual, for language is social" (1987: 729). In this manner, Latour and Bowker, however inadvertently, are developing a potential interdisciplinary connection between psychoanalysis and network theory, in so far as both are inherently "social" sciences.

What makes both psychoanalysis and Latourian network thinking social is that what compels the subject to act depends on the connections it is prompted to enter into by forces outside the self. For Lacan, encounters in the exterior world of relations – "first in the guise of the mirror stage...and later yet in the shape of a whole range of cultural representations" (Silverman, 1999: 56) – are internalized by the subject, who, in this way, becomes dependent on a networked environment of objects and other subjects. In *Reassembling the Social*, Latour asks if we "[s]hould...focus on the micro-level of interactions or [if we] should...consider the macro-level as more relevant?" (2005: 28). In the 1999 essay "Factures/Fractures," he chooses the micro-level, which consists of a 'network of attachments" (Latour, 1999: 31). This essay is crucial to the entire argument I am making in this chapter, as Latour, here, moves from thinking about networks as overarching systems that distribute forces between nodes to how individuals are made to act. The reason for this move is that to truly "understand the activity of subjects, their emotions, their passions, we must turn our attention to that which attaches and activates them" (1999: 27), allowing us to home in on all the "assistants, intermediaries, mediators" (1999: 25) that make us act in different ways. In relation to Eakins, the photographed nude body of his student, Wallace, in this way "assists" the viewer in forming a stronger attachment to the composition of *Swimming*.

Being neither in control of, nor controlled by, our attachments, we are "positioned to pursue a chain of mediators, each not being the exact cause of the next, but instead, each enabling the next to become, in turn, the originator of action" (Latour, 1999: 26). Latour, then, is not so much interested in subjects and objects, but rather in what he calls the "make-make" – the anglicization of the French *faire-faire*, the duality of which he captures as "to make one do" and "causing to be done" (1999: 29, 26). Latour argues: "The distinction between objects and subjects is not primordial, it does not designate different domains in the world: it is rooted in the fracture of action" (1999: 26). In Lacanian psychoanalysis, that distinction isn't primordial either; rather, the subject/object split doesn't occur until the mirror stage, or what Lacan also calls "the institution of the subject in the visible" (1998: 106). The outcome of this process is that "we purchase our social subjectivity at the price of narcissistic injury in the sense that we become culturally intelligible beings only insofar as we learn to love ourselves a bit less" (Ruti, 2010: 356). For Latour, in a similar way, the subject is marginalized to the extent that what matters finally is the outcome of our interactions with other subjects and objects; to become a social being is to become associated with others – be they persons or aesthetic agents like paintings and photographs.

To understand how the social process underpinning Latour's network of attachments works, we can turn to Lacan's definition of desire, which he refers to as "the metonymy of being" (2019: 23). Metonymy here refers to the fact that the subject is prompted to form attachments to a never-ending stream of displaced objects that stand in for a part of ourselves that is missing, even if we can't articulate what that part consists of (the missing part resides in the past, in fact, and we are continually looking for something that might make us feel as whole as before the self/other split occurred). It should be noted, however, that since we have obtained "social subjectivity," we tend to look for what is missing in or through what we think others want. As Slavoj Zizek puts it, the question is never "'What do I want?' but 'What do *others* want from me? What do they see in me? What am I for those others?'" (2007: 49); desire is clearly a social concept in psychoanalysis. To Latour, we might ask, what would prompt our "pursuit" in the first place if not desire for some new form of attachment? As with the Lacanian understanding, Latourian desire is social as well. However, Latour is not concerned with any kind of constitutive lack motivating the subject to seek out attachments; for him, although he doesn't tend to use it as a concept, desire seems simply to appear in the moment of mediation, when an action clarifies an attachment. Latour uses the example of smoking a cigarette as a key example in this regard: Cigarettes have a hold over the smoker; the smoker is effectively "smoked by [the] cigarette" (1999: 27). But instead of seeing this as a fundamental loss of control, Latour puts a more positive spin on addiction: The smoker is "attached to it [the cigarette], and if [s/he] cannot hope for any kind of emancipation from it, then perhaps other attachments will come to substitute for this one" (1999: 27). In an effort to quit smoking, it might be that the subject becomes attached to chocolate instead and then, perhaps, hypnosis, before becoming attached to yoga...and so on. What made the smoker take up smoking in the first places is much less interesting to Latour than what it makes him *do* henceforth.

For Lacan, as we have seen, the metonymy of being is set in motion by the self/other split incurred in the mirror stage. However, whether the engine of desire is run by some original bifurcation of the subject (Lacan) or the social itself (Latour), it seems clear that for both Lacan and Latour desire is marked by a logic of metonymy, as we attach to different others and objects based on how they make us feel and act; additionally, as we are always being acted on by, and prompted to respond in some way to, our surroundings, for Latour, "we cannot move from a state of attachment to that of unattachment" (1999: 27). For the self, as he puts it bluntly in *An Inquiry into Modes of Existence*, to "remain the same," one has to "pass" through "others" (2013: 41), meaning that when we engage with others we are always transformed in some way; that is the definition of being social for Latour. Interestingly, the notion of passing is also integral to the psychoanalytic concept of displacement, which is beholden to the German *eingeschoben*, where an object "passes through somewhere" (Lacan, 2015: 102). Whether in relation to a subject or an object, the concept of *passing through* prepares the way for "a relation that does not transport causality but induces two mediators into coexisting" (Latour, 2005: 108), enabling each other to act within the same field. What I am proposing here is that we do just that with regard to Latour and Lacan: establish a passage between them, to make them coexist. This coexistence – this *sliding* into view of one another – as I have been suggesting, is made possible on the basis of desire.

The conception of desire that I will follow for the remainder of this chapter is neither strictly Lacanian nor strictly Latourian, then. If, for Lacan, the objective and the subjective, however dialectically intimate, remain distinctive categories, for Latour, as all comes back to a question of action; in some sense, anything like a "material objective" or a "subjective symbolic" register is disregarded (2005: 107).[5] I retain the distinction between subject and object, but I allow that each can become a mediator in the metonymy of associations that forms the network.

An example from Roland Barthes's seminal text on photography, *Camera Lucida*, can help illustrate how a network of linked visual objects – a network of attachments – is established by desire. When Barthes found himself gazing upon a photo of Napoleon's younger brother, Jerome, taken in 1852, he was struck by an epiphany: "I am looking at eyes that looked at the emperor" (1981: 3). What has been captured by Jerome's eyes captivates Barthes in turn. The spectator's apparent object of desire may reveal itself to be linked to a non-apparent (both in terms of visibility and understanding) origin, which has been displaced onto the physical photograph; in Barthes's case, the origin is Napoleon's sovereign gaze. As Lacan puts it, "*what I look at is never what I wish to see*" (1998: 103; emphasis original). But does what I look at wish to see me? There is no sense, in Lacan, that objects can be captivated by the subject. However, we become attached to visual objects when they "solicit" (1998: 96) our attention through what Lacan calls the "gaze."

Although Lacan speaks of the gaze as being on the side of the object, he means by gaze here the mysterious feeling of being looked at by some inanimate thing. So, for instance, "a beam of light, a glint in someone's eye, a reflection in someone's hair, a jewel which shines can represent a gaze which is not in you" (Quinet, 1995: 143–44). This nonhuman gaze can also make its presence known when we catch sight of something unusual or enigmatic, which at once attracts and unsettles us. It might even be this unsettling feeling that causes us to attach to the object in the first place, as it stands in for another, invisible object, or node, in a network of attachments. For Barthes, the pupil of Napoleon's brother came to stand in for the gaze of Napoleon himself, although missing from the photograph. The photographic object, thus, can mediate a relation outside of itself; it becomes a metonym of desire, in other words. Here we can rewrite Latour's "made to do" as "made to see," which puts us into contact with a succession of visual intermediaries, and this network is mutually constituted by both subjects and objects.

Part of what makes Eakins's *Swimming* so powerful owes to how the insistent nudeness of especially the central male is "oriented toward the viewer *in order* for him to see it," as opposed to how "a viewer *happens* to see" "a conventional Adamic nakedness" (Davis, 1994: 317; emphasis original). The buttocks of Eakins's nude are especially hypnotic, and later in this chapter I will come back to how the networked forms of visual attention in the painting function to fix our gaze to this particular point in the composition. What is mainly important to grasp in this regard is that what a photographic object or a painting makes us see is based on a certain powerful trait that moves us beyond the work itself, so that we, in a sense, become the intermediary that causes it to coexist with that of another work. I am specifically, of course, interested in how visual attachments operate in Eakins's work according to a queer desire. I will show, therefore, how different representations pass through and between each other to create moments of aesthetic coexistence. This coexistence depends on the degree of intermediality that links Eakins's photography with his painting.

## Aesthetic Influence and the Geometry of Desire

Critics have frequently attempted to either qualify or diminish the relationship between Eakins and his desire as mediated by his photographic practice, sometimes with the aim of distinguishing it from his artistic one. In his article, Paul Myron Hillier takes great pains to specify, over and over, that Eakins's "motion photographs were not a part of his artistic practice, but a part of his positivist, scientific worldview" (2007: 34). In relation to Eakins's use of nudes, Hillier writes that the nudes in his motion photographs can be distinguished clearly from his artistic practice, "where the nude spoke to the splendor of the human body, the presence of beauty in modern American life" (2007: 34). His motion photography, informed by scientific principles, then, uses "the human body as an object to be studied, as a material item that can be calculated scientifically" (2007: 34). Whatever Eakins's intention, the aesthetics of the images and their appreciation are of course not beholden to the dichotomy of science and art. Nevertheless, Hillier dismisses every study of Eakins's photography that attempts to establish a link between this practice and his painting on the level of desire. His main "proof" is that Eakins described his photographic subjects as "objects" (2007: 35), a moniker that apparently connotes unambiguous scientific intent. Hillier is obsessive on this point, but I call for a more flexible analytic that takes into account the fact that Eakins's eye for anatomy was in itself not singularly focused on one subject or output. As Hillier concedes, "Eakins himself did not articulate what scientific use and value he thought his motion photographs could provide" (2007: 35). What network-thinking allows us to do is to reconsider the notion that use value is all that connects a "doer" with an "object." In the place of teleological causality, *avec* Latour, we should rather pursue the chain of mediators that connects Eakins's outputs.

The photographic models for *Swimming* were assembled in several stages. In the summer of 1884, he took seven students, including Wallace – but excluding Jessie Godley, the inspiration for the central male figure[6] – on a trip to Dove Lake, which is located in the vicinity of Philadelphia (Berger, 2000: 92). Here, Eakins choreographed a number of photographs depicting the students in different kinds of physical activities. However, both Godley's pose and the diving male were based on photographs and modelling sessions undertaken back in Eakins's Philadelphia studio. In the final painting, Eakins himself appears in the lower right corner, slowly emerging from the water in profile, only his head and left shoulder showing above the water's surface – and he appears to be looking either at the dog or the men and boys gathered on the rocks.

Three triangles make up the body of the standing nude. The hand of his left arm is resting on his hip, thereby bending his arm at the elbow to create an arrow-like figure. Albeit angled differently, his right arm creates a similar geometrical shape. His legs are spread apart, simulating the shape of a fan, or a pyramid (fig.4.4). In *Caravaggio's Secrets*, Leo Bersani and Ulysse Dutoit specifically show how pyramidal figures represent desire. In their discussion of Caravaggio's *St. John the Baptist with a Ram* (fig. 4.5), which features the saint as a naked youth in close contact with a male animal, Bersani and Dutoit say of the composition of the main figure that he is "half-reclining with legs spread and the right arm extending away from us, as if protecting or concealing something" (1998: 79). The authors comment on the "fanlike structures in the painting" that are formed variously by "the ram's horns"

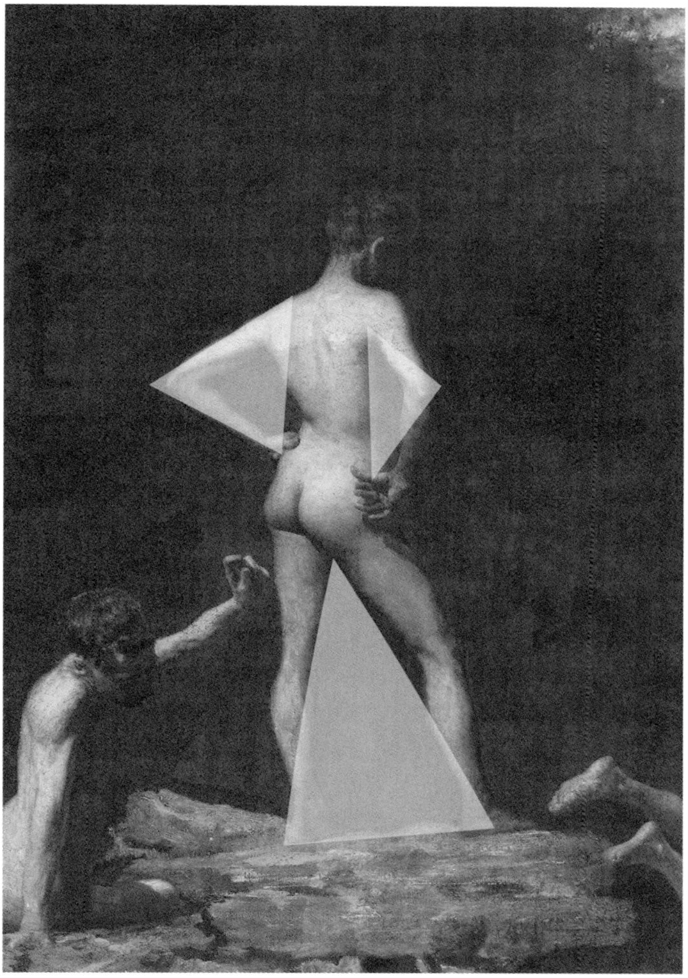

Fig. 4.4. Author's collage, showing the pyramidal shapes that make up the central nude of *Swimming*.

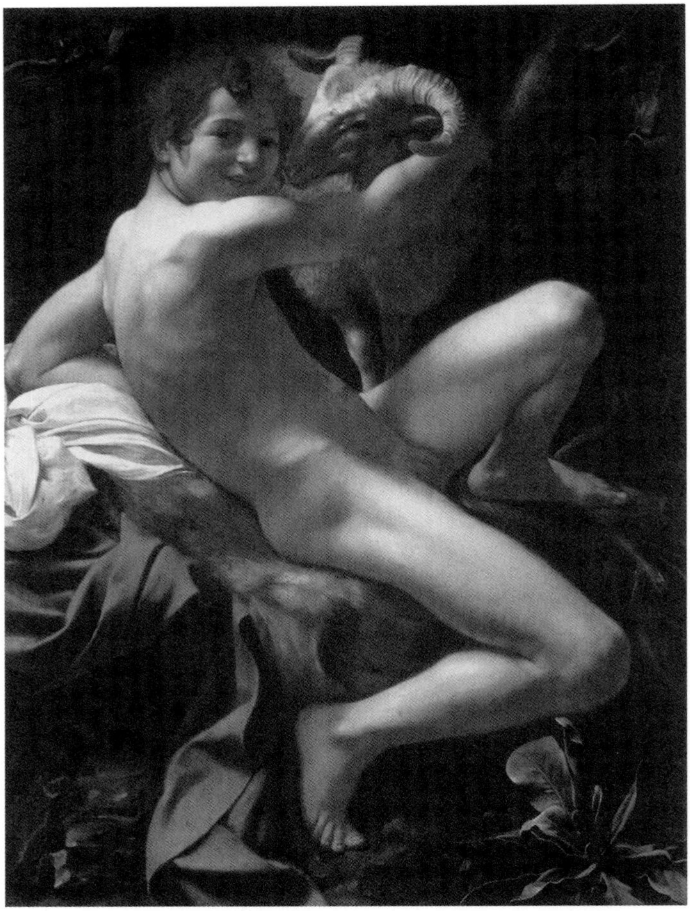

Fig. 4.5. Caravaggio, *St. John the Baptist with a* Ram, 1602–1603. Oil on canvas, 129 × 95 cm (50.8 × 37.4 in). On display at Musei Capitolini, Rome. Public Domain.

and "the boy's legs," and this has the effect of creating a tension between centrifugal repulsion and centripetal attraction (1998: 81). The fan created by the man's legs in *Swimming* introduces a similar relation between the viewer and the central part of the man's body, his buttocks. In this way, the Caravaggio painting introduces another aesthetic node in the network of attachments that is taking shape, and, in a certain sense, the pyramidal technique on display in *St. John* anticipates the network of desire that Eakins's establishes in *Swimming*. In fact, the homoerotics of Caravaggio's painting amplify the homoerotics of the Godley figure through patterned resemblance.

Pyramidal structures are prevalent in renaissance art, and this has offered critics a convenient way of reading Eakins's painting. In his seminal *American Renaissance*, F. O. Matthiessen says of the painting that, "The design is one of [Eakins's] most concentrated, and almost matches those of the Italian Renaissance in constructing a rhythmical pyramid" (1968: 610). Not surprisingly, then, a dominant triangle frames our viewing of *Swimming*. From the submerged Eakins in the lower right corner to the man "thigh-deep at the edge" of the rock formation, Matthiessen writes, "[t]he axis rises from the head of [the man spread out on the rock abutment] to the head of [the] standing figure," only to then carry the eye of the viewer, by way of the diving body, "back down into the water again" (1968: 610). Martin A. Berger calls this the "dominant compositional triangle" of the canvas – which the three triangular shapes of the central male nude are minor versions of – binding together the models (2000: 93). Eakins, relegated to the far-right corner of the canvas, himself an onlooker, diminishes the impact of his own masterly gaze.[7]

Whereas triangular patterns of the Italian Renaissance clearly contributed to the structuration and erotics of *Swimming*, arguably the most essential node in the network of attachments that lead to this painting is the photo of Eakins beside his student, Wallace. When examining the photographic portrait of Eakins and Wallace side-by-side with *Swimming*, the viewer cannot help but be struck by the power of interaction, across time and media, between Wallace in the former and the central nude in the latter (figs 4.6a & 4.6b). The portrait is from 1883, and production of *Swimming* began in 1884. In the painting, Wallace is kneeling on the rocks next to Godley, one arm raised. What is peculiar about the aforementioned portrait and *Swimming* is how similar Wallace, in the former, appears to Godley, in the latter. I want to draw attention here to the left arm in particular: the angles, lines, and musculature are almost identical; their gazes are also similarly down turned. However, the movement of each is different: In the photograph, Wallace's groin is thrust forward, whereas Godley, in *Swimming*, sticks his buttocks out to complete his pose of observation.

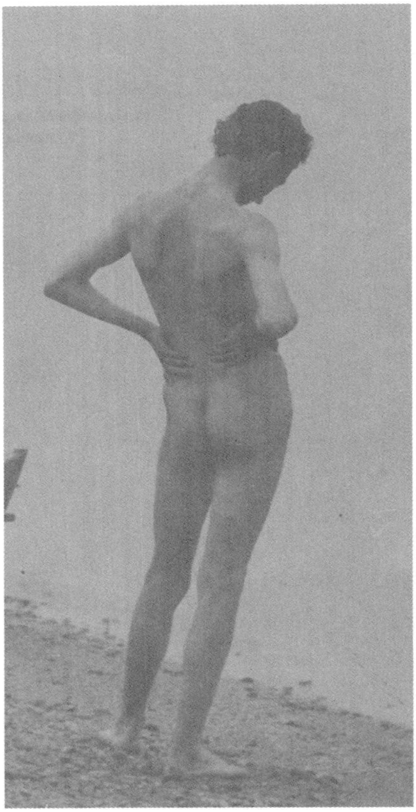

Fig. 4.6a. John Laurie Wallace (Unknown Photographer, *Thomas Eakins and John Laurie Wallace*, c. 1883, detail).

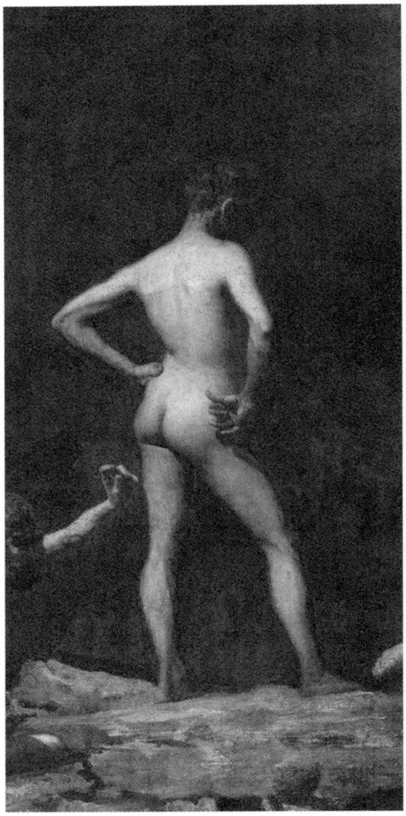

Fig. 4.6b. Jessie Godley (Thomas Eakins, *Swimming*, 1885, detail).

What we might call Eakins's object-oriented aesthetic finds its erotic pinnacle in *Swimming*, as Godley's buttocks assume central importance in this composition. Adams suggests that, "Buttocks are a major point of interest in Eakins's three most ambitious figure compositions: *The Gross Clinic*, *William Rush* (pl. 8), and *Swimming*" (2005: 306). However, the later sporting painting, *Salutat* (pl. 9), deserves to be added to this list. Buttocks, in this way, become a primary object form in the network of attachments that underpins the queer aesthetic of Eakins's work. Whether "attached" to a male or female subject, the gender of each pair of buttocks remains ambiguous. This ambiguity becomes clear when comparing the buttocks of *Salutat* with those of *Rush*; if anything, the male buttocks of *Salutat* are slightly fuller, as they are framed and emphasized by the jockstrap, which, to Michael Hatt, is what "leaves open the possibility of erotic delight" in the painting, making it "dangerous" in a late-19th-century setting (1993: 68).

Indeed, in *Swimming*, the standing man's face is completely shaded, and the most prominent part of his body is his buttocks, which, protruding left, are rendered slightly pink. As in the other two paintings that Adams mentions, in *Swimming*, "the sex of the naked figure is more than slightly ambiguous" (2005: 306). The sexual ambiguity of *Swimming* prompts Adams to state that "his painting seems to challenge the usual boundaries between the heterosexual, the homosocial, the homoerotic, and the homosexual. According to this view, we might suppose that Eakins's sexual identity was unstable, and open to reconstitution and revision" (2005: 310). But as Eakins seems to have been influenced in part by the physical-culture movement, which, in addition to a muscular physique, venerated full and firm buttocks (Davis, 1994: 315), the gender (if not the sex) of the male figure is rendered less ambiguous – thus amplifying the homoerotic quality of the painting.

In reality, the buttocks become a central actor in *Swimming*, as the centrifugal force of the painting stems from this very point, and it is what solicits our looking. Godley's buttocks positively radiate in *Swimming*, and this foregrounding of the lower part of the male body thus magnetizes as a central node in the network of queer attachments in Eakins. As Ruth E. Iskin puts it, "Light acts like a visual magnet" on the subject (1997: 57), and we have no control over when or whence a point of light might attract and, in turn, unsettle us. Once we are caught in a visual relation to an object, we start looking for what it says about us as subjects. However, a visual object, such as *Swimming*, does not reflect any kind of truth about the viewer; the point, instead, is that it leaves us wanting to see more, and as we grasp to locate the "beyond" of the painting – the place where our desire would intersect with Eakins's intention – we enter into a mediation between related visual objects. Specifically, the ontology of desire in Eakins is produced by the traversal of time, back and forth between two compositions: the 1883 photographic figure of Wallace and the 1885 painted figure of Godley.

As two frames of a moving picture, we can easily imagine the progression from Godley's protruding buttocks in *Swimming* to Wallace's thrust forward in the photograph with Eakins. This experiment of displaced chronography creates a visual unconscious connection between the two figures (fig. 4.7). We thereby encounter an intimacy between two different media – which are yet related in terms of Eakins's methodology – and two nude males, who nevertheless have almost the exact same dimensions. In this mash-up of compositions, Wallace appears both in a sitting position and as an active, central figure. Becoming actively involved in Eakins's compositions as spectator-*cum*-operator in this way allows for a more intimate appreciation and understanding of Eakins's sense of how one body can so deftly displace the one it mediates. The proximity between Wallace's and Godley's visual representations appears out of time, but, conceptually and affectively, these representations become intimate mediators of desire in the network of attachments that I am sketching in this chapter. The ghostly presence of Wallace's 1883 photographic form functions as the Lacanian trait in a network that forsakes temporal barriers to privilege a queer, intermedial space. As Raphaël Pirenne and Alexander Streitberger remind us, "intermediality occurs when a present medium takes recourse to an absent different medium" (2013: vii). The space between Wallace and Godley is thus magnetized by the metonymic spark of desire, which, in this intermedial way, compels the coexistence, if not copulation, of forms that translates the queerness of Eakins's work.

To get back to the original intent of this book, my inquiry has been focused on locating the real as the spatial attachment between two different bodies that nonetheless, as the outcome of an intermedial process of translation, merge into one creature, each representation being a synecdoche of the next or previous: a prototypical young, nude male of slim athletic build. The irony here is that the "spectra" of Wallace and Godley reach a higher degree of proximity in the comparative viewing of the earlier photograph and the later painting – separated by the chasm of time and physical media – than in the final image production of *Swimming*, where they are positioned side by side, one sitting, the other standing. In *Swimming*, Wallace and Godley do not interact, despite the fact that Wallace's hand is nearly touching Godley's thigh – not accounting for dimension.

The knowledge that Godley wasn't present for the sketching expedition to Dove Lake only renders the two figures more distant. Biographically, the affective

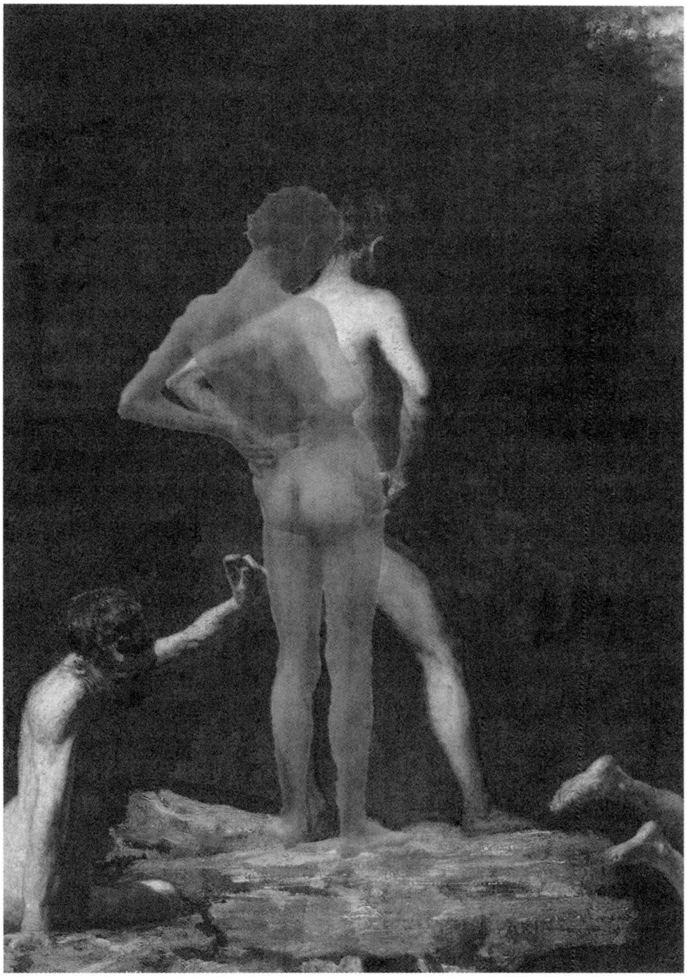

Fig. 4.7. Author's manipulation of *Swimming* and photographic portrait of Wallace. In *Swimming*, Wallace is sitting, arm raised, next to Godley's standing form.

distance is furthered by the fact that Wallace, but not Godley, sided with Eakins when he was fired from the Pennsylvania Academy of the Fine Arts. In fact, Godley took a stance against Eakins, and Adams gently hints that Godley's antagonism can be traced to some anxiety about how centrally Eakins featured his buttocks in *Swimming* (2005: 321). At only sixteen, with his "handsome physique and dark complexion" (Kirkpatrick, 2006: 253), Wallace had let Eakins, his senior by twenty years, strap him, in the nude, to a "massive cross" deep in the woods of New Jersey to model for *The Crucifixion*, completed in 1880 (fig. 4.8). Wallace also became one of three assistants that Eakins hired to photograph nude models every week for a period in 1883. The pictures became part of Eakins's so-called 'naked series" (Kirkpatrick, 2006: 273). That Eakins had a particular and enduring attachment to Wallace seems clear when examining their correspondence following Eakins's ouster from the Academy. In a letter dated June 26, 1886, Eakins addresses Wallace as "My dear Johnny" (Eakins, 1886), as was his custom. In that letter, he reports on the "infamous lies that were circulated" (Eakins, 1886) about him concerning, we must surmise, the different moral improprieties that had led to his forced resignation from the Academy in February of 1886 (Kirkpatrick, 2006: 313). But in the same letter, Eakins responds to Wallace's request to receive a sketch from him, and he returns to the topic of gifting his former student with "a little specimen of my work" in a later letter, dated January 12, 1887 (Eakins, 1887a). In a June 23, 1887, letter, he seems to have settled on a picture of a girl at a piano, finally. That letter begins with how "glad" Eakins is "to think of the pleasure I promise myself of seeing" Wallace in Chicago later in the summer (Eakins, 1887b). Unmistakably, Eakins was fond of Wallace, and the pleasure he takes in his company remains attached to his work as an artist, as evinced in his personal correspondence.

The ghostly displacement of Wallace with Godley that I have exposed in this chapter, then, intersects with the real-life attachment between Wallace and Eakins. The substitution of Wallace for Godley also signifies a wish to suture the rift between biography and representation. The distance by which we receive *Swimming* is greater still by virtue of the fact that it had passed through several media (sketches, photographs) before Eakins combines the images in the final composition. In other words, their ontologies only intersect by the force of the network of attachments that triggers the sensibility of the viewer. Our desire is inessential to Eakins's original intention, but the attachment we form to both images creates the opportunity for them to coexist. Furthermore, in *Swimming*, the line of sight between the sitting Wallace and Eakins, who is gliding through the water towards him, is rendered more significant by the ghostly appearance of Wallace's photographic form. The doubling

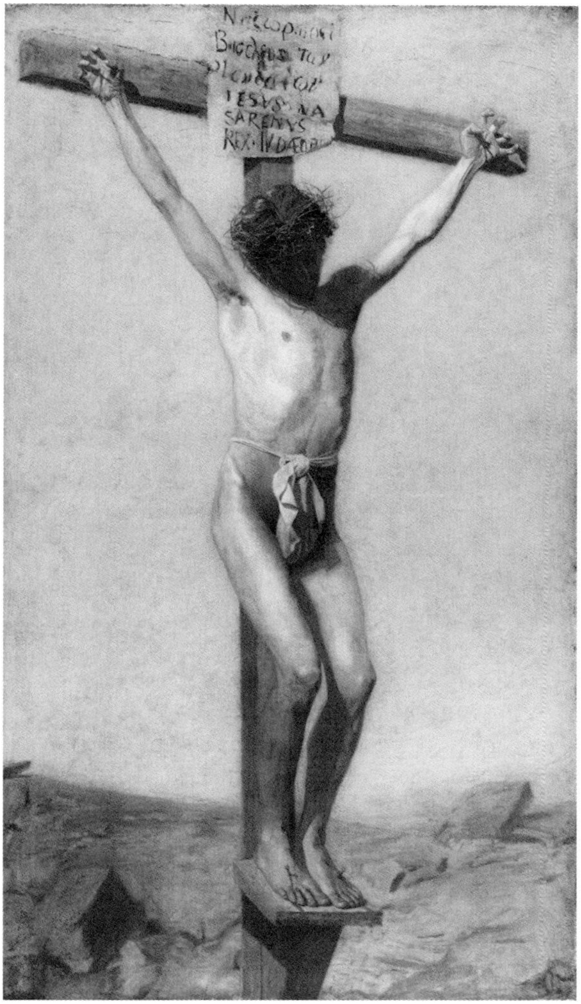


Fig. 4.8. Thomas Eakins, *The Crucifixion*, 1880. Oil on canvas, 243.8 × 137.2 cm (8 feet × 54 in). Philadelphia Museum of Art: Gift of Mrs. Thomas Eakins and Miss Mary Adeline Williams, 1929. 1929-184-24. Public Domain.

of Wallace also doubles the erotic energy of the painting, consequently making the "erotic delight" of the composition the more "dangerous," as Michael Hatt notes in relation to *Salutat* (1993: 68).

Whitney Davis ends his study of *Swimming* by suggesting that Eakins's gaze is trained on a "ghostly" reflection in the water, "about a foot away from his outstretched hands, where a slight perturbation, two circular strokes placed side by side, indicates where the diver's genitals are reflected" (1994: 332). This washed-out reflection – which becomes more clearly genital, apparently, "when the painting is turned upside down" (Davis, 1994: 332) – is the culminating point of Davis's Freudian reading, as it "restores...the homosexual relations of the swimming hole" (1994: 332). But his reading is limited by the idea that the queer gaze will always in the end center on "the penis of the most desirable boy" (1994: 332). However, Davis is right that *Swimming* is "not the 'end' nor resolution" of what he so poignantly, in regard to the aim of my chapter, calls "the *entire* network of revisions in transit" (1994: 332; emphasis original). Penis or buttocks? Repression or proliferation? The flexibility of what amounts to a psychoanalytic network theory means that we don't have to choose one or the other. The chain of mediation established between the two male nudes, Wallace and Godley, one photographed, the other caught in painting, allows us to share an intimate space with Eakins – one that elucidates, if not cements, his place in a queer visual American tradition.

## Notes

1 Important in this regard is, of course, Richard von Krafft-Ebing's work from 1886, *Psychopathia Sexualis*, but as Peter Coviello argues, drawing on Ed Cohen's *Talk on the Wilde Side*, Oscar Wilde's libel trial of 1895 is a more important event in the popular "solidification" of sexual identifies (2013: 3 and 207, note 3).

2 The idea, as Davis remarks, was to create a new class of young professional men. Aspiring to managerial positions and attending Ivy-League schools, the bodies of these men ought to be clearly distinguished from the "distorted bodies produced by manual labor" (1994: 315); to this end, colleges started athletic programs that would help the next generation of business leaders and lawyers mold themselves into the new ideal: "the torso of a Greek sculpture or a weightlifter's hefty frame, created on new machines devised to pack and puff a youth's 'lanky' or 'stringy' physique (hitherto associated with the sparseness of heroes like Lincoln) with new muscles" (1994: 315).

3 The primacy of the object in the Imaginary register of Lacan's theory of the subject prompts Crockett to suggest, boldly, that "[h]is psychoanalytic theory offers profound reflections on the nature of an object, which should inform these newer object-oriented realisms" He goes so far as to call Lacan "a theorist of OOO before the letter" (Crocket, 2018: 88).

4 The Imaginary and the Real registers were no less important to Lacan's thinking than the Symbolic (of course, Lacan's theory underwent different shifts between the registers over time).

5 In *Reassembling the Social*, Latour asserts that, "Social is nowhere in particular as a thing among other things but may circulate everywhere as a movement connecting non-social things" (2005: 107). Thus, for instance, "Scallops make the fisherman do things just as nets placed in the ocean lure the scallops into attaching themselves to the nets and just as data collectors bring together fishermen and scallops in oceanography" (Latour, 2005: 107).

6 Eakins photographed Godley for the painting on a separate trip to the boathouses at Bryn Mawr instead (Davis, 1994: 327).

7 Generally, Eakins was not too concerned with his own appearance, whether in real life or in representational form. In her essay "Ordering the Artist's Body: Thomas Eakins's Acts of Self-Portrayal," Sarah Burns examines a photographic portrait of the 24-year-old artist from ca. 1868. Eakins, almost handsome, is wearing a tattered vest, some buttons missing or broken, but this does not seem to bother the sitter, judging by the indifferent look on his face. The state of Eakins's attire combined with his defiant mien lead Burns to conclude, "Clothes, in his book, clearly did not (and never could) make the man" (2005: 84).

## Bibliography

Henry Adams, *Eakins Revealed: The Secret Life of an American Artist* (Oxford: Oxford University Press, 2005).

Roland Barthes, *Camera Lucida: Reflections on Photography*, trans. Richard Howard (New York: Hill and Wang, 1981).

Martin A. Berger, *Man Made: Thomas Eakins and the Construction of Gilded Age Manhood* (Berkeley: University of California Press, 2000).

Leo Bersani and Ulysse Dutoit, *Caravaggio's Secrets* (Cambridge, MA: MIT Press, 1998).

Geoff Bowker and Bruno Latour, "A Booming Discipline Short of Discipline: (Social) Studies of Science in France," *Social Studies of Science*, 1 (1987): 715–48.

Richard R. Brettell, "Thomas Eakins and the Male Nude in French Vanguard Painting, 1850–1890," in *Thomas Eakins and the Swimming Picture*, eds. Doreen Bolger and Sarah Cash (Fort Worth: Amon Carter Museum, 1996): 80–97.

Sarah Burns, "Ordering the Artist's Body: Thomas Eakins's Acts of Self-Portrayal," *American Art*, 19.1 (Spring 2005): 82–107.

Peter Coviello, *Tomorrow's Parties: Sex and the Untimely in Nineteenth-Century America* (New York: New York University Press, 2013).

Clayton Crockett, *Derrida after the End of Writing: Political Theology and New Materialism* (New York: Fordham University Press, 2018).

Whitney Davis, "Erotic Revision in Thomas Eakins's Narratives of Male Nudity," *Art History*, 17.3 (September 1994): 301–341.

Jennifer Doyle, "Sex, Scandal, and Thomas Eakins's *The Gross Clinic*," *Representations*, 68 (Autumn, 1999): 1–33.

Thomas Eakins, "Letter to John Laurie Wallace, June 26, 1886," *Thomas Eakins Letters,1866–1934*, Archives of American Art, Smithsonian Institution (1886) http://edan.si.edu/slideshow/viewer/?damspath=%2FCollectionsOnline%2Feakithom%2FBox_0001%2FFolder_005&keyword=-john (accessed September 10, 2020).

Thomas Eakins, "Letter to John Laurie Wallace, January 12, 1887," *Thomas Eakins Letters,1866–1934*, Archives of American Art, Smithsonian Institution (1887a), http://edan.si.edu/slideshow/viewer/?damspath=%2FCollectionsOnline%2Feakithom%2FBox_0001%2FFolder_005&keyword=john (accessed September 10, 2020).

Thomas Eakins, "Letter to John Laurie Wallace, June 23, 1887," *Thomas Eakins Letters,1866–1934*, Archives of American Art, Smithsonian Institution (1887b), http://edan.si.edu/slideshow/viewer/?damspath=%2FCollectionsOnline%2Feakithom%2FBox_0001%2FFolder_005&keyword=john (accessed September 10, 2020).

Rita Felski, "Latour and Literary Studies," *PMLA*, 130.3 (2015): 737–742.

Kathleen A. Foster, "The Making and Meaning of *Swimming*," in *Thomas Eakins and the Swimming Picture*, eds. Doreen Bolger and Sarah Cash (Fort Worth: Amon Carter Museum, 1996): 13–35.

Sigmund Freud, *Totem and Taboo: Some Points of Agreement between the Mental Lives of Savages and Neurotics*, trans. James Strachey (London: Routledge, 2001).

Michael Hatt, "Muscles, morals, mind: the male body in Thomas Eakins' *Salutat*," in *The Body Imaged: The Human Form and Visual Culture since the Renaissance*, eds. Kathleen Adler and Marcia Pointon (Cambridge: Cambridge University Press, 1993): 57–69.

Paul Myron Hillier, "Men and Horses in Motion: Thomas Eakins and Motion Photography," *Early Popular Visual Culture*, 5, 1 (2007): 25–40.

Ruth E. Iskin, "In the Light of Images and the Shadow of Technology: Lacan, Photography and Subjectivity," *Discourse*, 19, 3 (Spring 1997): 43–66.

Sidney D. Kirkpatrick, *The Revenge of Thomas Eakins* (New Haven: Yale University Press, 2006).

Jacques Lacan, *Anxiety: The Seminar of Jacques Lacan, Book X*, ed. Jacques-Alain Miller, trans. A. R. Price (Cambridge: Polity Press, 2015).

Jacques Lacan, *Desire and Its Interpretation: The Seminar of Jacques Lacan, Book VI*, ed. Jacques-Alain Miller, trans. Bruce Fink (Cambridge: Polity Press, 2019).

Jacques Lacan, *The Four Fundamental Concepts of Psychoanalysis: The Seminar of Jacques Lacan, Book XI*, ed. Jacques-Alain Miller, trans. Alan Sheridan (New York: W. W. Norton & Company, 1998).

Bruno Latour, "On Actor-Network Theory. A Few Clarifications Plus More than a Few Complications," *Soziale Welt*, 47 (1996): 369–381.

Bruno Latour, "Factures/Fractures: From the Concept of Network to the Concept of Attachment," *Res*, 36 (Autumn 1999): 20–31.

Bruno Latour, *Reassembling the Social: An Introduction to Actor-Network-Theory* (Oxford: Oxford University Press, 2005).

Josh Lehne, "The Question of the Homoerotic in Thomas Eakins' *The Swimming Hole*," *Lu Cerna*, 2, 1 (2007): 82–95.

F. O. Matthiessen, *American Renaissance: Art and Expression in the Age of Emerson and Whitman* (Oxford: Oxford University Press, 1968).

Elizabeth Milroy, "Points of Contact: Thomas Eakins, Robert Harris and the Art of Léon Bonnat," *The Journal of Canadian Art History*, 10, 2 (1987): 85–103.

Raphaël Pirenne and Alexander Streitberger, eds., *Heterogeneous Objects: Intermedia and Photography after Modernism* (Leuven: Leuven University Press, 2013).

Antonio Quinet, "The Gaze as an Object," in *Reading Seminar XI Lacan's Four Fundamental Concepts of Psychoanalysis*, eds. Richard Feldstein, Bruce Fink and Maire Jaanus (Albany: State University of New York, Albany, 1995): 139–148.

Jeff L. Rosenheim, "Thomas Eakins, Artist-Photographer, in The Metropolitan Museumof Art," in *Thomas Eakins and The Metropolitan Museum of* Art, ed. H. Barbara Weinberg (New York: The Metropolitan Museum of Art, 1994): 45–51.

Mari Ruti, "Winnicott with Lacan: Living Creatively in a Postmodern World," *American Imago*, 67, 3 (Fall 2010): 353–374.

Kaja Silverman, "Fassbinder and Lacan: A Reconsideration of Gaze, Look and Image," *Camera Obscura*, 7, 1 (1989): 54–85.

Susan Waller, "Professional Poseurs: The Male Model in the Ecole des Beaux-Arts and the Popular Imagination," *Oxford Art Journal*, 25, 2 (2002): 43–64.

Slavoj Zizek, *How to Read Lacan* (New York: W. W. Norton & Company, 2007).

# The Multilingualism of Jacob Riis's Imagetext

Christa Holm Vogelius

The contribution of Danish-American photojournalist Jacob Riis (1849–1914) to the history of photography and photojournalism is indisputable: as one of the first and most successful practitioners to experiment with the uses of flash photography to capture indoor and nighttime images, he brought broad visibility and social reform to Manhattan's poorest and most overcrowded immigrant districts. Nonetheless, he is often remembered primarily as an unwavering proponent of the melting-pot ideology of American assimilation, and as a photographer who in spite of his innovations to the medium, regarded imagery merely as an evidentiary supplement to his writing, research, and lectures. But Riis's own autobiography, *The Making of an American* (1901), forefronts the significance of his Danish upbringing and childhood home in shaping his later reform work, and frames his dual nationality as an important part of his adult identity. Similarly, his personal writings show a much more textured relationship to language and nationality, and invite new ways of reframing his imagery in relation to these terms. In private writings and letters home to his family in Denmark after his emigration in 1870, his use of code-switching and language alternation reveals his nuanced understanding of the particular resonances of both linguistic and national allegiance.

This lens on Riis as a linguistic and cultural pluralist reframes his phototextual work. In this chapter I read Riis's first and best-known photobook, *How the Other Half Lives* (1890), as a text that embraces transnational allegiances. It highlights – however problematically – linguistic and cultural diversity and achieves both through an equal interplay of text and image, or what W. J. T. Mitchell calls imagetexts: "composite, synthetic works (or concepts) that combine image and text" (2015: 39). Such composite texts necessarily contain what Mitchell calls "a third thing: the traumatic gap of the representable space between words and images," but the emphasis in Riis's text is not on the gaps between visual and verbal media so much as the differences within the categories of language and image themselves (2015: 39). I argue that Riis's work relies intimately on both textual and imagistic remediation, a term coined by Jay Bolter and Richard Grusin to describe the process by which a new medium references an older one to demonstrate its own unique capabilities (1999: 14–15). These phototexts remediate, or recirculate, the older form of the illustrated book to make their basic argument for the simultaneous, parallel existence of different immigrant groups. Riis's relation to language and Americanization is, like the remediation of older media, a non-linear system that mixes different forms diachronically and understands translation through a linguistic pluralism in which terms can be retranslated, mistranslated, and transferred from language to language, but are resistant to easy exchange.[1] Riis does not, either linguistically, culturally, or visually, make the argument for one-to-one translation, but frames each language, group, and medium as performing its own function within the system of the text. Attuned to the resonances of particular types of imagery for their linguistic and cultural difference, Riis's woodcuts and halftone photographs draw on the particular connotations of each form, resulting in a multimedial work that both gestures back to a history of reform texts and illustrated books at the same time as it emphasizes its own innovations to the genre in the form of evidentiary photographs.

In this chapter, I first demonstrate the relevance of Riis's mixed nationality and language background to his understanding of his identity and reform work, and then apply this same perspective to his new media aesthetics in *How the Other Half Lives*. Stressing cultural pluralism in both its language and its imagery, the text demonstrates the ways that ideological representations of populations and classes are also always aesthetic and reflected in the particular media of representation. Just as the text presents immigrant districts in New York as culturally distinct and, in their clear demarcations, transnational before the term, the different media of the text's illustrations assert their own unique functions as book-historical references or photographic evidence. My argument here is not that there is a strong conceptual connection between this transnationality and transmediality – not least because the mixed media aspects of the texts were largely out of Riis's personal control – but simply that a recognition of the text's fissures on both the national and medial levels are essential to a balanced understanding of how it functioned as, and in the context of other, reform work. The recovery of Riis as a figure both between nation and media reframes the complexities of this period's reform work, which was often neither simplistically invested in wholesale Americanization nor the purely evidentiary power of new media. Rather Riis, the editors who published his work, and the audiences who viewed it in its different formats, came to these visual and textual forms precisely for their diversity: their representation of the complex geographic, national, and linguistic fissures of the city enclosures, as well as media formats that both quote the familiarity of old forms and lean on the potentialities of new media. Riis exploited this space between familiarity and novelty to make work that was domesticated and unthreatening to his largely middle-class, white audiences, presenting difference as a consumable product. His reform work smoothed the edges of this difference without ever eradicating it, and the more recent presentation of Riis as an Americanizer, or as a photographer whose work is neatly enlarged in art prints, flattens the source of his appeal, which lay precisely in fissures and contradictions.

The backdrop to the cultural pluralism of *How the Other Half Lives* – and the media pluralism that constructs it – is Riis's own culturally pluralistic persona. This is a persona that he develops in greatest detail through his stress on bicultural identity in his autobiography, *Making of an American*.

## Americanization and Cultural Pluralism

Riis's close friend, Theodore Roosevelt, called Riis in his own autobiography "the best American I ever knew, although he was already a young man when he came hither from Denmark" (1913: 66). Later editions of Riis's autobiography, *The Making of an American* (1901), are prefaced by a variation of this statement in an excerpt from a 1914 magazine eulogy by Roosevelt shortly after Riis's death, where he concludes: "He did not come to this country until he was almost a young man; but if I were asked to name a fellow-man who came near to being the ideal American citizen, I should name Jacob Riis" (1947: xi). This understanding of Riis as model or assimilated immigrant extends into his later biographical and critical reception, which underplays his immigrant status and frames him as a wholesale proponent for the early 20th-century Americanization movement. The Danish title of Tom Buk-Swienty's biography of Riis, *Den Ideelle Amerikaner* [The Ideal American] (2005), gestures toward Roosevelt's declaration. Bonnie Yochelson, one of Riis's principal photographic critics, and Daniel Czitrom identify "urban poverty and the Americanization of the immigrant" as the "twin themes of his writing" (2007: xiii). For Katrina Irving (2000), who divides turn-of-the-century American attitudes to immigration between nativism (or scientific racism), Americanization discourses, and cultural pluralism or transnationalism, Riis's work falls predominantly within the second category, with occasional forays into the first. Additionally, Riis's advocacy and fundraising for the Children's Aid Society, which was behind the Orphan

Train Movement that between 1854 and 1929 migrated 100,000 Irish, German, and Italian American youth from Manhattan to rural homes as laborers with the explicit aim of national and racial assimilation, would seem to support this label of American and Americanizer (Schuller, 2017).

But Riis's politics were complicated and do not conform straightforwardly to an ideology of melting-pot assimilationism. His self-representation in the autobiographic *The Making of an American* is at odds with the basic principles of Americanization, evidenced from the first in his nostalgic reliance on his childhood in Denmark as sowing the seeds of his later life path. Riis begins the book with a vignette from his Danish hometown of Ribe, in which he recounts meeting his future wife as a young teenager on a bridge in the outskirts of town. In his memory, "it is all as it was that day nearly forty years ago" (1901/1947:1). The coexistence of past and present selves is essential to the story that Riis tells of his life and career in America. In this early romantic vignette, Riis also describes Ribe as the place where he had "my first collision with the tenement," a building that the town dubbed "Rag Hall" (1901/1947: 5), where the pre-adolescent Riis donates his Christmas money to "the poorest family there, on the express condition that they should tidy things up, especially those children, and generally change their way of living" (1901/1947: 9). The combination of self-distance and continuity that defines the narration of both Riis's romantic infatuation and his early charity work are essential to the structuring of the text as a whole. Riis distances himself from the methods of his early reform efforts, which "had at least the merit of directness, if they added nothing to the sum of human knowledge or happiness" (1901/1947: 9), and the misadventures of his youthful infatuation, but nonetheless frames both as setting into motion the concerns of his more mature work. In the case of the tenements, a concern for cleanliness and order continues into his adult work, but an understanding of the structural exploitations of the tenement system replaces his naïve sense of the inhabitants' need to "change their way of living," and in the case of romantic life, his blind infatuation with Elisabeth grows into a more mature love that, later in the autobiography, allows for the inclusion of his wife's first-person point of view in the form of a far-from-flattering chapter on their courtship.

In the light of this early vignette in Ribe, then, *The Making of an American* emerges as a love story to both Riis's nation of origin and family. A few pages into his drawn-out account of his first meeting with his wife, including meditations on her tasseled shoes and curled hair, Riis interrupts himself abruptly, asking, "And is this going to be a love story, then? Well, I have turned it over and over, and looked at it from every angle, but if I am to tell the truth, as I promised, I don't see how it can be helped. I stepped on [the bridge] that day a boy, and came off it with the fixed purpose of a man" (1901/1947: 3). The story of the couple's long and difficult courtship – eventually spanning continents as Riis traveled to New York, worked years in odd jobs, and established himself as a newspaperman before returning to Denmark to marry – plays a central practical and symbolic role in the story, explaining not only his early emigration, but also the motivation for much of his work, where so many of his ideas on tenement reform are based on the nuclear family structure and nostalgia for the safe enclosures of home. It is not surprising that this lifelong "love story" is dedicated to his wife, or as he calls her in the book's dedication, "Lammet" [the lamb].

But the love story is a layered one, a Riis consistently conflates nation, wife, and family. From the first page, where a description of Ribe's rural outskirts merges with the scene and description of seeing Elisabeth for the first time, Riis intertwines nostalgia for his homeland with his personal romance. This conflation is particularly marked at one point several pages into the first chapter, where after writing about Ribe's long-standing land disputes along its German border, Riis exclaims,

> Alas! I am afraid that thirty years in the land of my children's birth have left me as much of a Dane as ever.... Yet would you have it otherwise? What sort of a husband is the man going to make who begins by pitching his old mother out of the door to make room for his wife? And what sort of a wife would she be to ask or to stand it? (1901/1947: 7–8)

The metaphor frames mother and not wife as homeland, but the trope of familial nationality allows Riis to understand national allegiances as ones that are both loyal and expansive, primed for generational growth. In this sense, the narrative of his devotion to his wife frames not only the moment where the boy takes on "the purpose of a man" (1901/1947: 3), but also the moment that symbolically precipitates Riis's transnationality.

Riis's flexible understanding of nationality parallels his use of language and bilingualism in his early journals and letters to his family in Denmark. The pocket diaries that he kept for the first four years after his arrival in the U.S. are written primarily in Danish, but the lapses into English are meaningful, and often structured around this same identification with home. The diary, transcribed in *Ren Kjærlighed kan jo aldrig dø* [*True Love can never die*] (2007), at first glance seems to function primarily to record Riis's fluctuating and precarious financial situation, and in relation to this, his shifting employments and ambitions, from carpentry to traveling sales to telegraphy. But underlying these practical concerns, and often couched in his accounts of news from home, is the dominant concern of these early years and the most frequent cause of his entreaties to God: his desire to marry Elisabeth. The ambition seems a hopeless one. Not only does Elisabeth still live in Ribe, but her socially superior standing in the town means that there is little contact between her family and Riis's, and none between her and Riis. Further, Riis's long-standing infatuation seems never to have been reciprocated, and his decision at nineteen to leave Ribe for New York was precipitated largely by her refusal of his marriage proposal. A natural low-point in the entries thus occurs when Riis learns that Elisabeth is engaged. In an emotional entry that once again conflates Elisabeth and his home country, he writes: "Forlovet! Farvel Danmark, Farvel Alle I Kjære derhjemme. Farvel Elisabeth; O, Elisabeth!" [Engaged! Goodbye Denmark, goodbye all you loved ones at home. Goodbye Elisabeth; O Elisabeth!"] (2007: 97).[2]

This entry resonates as a clear turning-point in the diary both spatially and linguistically: the next page is left blank, and when the journal picks up again, Riis's first short entry ("went from Harrisburg to Syranton Lyrne county 135 miles") is the first full entry in English. Entries from this point on are increasingly scarce, but several of them are entirely in English, in sharp contrast to the earlier parts of the journal, where English is used only in untranslatable phrases, if at all. In the journal's last long entry, two years later, Riis in English records having bought the South Brooklyn News and, for the first time, being out of debt – and with the prospect of a steady income, again proposing to Elisabeth. With a sentiment that underlines the significance of the romantic narrative to his life's trajectory, Riis writes,

> In God's name, I wish and hope most tenderly that the answer [to the proposal] will be favorable.... If not, I think that in dead earnest I shall go to South America next year. I am tired of life in this Contry [sic] if I can not reach my only aim and object of so many years.... The next entry in my old diary will be the last and the decisive one. It is quite significant that on the last leaf of the book will be recorded the last word spoken in the drama that has been the drama of my life and whose acts are recorded here. (2007: 109)

It is also significant, though Riis does not comment on it, that this and many of the other entries after the time that Elisabeth became engaged are entirely in English. If Riis associates Elisabeth with home, he also associates her with the Danish language, and his emotional break from her prompts an abrupt switch, even in his personal writings, into the language of his adopted country. The "making of an

American" in a personal sense might be said to occur in the first May 1873 entry after Elisabeth's engagement, with Riis's prosaic English-language record about leaving Harrisburg.

In the next entry after Riis's final proposal to Elisabeth, he shifts back again to Danish to record receiving her reply of acceptance, almost exactly six years after her initial refusal: "Nu er hun min elskede Brud." [Now she is my beloved bride"] (2007: 110). Riis then affixes Elisabeth's reply in the diary and concludes with this final entry in Danish on December 7:

> Jeg skriver nu de sidste Ord i denne min gamle Bog, paa den anden Side skrev Jeg ogsaa det sidste Bogstav i den forunderligt brogede Historie Jeg her har skrevet ned for de sidste sex Aar. Nødvendigheden existerer ikke mere. Jeg tænker nu paa at rejse hjem til Foraaret, gifte mig med min egen Elisabeth og komme herover igjen. Forretningen trives til trods for daarlige Tider og Alt gaar godt. Til den gode Gud al Tak for hans Miskundhed. (2007: 112)
>
> [I now write the last words in this old book of mine, on the other side I also wrote the last letter of this wonderfully difficult story I have written down here for the last six years. The necessity no longer exists. I'm now thinking about traveling home in the spring, marrying my own Elisabeth and coming over here again. Business thrives in spite of the bad times and all goes well. To the good Father thanks for his mercy.]

In fact, though Riis was for the rest of his life a prolific letter writer, and though he kept account books, notes for his lectures, and some travel records from a trip to England in 1893, he would never again keep a personal diary of his emotional life. That he ends this one with a series of short entries in Danish, at a point when his writing in English was fluent enough that he was journalist, editor, and owner of a local New York newspaper suggests clearly what the first chapter of *The Making of an American* would likewise reinforce: that the central romantic narrative of his life had made him "as much a Dane as ever." Denmark, even after several years in the U.S., is still the "home" to which he travels, New York, the "over here" to which he brings his wife.

Riis's code-switching in his later correspondence similarly suggests at most a hyphenated identity rather than a wholesale Americanization. His correspondence with Americans is of course in English, but his letters home to family remain in Danish until the end of his life, with the exception primarily of the short greetings in English that his second, American wife sometimes appended to the margins of his letters. But while the main structure of these texts is Danish, Riis intermixes occasional English words and phrases that suggest a new cultural immersion. The letters to his sister in Ribe, collected in the Danish Emigration Archive in Aalborg, often use English phrases that are either untranslatable or just more convenient. One letter from July 1894, for instance, includes a long reflection on whether you can use the phrase "she's a brick" in Danish, with a meditation on the mythological origin of the phrase. Other letters use English words or phrases without commentary in a way that sounds contemporary to today's more globalized Danish, but was uncommon at the time. Riis's siblings, though, who went to secondary school at an institution where their father was both principal and English teacher, would not have had any trouble glossing English words such as "settled," "particulars," "light-hearted," or "manners," often, but not always, set apart from the Danish with quotation marks. The words and phrases that Riis uses are most often for convenience or fluency: "settled," for instance, in the domestic context that Riis uses it, would translate as the somewhat more cumbersome "slået os ned" (Jacob Riis Papers, Danish Emigration Archives: A90–1).

Riis shows a similarly relaxed relation to linguistic consistency writing to Danish-American associates. In letters between Riis and the Chicago-based brewer Max Henius, who, like Riis, emigrated in his early twenties, the two men alternate between texts primarily in Danish or in English. In their letters regarding Henius's founding of the Danish-American park in Rebild, Denmark, a cause to which Riis donated a small sum, Riis switches in alternating letters back and forth between Danish and English, though Henius, residing temporarily in Denmark, writes consistently in Danish. This fluidity suggests a natural and almost unthinking fluency in and between both languages. In Riis's mixed and alternating linguistic registers emerges a national identity that is both/and, transnational before the term (Jacob Riis Papers, Danish Emigration Archives: A90–2).

## The Cultural Pluralism of *How the Other Half Lives*

Riis's granular understanding of language and nationality in his personal writings is in both cases a form of cultural pluralism. Such pluralism comes into play in published reform texts such as *How the Other Half Lives* (1890) through an exaggerated, often racially stereotypical depiction of national and ethnic difference – but along with such cultural stereotypes, a sense that housing and immigration reform do not depend on the wholesale Americanization of immigrants. Although many critics and photo-historians understand Riis's work through the lens of Americanization – Katrina Irving for instance framing him as "concerned to speed assimilation through the improvement of the immigrants' environment" – there is little concrete evidence in this early text for this conflation of "improvement" with "assimilation" (2000: 75). In fact, Riis's representation of the immigrant, though it often depends on the racist trope of contagion and his readers' fears of crime and poverty spreading to non-immigrant neighborhoods, promotes not assimilation, but the clearer delineation of the (nationally and ethnically plural) domestic space.

Riis's description of the tenement quarters of New York, which he estimates as housing three-quarters of the city's inhabitants, relies centrally on racist stereotypes such as the hot-tempered Italian, the orderly German, and the thrifty Jew. But even with these cultural stereotypes, Riis stresses environmental adaptability to an extent that challenges contemporary scientific racism. In "Chinatown," for instance, he writes that "[w]hatever may be said about the Chinaman being a thousand years behind the age on his own shores, here he is distinctly abreast of it in his successful scheming to 'make it pay'" (1890/2014: 92). In spite of the negative racial stereotype, the idea that the Chinese laborer responds to the unregulated capitalism of the tenement district in which an older generation of immigrant landlords exploits a newer generation of tenants with egregious rents and substandard housing clearly underlines the cultural adaptability of this group. That the Chinese immigrant becomes "distinctly abreast of it" by taking advantage of the landlord role challenges one of scientific racism's central discourses, which flagged some races – Asians and Native Americans among them – as "older" and therefore less adaptable to cultural or environmental change than others (Schuller, 2017: 12).

It is similarly difficult to disengage the racially charged language of contagion from the toxic environment of the tenements that *How the Other Half Lives* portrays, but in this case as well, the target of the language is slightly different than it first appears. In "The Mixed Crowd," for instance, Riis describes an Arab district as "soiled by a dirty strain, spreading rapidly like a splash of ink on a sheet of blotting paper," and "the Russian and Polish Jew" as "having overrun the district...to the point of suffocation" (1890/2014: 27). Especially seen from the vantage point of contemporary political discourse, this language of infiltration seems strongly racialized, but Riis consistently frames the growth of the immigrant district not in terms of a demographic threat, but as a moral, epidemiological, and economic one caused by the structural evils of the tenement system – whose primary victims are the immigrants themselves. The immigrants, in other words, are not the plague, but the first victims of the disease. In the introduction to the text, Riis personifies the tenement district as an active threat to its inhabitants:

> in the tenements, all the influences make for evil; because they are the hot-beds of the epidemics that carry death to rich and poor alike; the nurseries of pauperism and crime that fill our jails and police courts; that throw off a scum of forty thousand human wrecks to the island asylums and workhouses year by year; that turned out in the last eight years a round half million beggars to prey upon our charities; that maintain a standing army of ten thousand tramps with all that that implies; because, above all, they touch the family life with deadly moral contagion. (1890/2014: 3)

In this bird's eye view of the system, infiltration assaults rich and poor alike, but the tenement is the agent, the "splash of ink," and its inhabitants the passive carriers.

The chapter on Chinatown is particularly illustrative of Riis's larger values in terms of pluralism and immigration, as it underlines both this community's especially dangerous species of contagion, drug addiction, and Riis's surprising solution to it. This chapter, which is one of Riis's most rampantly racist, documents the threat that the Chinese immigrant brings to New York through the opium trade, an industry that spreads through non-immigrant districts and, as Riis chronicles it at least, to white, underage women, who become some combination of enslaved addict and mistress to older Chinese men. The spreading of opium addiction beyond the border of Chinatown and the entrapment of young white girls within it represents, for Riis, the particular danger of this community, but also demonstrates the entanglement of seemingly isolated immigrant neighborhoods with the larger city. In the case of Chinatown, this entanglement takes place through the Chinese laundry, which employs white women and lures victims in through the "hundred outposts of Chinatown that are scattered all over the city, as the outer threads of the spider's web that holds its prey fast" (1890/2014: 98).

Riis's solution to the problem calls for an expansion of immigration rather than its curtailment. After the first major wave of Chinese immigration in the mid-19th century, which often brought laborers to work on the transcontinental railroads, the Chinese Exclusion Act of 1882 prohibited immigration from China for 10 years, an act that was extended by the Geary Act in 1892. These acts, the first immigration restrictions to be based on ethnicity, not only curtailed immigration, but skewed their demographics, as the earlier generation of immigrants, most of whom were single males, could not reunite with their wives or other family members. Anti-miscegenation laws in some states (and social stricture in the rest) also prevented Chinese men from marrying white women and created an environment, as Riis describes it, of single Chinese men and their common-law white "wives" (1890/2014: 98).

In conversation with this representation, the pictures in "Chinatown" are solitary: an artist's rendering of Riis's photograph of a single man passed out on a bench in an opium joint (fig. 5.1); a halftone photograph of a man facing the camera standing by a telegraph pole, hands in pockets (fig. 5.2); even the artist's woodcut illustration of a single opium pipe to mark the end of the chapter (fig. 5.3). In the first two cases, the reproductive process cropped out or obscured additional figures from the images; illustrator Kenyon Cox's rendering of Riis's opium smoker eliminates a standing man from the right foreground, while the halftone image of the telegraph pole is sufficiently dark to efface a bent-over figure from the right background. The effect is a heightening of the solitary feeling of the neighborhood that Riis's text emphasizes.

Riis's single or undomesticated man is here as elsewhere a principal source of the immigrant neighborhoods' problems. In this case, Riis's solution to the Chinese immigrant's bachelorhood, which he describes through the lens of addiction and exploitation, is to relax immigration strictures: "Rather than banish the Chinaman, I would have the door opened wider – for his wife; make it a condition of his coming or staying that he bring his wife with him. Then, at least, he might not be what he now is and remains, a homeless stranger among us" (1890/2014: 103). In this passage as in many others, Riis presents the domestic space – and implicitly the ethnically closed domestic space – as a direct means of counteracting the spread of the tenement's ills.

Riis makes similar moves to connect "homelessness" and the ills of these neighborhoods throughout the text. On the first page of the first chapter, after denouncing the tenements as "hot-beds of the epidemics," he underlines precisely what these districts lack, quoting from a report of the Secretary of the Prison Association in New York:

> By far the largest part – eighty per cent at least – of crimes against property and against the person are perpetrated by individuals who have either lost connection with home life, or never had any, or whose *homes had ceased to be sufficiently separate, decent, and desirable to afford what are regarded as ordinary wholesome*

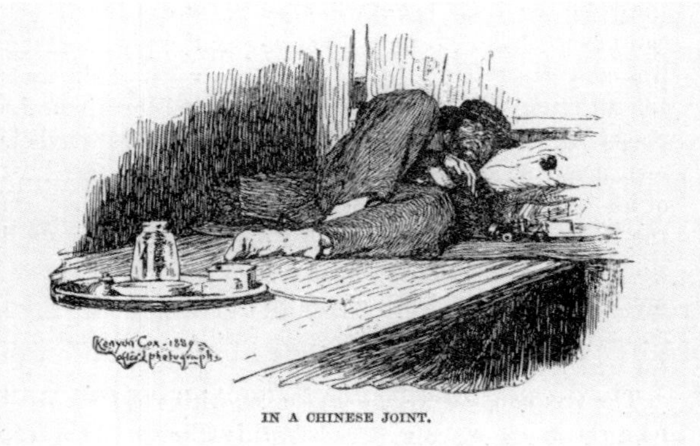


Fig. 5.1. Kenyon Cox, *In a Chinese Joint*, 1889. Jacob Riis, *How the Other Half Lives: Studies Among the Tenements of New York* (ebook, Project Gutenberg,1890/2014): 98.

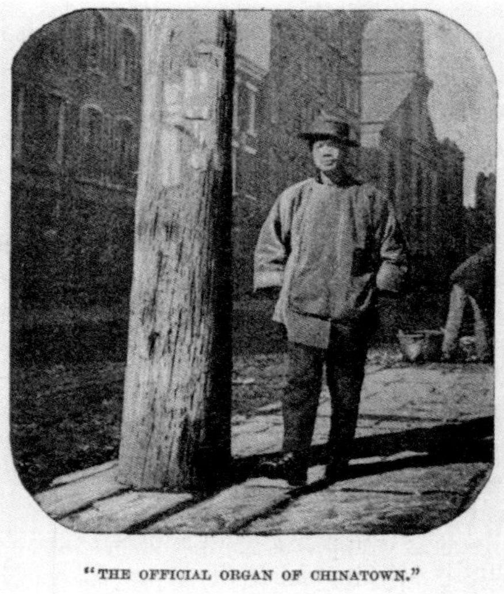


Fig. 5.2. Jacob Riis, *The Official Organ of Chinatown*, 1890. Riis, *How the Other Half Lives: Studies Among the Tenements of New York* (ebook, Project Gutenberg,1890/2014): 100.

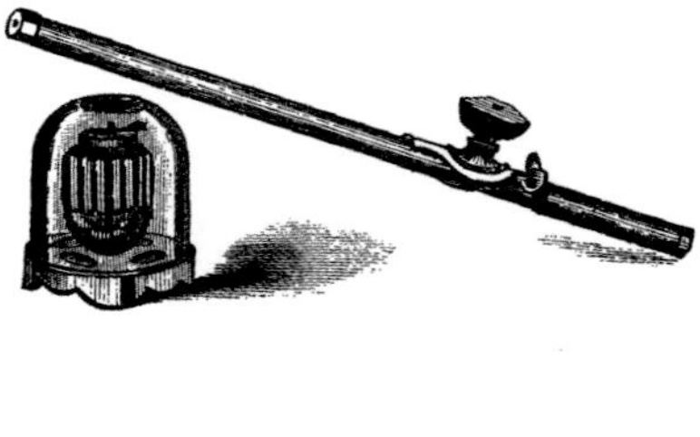

Fig. 5.3. Kenyon Cox, *Opium Pipe*, 1889. Jacob Riis, *How the Other Half Lives: Studies Among the Tenements of New York* (ebook, Project Gutenberg,1890/2014): 103.

> *influences of home and family*.... The younger criminals seem to come almost exclusively from the worst tenement house districts. (1890/2014: 2; emphasis original)

This focus on the home – and the home specifically as "sufficiently separate" – recurs in Riis's text through his detailing of the tenement's failings: its lack of locks on the external doors to apartments; its routine lodging of several families (rather than one nuclear family) in each apartment; its housing of lodgers, usually single males; its enmeshing of domestic and work life through the domestic labors of cigar- and suit-making families; and the permeability of home life onto the staircases and front stoops of buildings.

The innovation of Riis's flash photography was that it supported the text in a way that had not yet been possible in the history of this reform literature, by bringing these small dark enclosures and this insufficiently private space for the first time to a wider public. Riis's photographs show not just the crowded alleyways between buildings, but the dirty staircases that serve as children's play areas, the lodging house rooms in which several men sleep next to one another in cramped cots, and the encroachment of work into the living rooms of laboring families. Kenyon Cox's illustration from Riis's photograph, *Lodgers in a Crowded Bayard Street Tenement* (fig. 5.4), for instance, shows at least five men resting closely together in a lodging house. The illustration, as the original photograph, is brightly lit from an unseen source, but the closed eyes of all of the lodgers suggests this to be one of the photographs that Riis took on his nighttime raids of the district. On these excursions, he and his assistants broke into different bars and sleeping quarters, created illumination for a photograph through a flash gun or lighting of chemicals in a pan and fled often before their subjects were fully aware of what had taken place (Yochelson and Czitrom, 2007: 141–142). In this way, the very practice of Riis's photography, as well as the scenes that it depicts, supports the idea that these districts and their private spaces are not "sufficiently separate" – and with this insufficiency, the failure to contain "the evil they breed" (1890/2014: 3).

The ideal of domestic boundedness may also entail ethnic boundaries, as in the case of the marriage of Chinese immigrants: Riis's vision of New York is a multi-ethnic one, but not necessarily one of cultural intermixing. Nonetheless, Riis arguably suggests, as Randolph Bourne would more explicitly state a few decades later, that this variegated cultural landscape is itself American, and the concept of a more uniform American identity is an illusion (Bourne, 1916). The third chapter, "The Mixed Crowd," the first of many to lay out the demographics of the tenement

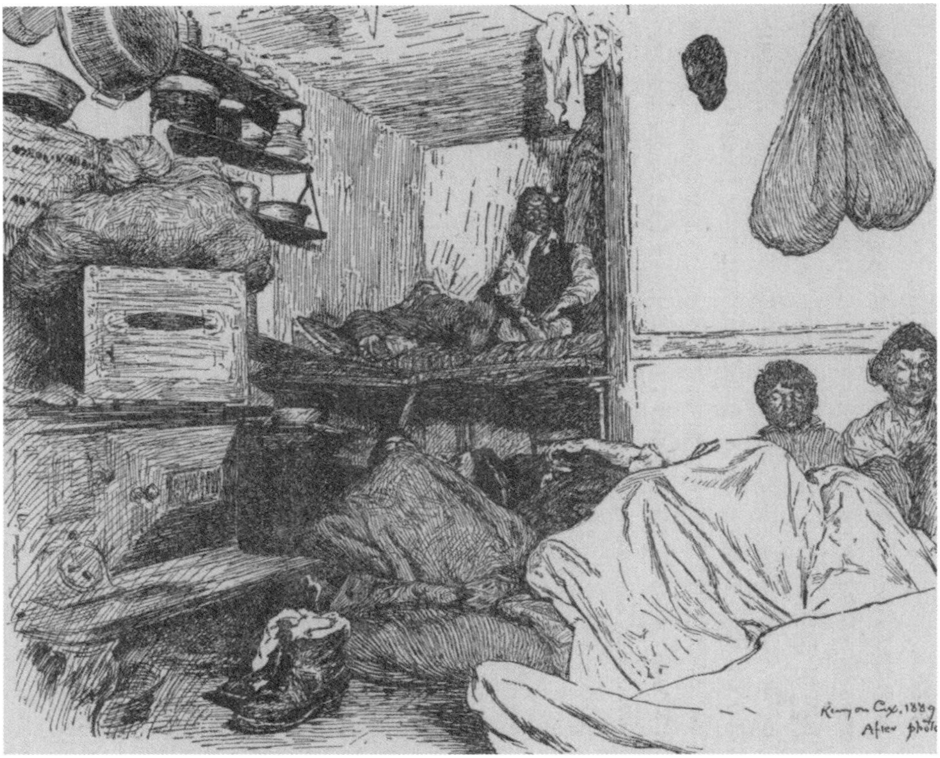

Fig. 5.4. Kenyon Cox, *Lodgers in a Crowded Bayard Street Tenement – "Five Cents a Spot,"* 1889. Jacob Riis, *How the Other Half Lives: Studies Among the Tenements of New York* (ebook, Project Gutenberg,1890/2014): 69.

blocks, begins by announcing that "[t]he one thing you shall vainly ask for in the chief city of America is a distinctively American community. There is none; certainly not among the tenements" (1890/2014: 21). This statement seems at first glance to be drawing a perhaps disparaging contrast between the immigrant groups that Riis will outline and true "Americans." But the clause "there is none" in fact denies the existence of a "distinctively American community" anywhere in New York – or possibly anywhere at all. The dialogue that follows emphasizes this elusiveness:

> Where have they gone to, the old inhabitants? I put the question to one who might fairly be presumed to be of the number, since I had found him sighing for the "good old days" when the legend 'no Irish need apply" was familiar in the

> advertising columns of the newspapers. He looked at me with a puzzled air. "I don't know," he said. "I wish I did. Some went to California in '49, some to the war and never came back. The rest, I expect, have gone to heaven, or somewhere. I don't see them 'round here." (1890/2014: 21)

That even "one who might fairly be presumed to be of the number" cannot locate a "distinctive American community" does not present a strong argument for assimilation (1890.2014: 21). In the landscape that Riis lays out, there is no uniformly American identity to assimilate to, only a patchwork of immigrant communities that emphasize each other's characteristics in the lines between their districts.

## How the Other Half Lives as Imagetext

If Riis's text emphasizes the "mixed crowd" over more homogeneous Americanization, this ethos likewise echoes through the media of his text, which depends on an interplay of the visual and the textual. The first pages of the text establish this dialogue by citing the last five stanzas of a twelve-stanza poem by James Russell Lowell, "A Parable." The poem as a whole narrates Christ's earthly descent to witness "[h]ow the men, my brethren, believe in me." The early stanzas document the pomp with which Christ is received, while the concluding stanzas, which Riis cites, contrast this finery to the poverty of many of its citizens. These last stanzas in particular represent humans as images of both spiritual and material construction, or as Christ exclaims in encountering the effects of poverty on men: "Lo, here.... The *images* ye have made of me!" (1890/2014: n.p.; emphasis original). The italicization of the word "image" is Riis's own rather than Lowell's, and these lines reflect Riis's photographic images, which like Lowell's poor – "A low-browed, stunted, haggard man, /And a motherless girl, whose fingers thin / Pushed from her faintly want and sin" (1890/2014: n.p.) – are very directly the products of their environments. Lowell's poem, in the context of Riis's text, also plays on a connection between the social and architectural environment, as the men who welcome Christ respond to his criticism of inequalities by protesting, "O Lord and Master, not ours the guilt, / We build but as our fathers built" (1890/2014: n.p.). The resonance between social and physical constructions in these lines appropriately introduces Riis's text, with its focus on the details of tenement construction and the disadvantages of poverty both as essential to the shaping of the lives within. And in staging people as images, Lowell's poem also frames the photographic images in the pages to come not

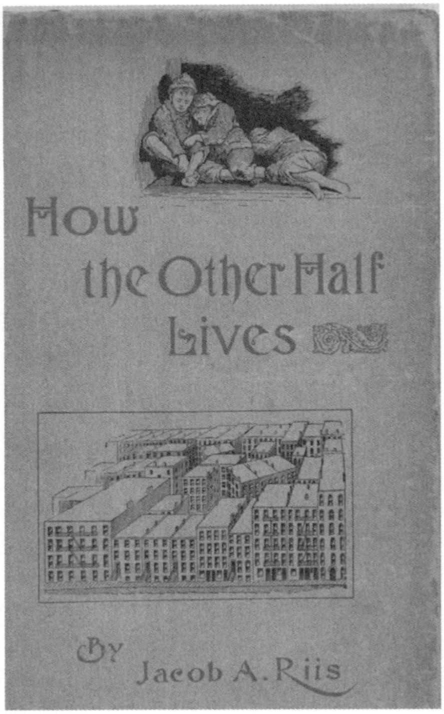


Fig. 5.5. Jacob Riis, Cover Image, 1890. Riis, *How the Other Half Lives, Studies Among the Tenements of New York* (New York: Charles Scribner's Sons, 1890). Rare Book and Special Collections Division, Library of Congress. 063.00.00.

only as representations of a social reality but also as representations, in various forms, of Christ.

The pictures in the pages that follow, though, are no more a singular entity than Riis's textual representation of the immigrant scene in New York. The attribution on the title page – "with illustrations chiefly from photographs taken by the author" – belies the work's imagistic plurality. Not only does the text include illustrations based on photographs other than Riis's own, as well as illustrations not based on photographs, but it also includes images that are not technically illustrations at all. The original cover of the book displays two different types of woodcut prints: the top a rendering of a Riis photograph of three boys huddled together on the street, the bottom an artist's illustration of a bird's eye view of tenement buildings (fig. 5.5). By the cover page of the first chapter, there is a third type of image: a full-page dark halftone print of Riis's photograph *Hell's Kitchen and Sabastopol* (fig. 5.6), taken from the outside of a tenement block. The different media of these works result in very different types of legibility, even though two of the three works are reproductions of Riis's images.

Many of the images began in a single form, as Riis captured his original photographic images for the text as glass-plate negatives in 1888. He first displayed them through stereopticon (or magic lantern) slide projections that he used to accompany his lectures on the need for tenement reform. The popularity of these lectures, which like Riis's later texts combined firsthand descriptions of the tenements, sentimentalized language, and statistical information, led to the commission of a magazine article in *Scribner's* later in 1888 and to the publication of Riis's book two years later. But both of these printed texts reproduced Riis's photographs alternately as woodcut illustrations and halftone prints, with significant differences in style and conceptual significance, and both also included reproductions from other photographs as well as artists' illustrations not based on photographs (Yochelson and Czitrom, 2007: 86–120).

The dominant form of imagery in the magazine article – though not the book – is the artist-signed woodcut illustration, based primarily on Riis's photographs, and in a few cases on the work of other photographers (e.g., fig. 5.1). Fifteen out of twenty-one images in the magazine piece were woodcuts by one of several commissioned illustrators; the book reused all twenty-one of these images, but also included seventeen new photographs, rendered not as woodcuts, but as halftone images. The woodcuts represent the original images fairly faithfully, though they often lighten or increase the contrast of the photographs for legibility, as we can see for instance in the sharply defined cover images. In other cases, they slightly simplify scenes, remove peripheral objects to increase the clarity of the main scenes, or even add figures for a more balanced composition. In one relatively dramatic example of

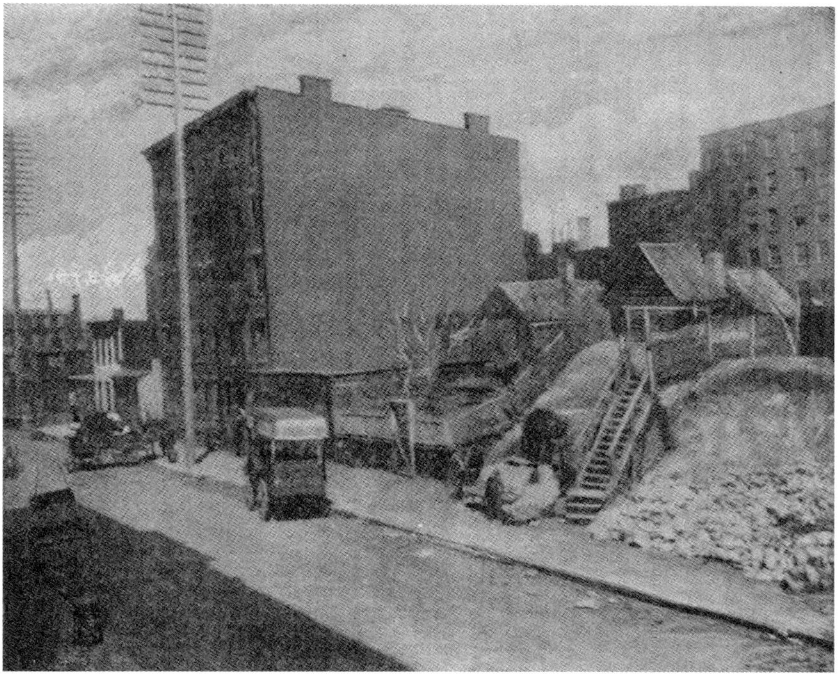

Fig. 5.6. Jacob Riis, *Hell's Kitchen and Sabastapol*, 1890. Riis, *How the Other Half Lives: Studies Among the Tenements of New York* (ebook, Project Gutenberg,1890/2014): 6.

artistic license, illustrator Otto Bacher manipulates a photograph by Riis (fig. 5.7) by adding a child and baby to the left side of the visual scene in *At the Cradle of the Tenement – Doorway of an Old Fashioned Dwelling on Cherry Hill*, balancing out and adjusting the figures crowded to the extreme right of the original image (Yochelson and Czitrom, 2007: 155–158) (fig. 5.8). The main function of these artists' interpretations, then, is to heighten the expression and impact of Riis's original images, but they also confer the text with the collaborative ethos of the artist-illustrated book through signed woodblock illustrations. By remediating the appearance and layout of the illustrated book (with images for the most part inlaid between columns of text, rather than as separate page plates), but emphasizing the images' origin "from photographs taken by the author" in the still-novel form of the photobook, the text pivots between tradition and innovation, relying on readers' associations with each.

The illustrated book had by the late 19th century lost some of the cultural cachet of earlier periods, but still often assumed a close interrelation between image and text. In earlier decades of the century, the expense of commissioning and printing illustrations was such that editors of illustrated books and periodicals often commissioned writers to produce texts to accompany illustrations, rather than the other way around. Meanwhile, the quarter-century from 1825 to 1850 saw the publication of four to five thousand magazines in America, the most widely circulated of which owed much of their readership to their illustrations, with editors boasting about the quantity, quality, and general renown of the images that they obtained (Williams, 1997: 32). But during the second half of the century, the cost of printing images fell steadily, and the relationship between text and image was more likely to be one of equality. Charles Dickens, whose lavishly illustrated canon was central to the development of the Victorian illustrated book, worked in close collaboration with his illustrators, often supplying summaries and choosing textual scenes for illustration (Golden, 2017). Riis, who devoured Dickens's works as a young man in Ribe, was clearly influenced by the author's social commentary, but the conversation between text and image may likewise have influenced his own illustrated works.

Certainly, Riis shows more concern for the thematic resonance between text and image than his own authorship of the images. He appears to have raised no concern, for instance, about the number of illustrations not based on photographs at all. The text includes several woodcut details from the illustrators' own compositions that mark and thematize space, as for instance the detail of the opium pipe at the end of the chapter on Chinatown that dwells so insistently on addiction. Similarly, three of the woodcuts are reproduced from photographs other than Riis's, but he flagged only one of them, Victor Perard's rendering of boys and men lining up at a coffee

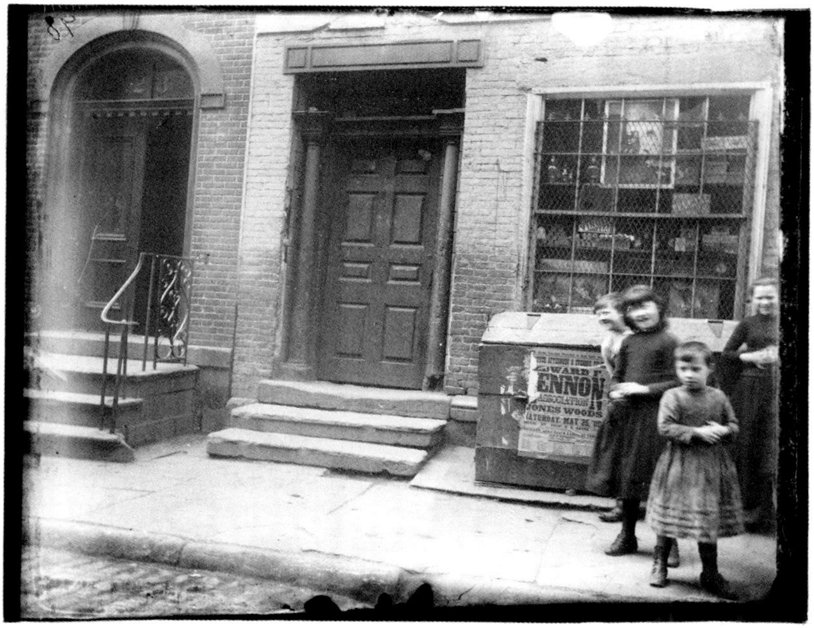


Fig. 5.7. Jacob Riis, *At the Cradle of the Tenement – Doorway of an Old Fashioned Dwelling on Cherry Hill*, 1888-89, Jacob A. Riis Collection, MCNY, 90.13.4.101.

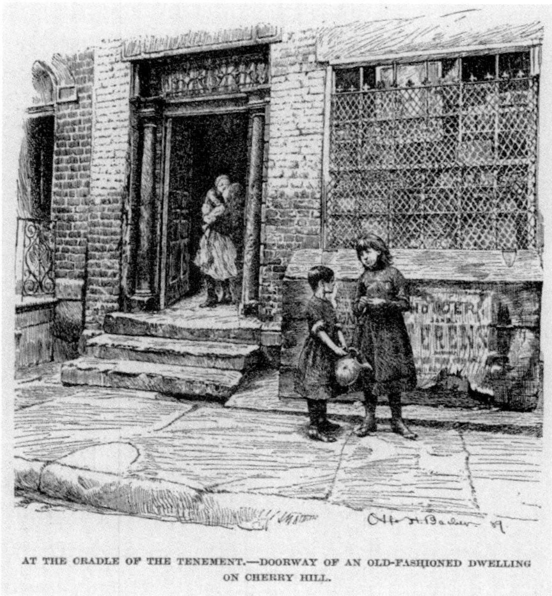


Fig. 5.8. Otto Bacher, *At the Cradle of the Tenement – Doorway of an Old Fashioned Dwelling on Cherry Hill*, 1890. Jacob Riis, *How the Other Half Lives: Studies Among the Tenements of New York* (ebook, Project Gutenberg,1890/2014): 31.

stand, not for its being based on another photographer's work, but for its thematic inappropriateness to the text. Riis wrote on his copy of the magazine piece: "This picture was smuggled into the story. It was not mine and had nothing to do with it" (Yochelson and Czitrom, 2007: 157–159).

At other moments, Riis's writing gestures explicitly to images that are included in the text, emphasizing the collaboration between the media. One particularly direct example is a photograph of a tramp seated outside of a building, smoking a pipe (fig. 5.9). In the text that appears on the opposite page of the full-page image, Riis writes,

> I bade him sit for a picture, offering him ten cents for the job.... He took the pipe out of his mouth and put it in his pocket, calmly declaring that it was not included in the contract, and that it was worth a quarter to have it go in the picture. The pipe, by the way, was of clay, and of the two-for-a-cent kind. But I had to give in. (1890/2014: 78)

This conversation, which Riis uses to support his unsympathetic view of tramps, and his sense in this case that the man, "scarce ten seconds employed at honest labor" (1890/2014: 78), was already on strike out of sheer laziness, also showcases the text and image as co-creative. This is a collaboration that gestures back to Riis's original presentation of the images in the form of first-person lectures that he structured as tours of the tenements, but it is also in line with the period's co-creative conventions of book illustration.

In printing images such as this last one, the halftone process offers a documentary and evidentiary function that goes well beyond that of conventional illustration. *How the Other Half Lives* was the first book to rely significantly on the halftone photographic process, which had only become commercially available during the same year that Riis's text was published and which made the reproduction of photographs possible by mechanical means on a larger scale. By exposing a photograph through a screen of gradient dots, the process reproduced the grayscale of an image or photograph with a varying degree of tonal range and would become widely used for magazine and newspaper printing. It was still in its early stages in 1889 and 1890, and as a result the halftone images in Riis's magazine text were of poor quality, and manually touched-up by an artist to the extent that they looked more like ink wash drawings than photographs. The book printing made improvements to the quality of the halftones and increased their quantity to where they clearly dominated the text: all seventeen new images were halftones, in addition to the six imported from the magazine piece (Yochelson and Czitrom, 2007: 154–160).

These halftone prints, though still dark and unclear by today's standards, were a large part of what set the text apart at the time of its publication. Tenement housing in New York had been considered a public health and safety risk since the 1840s, when these three- or four-story buildings, sometimes former middle-class family homes or warehouses, were first subdivided into much smaller apartments. Often these apartments were railroad flats in which rooms were connected along a line, making the interior rooms windowless. The absence of light and air in the tenements, exacerbated by the narrow alleys that separated the buildings, contributed to their tendency to spread disease, as did their frequent lack of indoor plumbing as well as their extreme overcrowding. Cholera and tuberculosis epidemics were common, and the mortality rate was much higher than the average for New York, especially among infants. These are all points that Riis makes in his text in advocating for tenement reform – but he was far from the first to make them. In fact, as Riis documents in *How the Other Half Lives*, these efforts at reform had been in steady progress for much of the second half of the 19th century, beginning in the 1840s, but to little lasting or widespread effect. Preceding Riis's writing were decades of sanitary inspection reports, analyses by charities, and journalistic accounts on a housing district that had been long overcrowded and dangerous. In fact, the introductory line to Riis's book, which reads, "Long ago, it was said 'one half of the world does not know how the other half lives'" (1890/2014: 1), is taken from an 1845 report by the city inspector of New York on the overcrowding of this same district (Yochelson and Czitrom, 2007: 25).

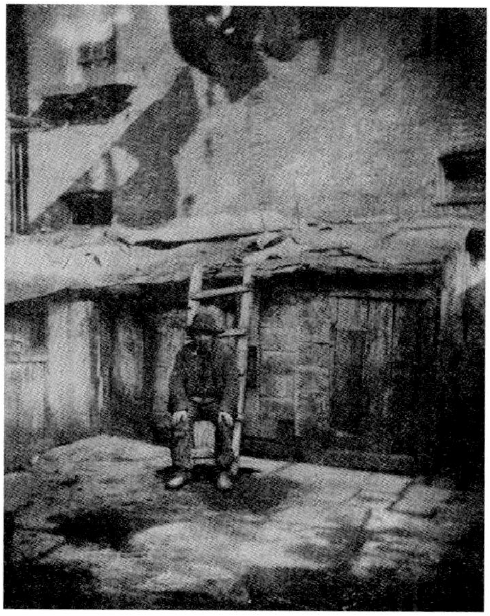

Fig. 5.9. Jacob Riis, The Tramp, 1890. Riis, *How the Other Half Lives: Studies Among the Tenements of New York* (ebook, Project Gutenberg,1890/2014): 77.

A significant part of Riis's contribution, then, lay in the photographs themselves, and the particular evidentiary power associated with photography's earliest days.

Early photography, which was sometimes called "light painting," was regarded as the direct imprint of nature, or as William Henry Fox Talbot, one of the medium's early founders, titled it in the first commercially-produced photography book, *The Pencil of Nature* (1844). The photograph, unlike painting, was not considered capable of falsifying reality. As critic Oliver Wendell Holmes wrote in 1859, "The sun is no respecter of persons or things.... The very things an artist would leave out, or render imperfectly, the photograph takes infinite care with, and so makes its illusions perfect" (1859/1980: 77–80). The photobook form often cataloged visual evidence in the service of sciences and pseudo-sciences such as astronomy, zoology, anthropology, and phrenology; as photography critic Gerry Badger writes, "The primary task of the nineteenth-century photobook was taxonomic, to collect and classify" (2004: 40). The sense that the photograph was unable to tell a lie was central to the popularity and impact of Riis's work, from his slide-based lectures, to his later photographic texts. When he first sent his article text out to *Harpers* in 1888, the editors immediately recognized the novelty of the images, which they offered to print with another writer's text. (Riis, who saw himself foremost as a writer rather than photographer, refused indignantly, and published the article in *Scribner's*, which also commissioned the extended book.)

The novelty of these images had little to do with their content and much to do with their medium. Images of scenes very similar to those that Riis depicted had become a staple of magazine and reform literature, to the extent that Riis's choice of scenes and characters was shaped by these imagistic conventions. The fruit vendor, the street urchin, and various forms of home-labor, from the cigar roller to the tailor's workshop were, by the time that Riis made his first forays into the Lower East Side, genre conventions of tenement reform writing. Riis took direct inspiration from many of the scenes that earlier artists had depicted in woodcuts or lithographs, remediating these scenes in a new format that was itself evidence of factuality. Even though Riis, like many other documentary photographers, cropped and staged images, the resulting photographs were nevertheless widely regarded as novel for their evidentiary power. As one reviewer wrote, "The illustration by means of photographs secures fidelity to facts and the sad realities with which the book deals" (Yochelson and Czitrom, 2007: 162).

At the same time, the photobook's reference to the older form of the illustrated book was what allowed it to showcase this evidentiary power. If the novelty of Riis's accomplishment lay in the halftone image's ability to reproduce the photograph mechanically and affordably, it operated nonetheless within many of the older conventions of book illustration, such as its inclusion of decorative chapter-markers and its reliance on artist-signed woodcut illustrations. In this sense, the text also functions within the purview of 'new media," following Jay Bolter and Richard Grusin's definition of the operations of digital technology:

> New media are doing exactly what their predecessors have done: presenting themselves as refashioned and improved versions of other media.... What is new about new media comes from the particular ways in which they refashion older media and the ways in which older media refashion themselves to answer the challenges of new media. (1999: 14–15)

This process of implicit or explicit citation is what Grusin and Bolter call remediation. Riis's photobook remediates the older medium of the illustrated book in order to showcase the greater evidentiary power of the new medium, at the same time as it relies on the conventions of illustration to provide clearly legible scenes and the cachet of an artist's signature. The goal of all media, according to Grusin and Bolter, is what they call immediacy, or a viewer/reader's complete immersion in a scene through the particular strengths of the medium. This immediacy is ironically achieved through a composite collage of older and newer media, or as they write from a contemporary perspective: "The desire for immediacy leads digital media to borrow avidly from each other as well as from their analog predecessors such as film, television, and photography" (1999: 9). Riis's narration of a tour through the tenements, alongside of images that depict daily realities directly, was arguably as successful as it was precisely because it created a greater effect of immediacy – of really being there – than any of the depictions of the tenements that preceded it. The connection to an earlier media history in the context of reform writing serves the purpose of underlining the depth and history of the problem, while the new medium places the argument insistently within the present.

In this sense, the imagistic language of the text is, like Riis's language itself, multivocal and multilingual rather than dependent on a single register. The evidentiary power of Riis's photographs is dependent on the different signaling of the illustrated media that came before – but also on the illustrations within Riis's own text. The lines of demarcation defining the borders across Riis's mixed-media work mark the unique capabilities of each medium as it converses with others, just as the lines between the different immigrant neighborhoods in the Lower East Side mark different contributions to the landscape, and as Riis's own alternation between English and Danish in his personal texts marks a productive divide in his identity. But if media and nationality define one another by contrast, what is striking about Riis's early writing on immigrant communities – and his own status as an immigrant – is that the broad concept of the American and Americanization, with which Riis is so closely connected in most narratives of tenement reform, is an empty signifier in his earliest and most famous work on the Lower East Side. Italians, Bohemians, and the Chinese are described in a manner that depends on the language of cultural stereotype, but to a level of differentiation and detail that contrasts with the undefined Americans who have "gone to heaven, or somewhere" (1890/2014: 21). Riis's later work with the (often American-born) children of immigrants in *Children of the Poor* (1892), and with the Children's Aid Society, complicates his place in narratives of Americanization, but even in this later work he arguably uses second-generation groups to shape a new definition of the American. In this sense, Riis employs the new medium of the photobook strategically to define changing categories of American life and transnational identities that are both fissured and whole.

## Notes

1 For a survey of the notion of untranslateability in translation studies, see Emily Apter, Against World Literature: On the Politics of Untranslateability: 1–27.

2 All translations from Danish are my own unless otherwise noted.

## Bibliography

Emily Apter, *Against World Literature: On the Politics of Untranslateability* (London: Verso, 2013).

Jay Bolter and Richard Grusin, *Remediation: Understanding New Media* (Cambridge, MA: The MIT Press, 1999).

Randolph Bourne, "Trans-national America," *The Atlantic*, July 1916, https://www.theatlantic.com/magazine/archive/1916/07/trans-national-america/304838 (accessed December 18, 2020).

Tom Buk-Swienty, *Den Ideelle Amerikaner* (Copenhagen: Gyldendal, 2005).

Tom Buk-Swienty, ed., *Ren Kjærlighed kan jo aldrig dø: Dagbøger fra Amerika*, (Copenhagen: Gyldendal, 2007).

Oliver Wendell Holmes, "The Stereoscope and the Stereograph," in *Classic Essays on Photototography*, ed. Alan Trachtenberg (New Haven: Leete's Island Books, 1859/1980): 79–81.

Catherine Golden, *Serials to Graphic Novels: The Evolution of the Victorian Illustrated Book* (Gainesville: University of Florida Press, 2017).

Katrina Irving, *Immigrant Mothers: Narratives of Race and Maternity, 1890–1925*, (Urbana and Chicago: University of Illinois Press, 2000).

W. J. T. Mitchell, *Image Science*, (Chicago and London: University of Chicago Press, 2015).

Martin Parr and Gerry Badger, *The Photobook: A History*, Vol. 1 (New York and London: Phaidon Press, 2004).

Jacob Riis, *How the Other Half Lives: Studies Among the Tenements of New York*, (ebook, Project Gutenberg, 1890/2014).

Jacob Riis, *The Children of the Poor* (New York and London: Johnson Reprint Corporation, 1892/1970).

Jacob Riis, *The Making of an American* (New York: The Macmillan Company, 1901/1947).

Jacob Riis Papers, Danish Emigration Archives, A90–1–2, Aalborg.

Theodore Roosevelt, *Theodore Roosevelt: An Autobiography* (New York: The Macmillian Company, 1913/2006).

Kyla Schuller, *The Biopolitics of Feeling: Race, Sex, and Science in the Nineteenth Century* (Durham: Duke University Press, 2017).

[William] H[enry] Fox Talbot, *The Pencil of Nature* (London: Longman, Brown, Green, and Longmans, 1844).

Susan Williams, *Confounding Images: Photography and Portraiture in Antebellum American Fiction* (Philadelphia: University of Pennsylvania Press, 1997).

Bonnie Yochelson and Daniel Czitrom, *Rediscovering Jacob Riis: Exposure Journalism and Photography in Turn-of-the-Century New York* (New York: The New Press, 2007).

Section III

# Human-Posthuman Materialities

# Composita, the "Mascot" of the Class of 1886: A (Fictional) Picture of "Real" Victorian-era College Sisterhood and Social-Caste Expectations

Kris Belden-Adams

In an essay about composite portraiture published in *The Boston Daily Globe*, W. I. Lincoln Adams mused:

> A person was shown the photograph of a young lady who impressed him greatly. The expression of the countenance denoted a strong will and a serene, if not a volatile, disposition. It was the face of a young woman whom one would like to know. "Who is the original of this portrait?" it was asked [...]. "The graduating class of Smith College," came the reply. (1890: 8)

Adams continued: "And the young man realized the fact that there was in reality no such lady as the one whose face he so greatly admired, or, rather, that there were 49 of her!" (1890: 8).

The woman with whom this "young man" was so smitten was a woman who never existed. "She" was a composite photograph made by Charles O. Lovell by separately and sequentially exposing 49 individual portraits of the graduating seniors from the Smith College Class of 1886 to create a single image – with the aid of generous retouching – of the "average" appearance of the women of the graduating class (fig. 6.1). The resulting portrait, nicknamed *Composita* by members of the Class of 1886, became an unofficial mascot for the group, which was among the first generations of women in the U.S. to gain access to a college education. *Composita* inspired the writing of poems, a graduation toast, was mentioned in alumni publications, joined group pictures at reunions, and was the main character in a play by Zulema Ruble that was performed at graduation (Ruble, 1887). Reproductions of the Class

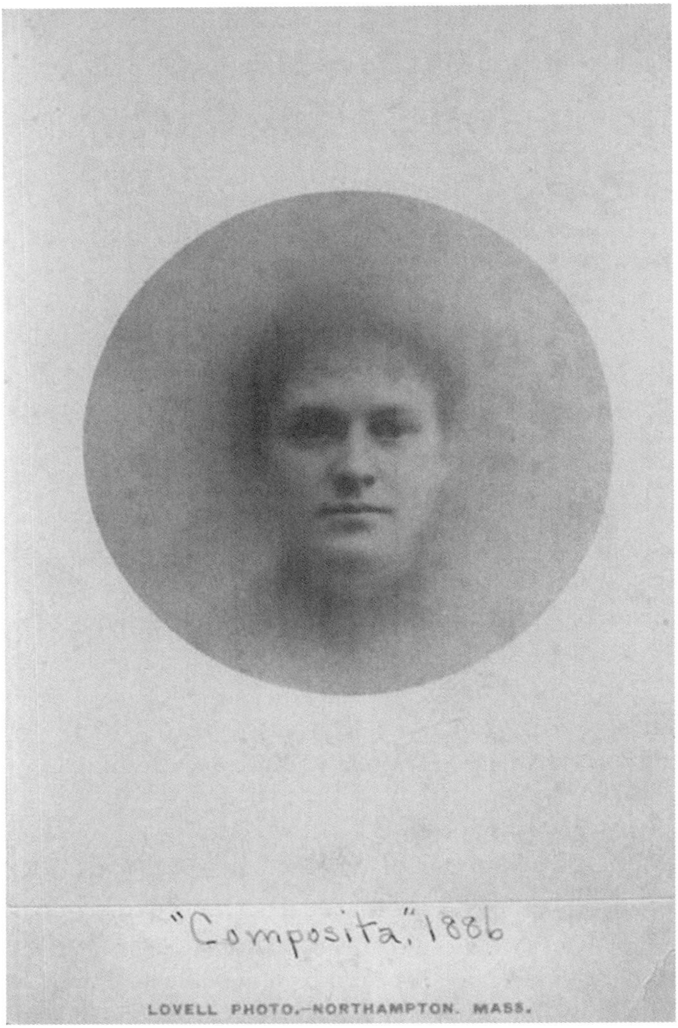


Fig. 6.1. Charles O. Lovell, *Composita*, Composite Portrait of the Smith College Class of 1886, 1885-1886. Smith College University Archives. Public Domain.

of 1886's beloved "child of Ether and of Light" were sold by Lovell's studio to members of the graduating class and their families as a keepsake, and archived by Smith College (Unknown, 1886: 6).

For the all-female Smith College Class of 1886, *Composita* offered a literal, materialized, yet metaphorical, symbol of group cohesion – because, as one member of the class wrote in a poem published with commencement proceedings, "In Union is strength" (Unknown, 1886: 89). Everything about the Smith College education was designed to encourage student bonding and cohesion: from the group's selection of their own unique sash, symbol, and class pin, to the establishment of social rituals such as dances, high teas, sleigh rides, and serenades. Even location and design of the dormitories as a series of individual homes served to simulate life at home for the students, and to encourage bonding to provide a setting that would "alleviate the fears of parents who had difficulty in sending their daughters away from home" (Young, 2011: n.p.).

But as Smith College archivist and librarian Nanci Young points out, creating graduating-class unity was a means of guiding the women of the Class of 1886 toward their social-caste-dictated destinies. Young notes that parents "were fearful that these young women would end up thinking more about careers than preparing for marriage" (Young, 2011: n.p.). Like most women of the upper classes, the women of Smith were expected to lead a "proper" social life, which involved marrying well (within their social caste), supporting their husbands, and maintaining the family's social stature within the upper-class community. This mission was particularly important for the established upper classes of Massachusetts, which saw their position threatened by the arrival of waves of immigrants and consequently coveted a leadership role in the development of eugenics as a solution to protecting the status quo (Southard, 1910). The women of Smith also were reminded of their critical roles as mothers whose shared destiny included raising "well-bred" offspring to preserve their own elevated social caste in faithful adherence to the mission of the Positive Eugenics movement (Smith College Archives, 1886). Thus, Smith College, along with other Massachusetts elite institutions such as Harvard University, fittingly adopted the composite photography – a technique invented by Francis Galton, the founding father of eugenics – to subtly underscore the importance of conforming and upholding the established social order in the late 19th century.

This chapter examines the rhetorical functions of this photographic symbol of group cohesion: to communicate graduating-class unity while also upholding social-caste, eugenics-related, and gender-norm expectations. However, when positioned within the context of first-wave feminism, and in relation to the individual stories and portraits of members of the class, *Composita* reveals problems and aspects of non-conformity with its own rhetorical message. Similar pressures were palpable to the women of the Smith College Class of 1886, who were torn between adherence to their social-class expectations, and the promise of new liberty offered not only by their education, but also by the unevenly spreading New Woman and suffrage movements. Thus, *Composita* gave material expression to unquantifiable pressures the Smith College Class of 1886 faced.

## "There were 49 of her!": *The Creation of Composita, Picturing a "Superior Bloodline"*

The hazy dark eyes of *Composita* meet, but do not challenge, the viewer's gaze. They hint at a sharpness of mind that lies beneath *Composita*'s fair-skinned surface – as the admiring "young man" quoted earlier by Adams observed – to denote "a strong will and a serene, if not a volatile, disposition" (Adams, 1890: 8). Composite portraits like this one typically featured a distinctive haze around the subject's eyes. Despite a photographer's best efforts to align the eyes of each constituent portrait, the area surrounding each subject's eyes inevitably varied in expression and shape, and thus, created less-than-crisp results on the composite. *Composita*'s dark hair is pulled back and falls into bangs on her forehead. The high neckline of a dress meets the base of her neck, preserving her modesty in accord with upper-class societal expectations. *Composita*'s mouth and nose are proportional and do not dominate her visage. She is a picture of tempered vigor.

To make *Composita*, Northampton-based commercial photographer Lovell carefully aligned and re-photographed forty-nine front-facing portraits on a single negative using a technique pioneered in 1878 by respected eugenicist/statistician/criminologist Francis Galton. As Galton articulated in articles published to audiences in the U.S. and Europe, any archive of up to 500 photographs could be combined to make a single group portrait as long as each image had consistent facial shapes, proportions, and pupil sizes/axes (figs. 6.2a & 6.2b) (Galton, 1879: 132–144). Facial size could be altered for conformity by the photographer by adjusting the distance between the portrait and the camera. Exposure times for each constituent portrait were equal to the total length of the exposure divided by the number of photographs to be included in the composite. For example, if the total exposure time for *Composita* were to have been 49 seconds, a portrait of each member of the Class of 1886 would be exposed for one second on the light-sensitive plate.

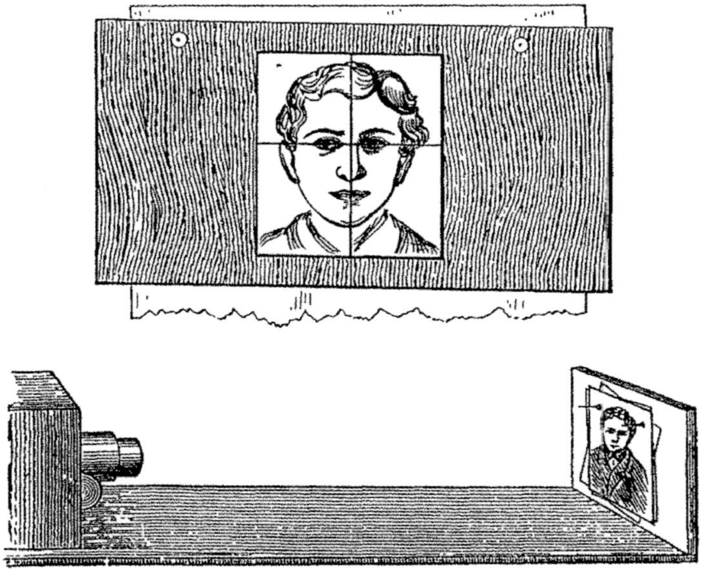

Figs. 6.2a & 6.2b. Diagrams for the Making of a Composite Portrait. Francis Galton, "Composite Portraits," *Nature*, 18 (1878): 97-100. Public Domain.

None of Lovell's notes about the making of *Composita* have survived, nor have its constituent portraits. However, a distinct typology of the collegiate upper class did exist and was discussed in the mass press. The women of the Class of 1886 were associated with a unique New-England-based aristocracy described by Bostonian Oliver Wendell Holmes in an article for *The Atlantic Monthly*:

> What our people mean by "aristocracy" is merely the richer part of the community, that live in the tallest houses, drive real carriages (not "kerridges,") kid-glove their hands, and French-bonnet their ladies' heads, give parties where the persons who call them by the above title are not invited, and have a provokingly easy way of dressing, walking, talking, and nodding to people, as if they felt entirely at home, and would not be embarrassed in the least, if they met the Governor, or even the President of the United States, face to face. (1860: 91–92)

Holmes further suggested that this social caste (to which he was fortunate to belong) possessed "excellent moral character, of high intelligence and good education" (1860: 98). He even described their appearance: "commonly slender," with a "smooth" face "apt to be pallid," possessing facial features that are "regular and of a certain delicacy," with "bright and quick" eyes (1860: 92). While members of this social caste "may be timid," they nonetheless are keen of mind and diligent at academic studies, Holmes adds (1860: 92). The unnamed "young man" at the start of this essay was drawn to *Composita*'s perceived possession of such "a serene, if not a volatile, disposition," demeanors that Holmes described as "bright and quick" (1860: 92). Likewise, *Composita* represented this smooth-faced, socially sophisticated, educated young class of New England semi-"aristocrats."

As members of a "superior" upper-caste of New Englanders of Anglo-Saxon origin, the women of the Class of 1886 were consistently reminded of their collective responsibility to breed and to expand their social caste and bloodline, which was stressed as being as important as their academic courses – if not more so. Their mission as future mothers was aligned with "Positive Eugenics," which supported the "better" breeding of people who possessed desirable hereditary traits, as a means to improve the humanity and combat poverty, mental illness, and crime (Burke and Castaneda, 2007: 6). "Fit" and "unfit" individuals were cataloged using means such as composite photography and were praised in journals and promotional materials produced by the Eugenics Record Office. Specifically, the Eugenics Record Office told the public that physical appearance was revealing of a great many attributes, including one's sexual promiscuity and orientation, trustworthiness, optimism or pessimism, popularity, political leanings and degree of patriotism, management of money, tendencies for eavesdropping, whether someone genuinely likes children, and is predisposed for tumors, gastritis, appendicitis, hay fever, sinusitis, asthma, and/or impotence (Davenport, 1912: n.p.). The American Eugenics Society worked to spread the message through political activism and education and awarded prizes to "healthy" families and "fit" couples for scoring well on a series of eugenic measures (Stier, 2010: 478). Mass-circulated women's magazines featured stories with eugenics-based morals, in which women were told that they had to make a choice between having children that were "bright, healthy," and "robust" or "sickly," "depraved," and "unintelligent" (Hasian, 1996: 83).

Smith College played a role in promoting Positive Eugenics, which was taught as a scientific fact and "urgent social necessity" in the college's biology, sociology, and economics curriculum and was accepted as "truth" (Auger-Day, 2011: 60). The discourse of eugenics thus shifted from being the domain and academic study of white Anglo-Saxon men to being a social imperative for women of child-bearing years, its primary (mute) actors. Smith College was adjacent to the hilltop grounds of Northampton State Hospital, an institution for the mentally ill that received its first patients in 1858 and reached a population of nearly 500 by 1886. At this time, eugenics promoted the isolation of the "unfit" such as the Northampton patients, who were deemed the unfortunate recipients of "bad genes" (Auger-Day, 2011: 60). The women of the Class of 1886 would regularly see these patients tending their communal gardens and other parts of the grounds of the institution and were instructed to regard them as living examples of the importance of expanding their "fit" and "superior" bloodline for the good of humanity.

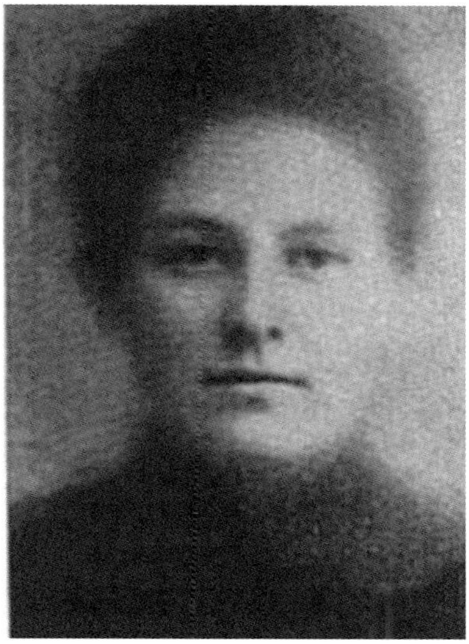

Fig. 6.3. John Tappan Stoddard, *Co-Composite of the Women of the Harvard "Annex," Mount Holyoke, Smith, Wellesley, Wells, and Vassar*, 1887, "College Composites," *The Century Illustrated Monthly Magazine*, 35, 13 (Nov. 1887-April 1888): 125. Public Domain.

Holmes's description of this unique, intelligent, capable, serene, and idealized regional U.S. social caste also was given a lasting visual form in the photographs of John Tappan Stoddard, who taught chemistry and physics at Smith College from 1878–1919. Stoddard was an enthusiast of both composite techniques and eugenics. He created his own camera system and included *Composita* in what he called a "co-composite"– his term for a "super-composite" in which the composites of the 1887 graduating classes of the Harvard "Annex," Mount Holyoke College, Smith College, Wellesley College, Wells College, and Vassar College were combined (fig. 6.3). Stoddard unveiled this co-composite in the mass-press magazine *The Century Illustrated Monthly Magazine* and argued that it offered a more accurate view of the upper social caste than any single composite, such as *Composita*, could because co-composites were based on a larger archive of 287 portraits of women from New England upper-class institutions of higher learning. Stoddard's co-composite, as well as *Composita*, are both consistent with Holmes's description of the general physiognomy of the New England upper class, including an overall serenity, pale complexion, facial features that are "regular" and sometimes "delicate," and "bright and quick" eyes.

In his essays on composite photography, Henry Pickering Bowditch, a physician/eugenicist and advocate of Galton's composite photography who taught at nearby Harvard University, asserted that constituent images should be "carefully chosen for their conformity to what may be regarded as the average size, proportions, and general appearance of the group to which they belong" (1894: 331). Bowditch mentions that this was a common practice for accuracy's sake, "to remove this subjective source of error and to give to the typical form a truly objective character" (1894: 331). Practically speaking, a greater uniformity in the constituent portrait set made for a finished composite with less blur, greater clarity in its articulation of facial features, and an enhanced degree of "truth value."

The resulting "objective character" in a composite, Galton suggests, also was a subjective visual encapsulation of the image maker's preconception of the common physical features shared by a set of individuals. Galton called such typological judgments of sets of people "generic mental images" and conflated the manner in which a photographic plate impresses multiple exposures with the way in which the human sensorium forms impressions of others: "A generic mental image may be considered...nothing more than a generic portrait stamped on the brain by the cumulative, successive impressions made by its component images" (Galton, 1879: 166). Galton here ascribes the human eye and mind with the capacity to isolate visualized, atomized bits of time from the lived continuum, while conflating photography with the temporal process of forming stereotypes.

In the late 19th and early 20th century, historian of data visualization Ingrid Kallick-Wakker observes, knowledge was thought to be obtained through a process called "*anschauung*." It was characterized as "the intuition through pictures formed in the mind's eye from previous visualizations of physical processes in the world of perceptions" (Kallick-Wakker, 1994: 310). Kallick-Wakker further suggests that such subjective images were "often treated as factual reports independent of social and cultural circumstances" by members of various scientific communities (1994: 310). Thus, the denial of societal and cultural influence over the photographer's preconception of "generic mental images" for a finished composite was critical to upholding the image's perceived objectivity, as well as the photographer's. Galton's technique of composite photography enjoyed credibility as a means of translating perceived typologies and stereotypes into tangible pictures that also functioned as statistical averages, in accord with then-prevailing *anschauung* processes of knowledge-creation.

*Composita*, as well as other New England college and university composite portraits, were prominently displayed as proof of the merits of Positive Eugenics.

For instance, Bowditch published more than a dozen – including the composite portrait of the Smith College Class of 1887 – in the official publication of the Second International Exhibition of Eugenics, alongside images of practicing physicians, mathematicians, members of Bowditch's family, members of the National Academy of Science, Harvard faculty, and "horse-car" drivers (fig. 6.4). "Generic mental images" – to use Galton's term – of the educated upper caste of New England functioned as symbols of the desirable hereditary traits of reproductively "fit" individuals and gained credibility from the perceived "truth value" of photography's indexicality. This is to say, composite portraits gave the intellectual heft of "science" to the social castes of the "ill-bred" and "well-bred." The portraits' truth value was premised on what Allan Sekula argues was its status as a condensed version of an archive, one that "attempts to exist as a potent single image, and the single image attempts to achieve the authority of the archive" (1986: 54). Galton's process of making a composite was exacting, rigorous, and even "scientific" in its precision – and by extension, its perceived "objectivity." It strove to take the subjective process of *anschauung*

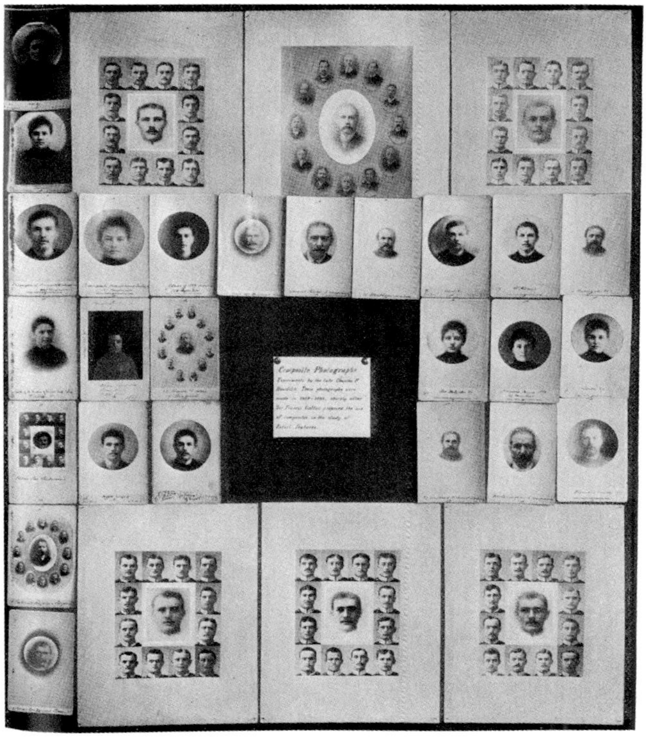

Fig. 6.4. Henry Pickering Bowditch, *An Arrangement of College/University Class Photographs,* Publication of the Second International Eugenics Congress (1921): 130-131. Public Domain.

"out of the hands of erring judgment and vague imagination and reduce the art of type-getting to a mechanical one of combining photographs" (Jastrow, 1885: 165).

Fidelity to the full archive would therefore be a prerequisite to a composite photograph's objective integrity. In the mid-to-late 19th century, photographers had no means of adjusting constituent portraits that were not frontal, or in which the subject's appearance was in any way divergent from the "norm." Instead, without announcing that they were doing so, photographers omitted non-conformist constituent images from the composite, out of concern for producing the most lucid – and therefore, convincing – image of that "norm." Galton notes in his biography that his most successful composite images were comprised almost completely of photographs that "were not greatly unlike, and were of the same size, as judged by measuring the vertical distance between the pupils of the eyes and the parting of the lips" (1908: 260).

While tinkering with recombining images from *Composita*, composite photography enthusiast/Smith professor Stoddard was first to suggest that the Class of 1886 did not resemble its composite. Using constituent portraits gleaned from Lovell, who also lived and worked in Northampton, Stoddard experimented with recombining different portraits of the Class of 1886 to achieve various results that differed noticeably from Lovell's (Stoddard, 1886: frontispiece). To the unaided eye, the Stoddard composite using all of the class portraits has a thinner face, and "her" features are not as full and rounded. A comparison of *Composita* to Stoddard's image using facial-recognition applications suggests that while the images are similar, they fall short of being a "positive" match, using the threshold of a 96% or greater visual similarity required in criminology.[1] Stoddard's composite was determined to be that of an 18-year-old, brown-haired, Caucasian female. *Composita* was identified as a 33-year-old masculine-leaning, gender-fluid, Caucasian person. His experiments affirmed Galton's claims that the outcome of a composite portrait can be skewed by altering its components, and also suggested that Lovell may have changed his usual inclusivity-inclined working methods to make *Composita*. Stoddard thus unveils the subjective practice of compositry.

As a way to possibly determine whether Lovell would have omitted several of the constituent portraits from *Composita*, a portrait – usually a ¾-turned view – of each member of the Class of 1886 was scanned digitally. Each portrait was imported to a separate layer in Photoshop, resized according to the size of the subject's left eye, toned to a relatively uniform range, positioned to line up the eyes as closely as possible, and each layer was assigned an equal opacity. No portraits were omitted. The resulting portrait appears here, in relation to *Composita* (figs 6.5a & 6.5b).

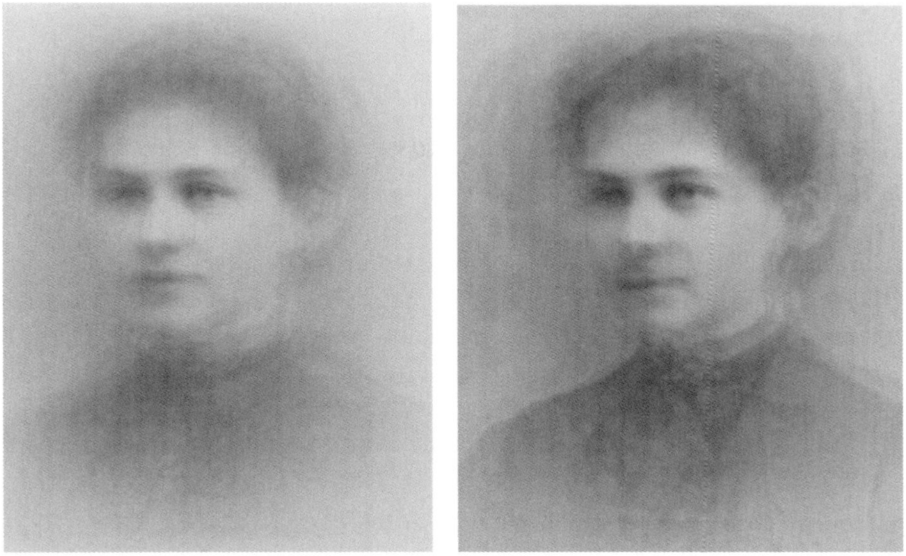

Fig. 6.5a. Kris Belden-Adams, *Photoshop Re-Composita*, 2016. Left: 2.04 percent opacity per layer, with right-facing photographs horizontally flipped for uniformity. Right: Without right-facing images flipped for uniformity; first layer 2.04 percent, with sequential layers darkened +2.04 percent. Both images based on 49 portraits from the Smith College Archives. Public Domain.

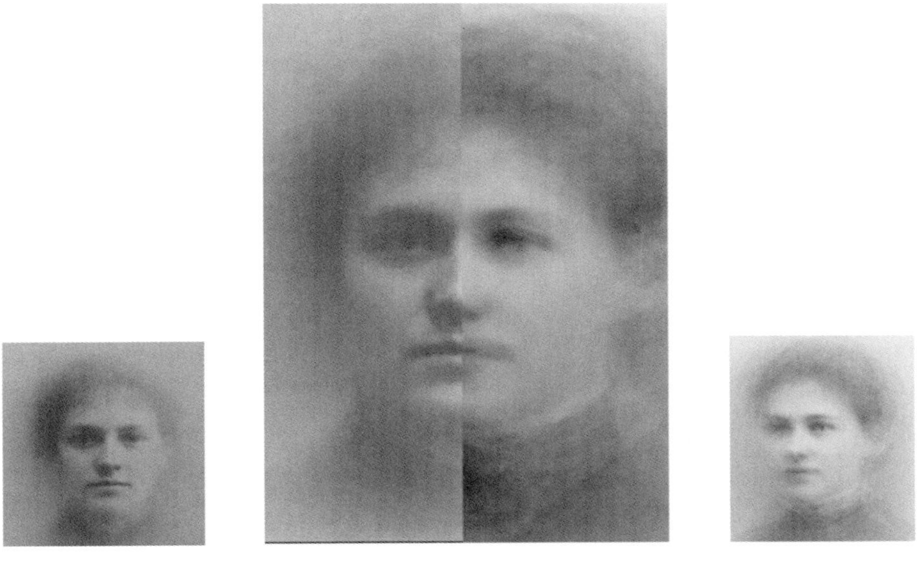

Fig. 6.5b. Kris Belden-Adams, *Composita/Re-Composita Comparison*, 2016.

The digital composite notably has lighter eyes, a slightly slimmer nose, and a less prominent chin than its analog counterpart. While *Composita*'s eyes are wide, horizontal, and almond-shaped, the digital image's eyes – especially the most clearly defined one to the viewer's right – are smaller and teardrop-shaped, tapering toward the ear. Although it is difficult to compare a ¾-skew composite to a frontal one, the Photoshopped composite's facial structure is thinner and more delicate. *Composita*'s jaw is more square in comparison, and her mouth is wider. When both composites were processed using the online PicTriev application's facial-recognition algorithm, *Composita*'s attributes interestingly were characterized as 67-percent "masculine," while the digital composite scored 83-percent feminine. When both images are digitally compared in PicTriev, they were found to bear only a 52-percent similarity to each other. It can be concluded, perhaps, that Lovell did not use all 49 of the class portraits to make *Composita*.

This would not have been unusual. Joseph Jastrow has suggested that composite portraits inevitably strongly represent at least one member of the group and are skewed by the photographer to do so (1885: 166–167). Indeed, "hiding" layers of the Photoshop composite greatly influenced the final product to resemble the likenesses of the included portraits. The more "alike" those constituent portraits appeared to be, the more coherent the composite became. Because the analog *Composita* was composed from a partial data set, the photograph calls for a revised view of Sekula's ideas about composite photography's relationship to the archive, which relies on its sample size and archival inclusiveness for its statistical potency.

Yet *Composita* possesses a more nuanced relation to "the real." Charles Sanders Peirce's trichotomy of signs posits that an individual archival image possesses an indexical relationship to its referent (Peirce, 1985: 1–23). While the "index" is frequently interpreted within photographic discourse as a photograph's absolute fidelity (as the product of light recording on a sensitive surface) to reproducing the appearance of its subject, Peirce's original definition allowed a photograph some freedom to slip in and out of semiosis with its referent as an inferred signal, while also allowing the photograph iconic and symbolic functions. As the constituent portraits of a composite are exposed sequentially on the photographic plate, and a composite image is formed, the finished image takes on the function of a Peirceian symbol for an entire mid-to-late-19th-century New England class of semi-aristocrats. Its referent is imaginary – a Galtonian "generic mental image," typology, or "average" of the recurring physical traits of female members of its group. In his study of 19th-century composite photography, James Emmott suggests that this way of "knowing" was a central objective of 19th-century statistics, which focused on "describing the states of things by the marshaling and filtering of huge amounts of data into the production of regularities, patterns, and averages" (2011: 476). Moreover, historian of data visualization Richard Wright suggests that making a visual average – as a composite portrait does – is one way of gleaning information from an archive:

> [T]he database can be said to remain undefined as an accessible object until a process to externalise it has been applied. Then it is realised, made real before our eyes. Visualisation provides accessibility to abstruse logical structures and a means of forming an intuitive conception of the subject. (1990: 69)

Any singular visual manifestation of an archive, then, is destined to function subjectively, as an allegory, aggregate, or symbol (Wright, 1990: 72). In the discursive field of data visualization studies, composite images are considered "data portraits" that seek to objectively report the data gleaned from an archive. Such images, Judith Donath argues, straddle the worlds of science and art, and the languages of objectivity and subjectivity:

> [T]heir techniques come from the world of statistical analysis, but their purpose is artistic. Some may be closer to one extreme or the other – neither is 'right' – but understanding where a particular portrait falls in this subjectivity continuum is a key element in understanding its function. (2010: 381)

As Matthew Biro has suggested, such vacillations between subjective and objective representations are also indicative of the challenging task of locating one's identity, especially during periods of social/cultural/economic change (Biro, 2009: 67). The young women of the Class of 1886 were enculturated to respect and fulfill their social-caste-dictated expectations, yet were educated to be independent, critical thinkers. They were among the first generation of pioneering women to gain access to a college education and grew to adulthood as the projects of suffrage and the New Woman movement stumbled to find momentum. *Composita*, perhaps fittingly, is described as serene, yet possessing a spark in her eye.

## Composita: A Problematic Symbol of Heteronormativity

*Composita* identified and unified the Class of 1886 at Smith College, not only as members of the New England upper-class, but also as exemplars of the merits of providing higher education for women in a climate in which they were "treated as rationally as men and allowed the same freedom" (Sanborn, 1881: 539). As such, these women collectively straddled a divide between the social caste system of their parents' generation and the potential for independence from class-dictated expectations that a college education might bring. The women of the Class of 1886 faced these challenges together, as a cohesive group of upper-class New England women who were united rhetorically as *Composita*: calm, conformist, yet possessing the enlivened eyes of one who can think and potentially act independently.

*Composita* was only one of several means by which Smith College encouraged cohesion (albeit platonic and heterosexual, in its orientation) among members of the Class of 1886. Instead of conventional dormitories, the women lived in a series of separate residential homes – with bedrooms, dining rooms, parlors, and kitchens – that were clustered around the college's academic buildings, so that the "young ladies [could] enjoy the quiet and comfort of a private home, and at the same time, the advantages of a great [literary] institution" (Young, 2011: n.p.). Each home had a "lady in charge" who was the "social and moral arbiter of student life," and who also handled direction of each house's servants (Young, 2011: n.p.; Sanborn, 1881: 539). To discourage the formation of house-based cliques, each academic building had a large social hall for "the purpose of bringing together as often as may be deemed profitable, all members of the College and their friends, in social intercourse" (Young, 2011: n.p.). The women of the Class of 1886 were thus schooled in the social graces of their New England class of semi-aristocrats, in anticipation of their assumption of the role of the "lady in charge" of their own homes after graduation.

Among the complex challenges faced by the women of Smith College was the task of changing conservative opinions about women's access to higher education. Many members of the upper classes opposed women's access to a college education, which for decades was considered a masculine endeavor. Historian Allan Johnson notes:

> For more than two-hundred years after the first colleges were established in America their doors were barred against women. Even the rudiments of education were grudgingly granted in colonial days; and, if any women were bold enough to claim the privilege of learning the things that men were encouraged to know, it was at the peril of social disapprobation. (1921: 233)

Patriarchal domination of U.S. colleges and universities persisted until the end of the Civil War, when women of the upper class began to take interest, under the guise of "bettering" themselves for marriage – their most important duty to society. Still, so few women sought the opportunity, in part because it was still stigmatized as "offensively masculine" (Johnson, 1921: 237). Historian Allen Johnson argues that "the better she did it, the worse for her reputation" (1921: 237). Katherine Hulburt, one of several women of the Class of 1886 who continued her education in graduate school at Yale University, described what it was like to be one of very few female students at a co-ed school: "Here...Kant lives, and groans, I fancy, in the undisturbed soil of some twenty graduate minds, while the feminine portion of the class challenges in silence and discreetly holds its peace" (Hurlburt, 1888). Smith classmate Leona Peirce noted that female graduate students were addressed as "gentlemen" in co-ed classrooms at Yale and Cambridge University and then ignored altogether (Peirce, 1888). Women who might deviate from heteronormativity – and educated women often were categorized as such – were labeled "degenerate" in the mass press and by eugenicists. The fear of an educated, "masculinized" female population reached a fever pitch in 1890, just four years after the Class of 1886 graduated, as the first "bold New Women" began appearing "unescorted in Boston streets, using big vocabularies to defend themselves from forward strangers" (Hunter, 2002: 273).

Many members of the New England upper class voiced fears that granting women access to advanced education also would sap "the energy necessary for intellectual activity [and] would divert vitality away from women's reproductive organs" (Curs, 2014: 210). Higher education, they further argued, was a threat not only to students' "own bodies and (presupposed) families but also to a nation apparently overrun by births of the wrong kind – those among black and immigrant populations" (Curs, 2014: 210). In reaction to this fear, many members of the upper class, as well as the faculty and staff at Smith College, impressed upon their daughters and students that they had a personal responsibility to do their part "to shield American blood from 'inferior' racial traits" and to help New England avoid its much-feared fate of becoming "a veritable Babel," filled with streets of "gross little foreigners" (Haller, 1963: 40; Johnson, 1921: 162–163).

*If* a woman *must feel so inclined* to work (despite heavy discouragement), acceptable vocations to fill the time of the Smith College graduate before marriage perhaps were best exemplified by the entries in the 1883 volume, *Our Famous Women: Comprising the Lives and Deeds of American Women*, which included essays, anecdotes, personal notes honoring female writers, teachers, suffragettes, women who started schools, nurses, and editors/authors of publications about child-rearing and cooking. Typical of most of the entries, Lucretia Mott's biography, titled "A Great Philanthropist, Great Preacher, and Perfect Woman," discussed her "perfect wedded life" and her devotion to her children at much greater length than her work to further the rights of women at Seneca Falls (*Our Famous Women*, 1883).

This is to say, the women of the Smith College Class of 1886 were provided with examples of "appropriate" job tracks that only were supposed to supplement, not replace, their expected role as mothers. Of the 49 graduating women in the Class of 1886, 41 became high-school or college teachers (Smith College, College Archives). Almost all of those women who married (and the majority did) stopped teaching as soon as they did and became mothers, keepers-of-the-house (and its staff), and took charge of the family's social profile in the community. Four graduates assumed those roles immediately, without entering the workforce (Smith College, College Archives). Encouraging the women to turn their backs on motherhood, after all, would not only wreak havoc for Smith College for encouraging the women to rebel against their plight, but it would also greatly harm the college's relationship with the community it intended to serve, and from which it recruited students.

To assuage fears that giving women access to a college education would distract them from their society-dictated mission as mothers, Smith College also assigned its women a required diet, a set routine of hygiene, scheduled rest, and exercise, and the women were subject to rigorous data collection about their health and genetic background:

> [D]ata were collected on breath (the strength and capacity of her lungs), height, weight, hair color, eye color, "temperament," whether she wore corsets, if she had ever "taken gym," her birthplace, her father's occupation, the nationality of her parents and grandparents, and if she had any hereditary diseases. Measurements were similarly recorded of each woman's waist, "wingspan," vision, hearing, head circumference, chest (in repose and expanded), hips, knees, calves, ankles, instep, elbows, wrists, and on and on. This information was reported regularly to attest to the fitness of the students, and Smith College frequently reported that students' health improved over their tenure at the college. (Bowditch, 1890: 287–304; Young, 2011: n.p.)

Composite photography and eugenics promoter Bowditch aided the state of Massachusetts in its development of a system to track the personal health and genetic data of each female student at private schools in the state, including Smith College (Bowditch, 1890: 287–304). This manner of cataloging female students was not unlike the one developed in 1879 by French criminologist Alphonse Bertillon, who created a system of measuring various body parts of criminals (including hair and eye color, head length and breadth, the length of the middle and small fingers, left foot, and forearm) in order to (reportedly) help police catch repeat offenders. In 1888, Bertillon added standard frontal and side-view "mugshots" – a means of conveying "pictorial statistics" – to his forensic anthropometric system cards for each criminal.

Inspired by Bertillon's anthropometry, which enjoyed enormous credibility and is still used in law enforcement today, Galton began using composite photography in the 1880s to create composite images of "mental images" of criminals (figs. 6.6 & 6.7), often comparing these "coarse and low types" to composite pictures of Royal Engineers for contrast (Galton, 1883: 10, 75, 77). Of particular note is Galton's arrangement of four "men convicted of larceny" (shown in upper-torso and frontal facial views) beside face-view-only composites of four men from the "normal population" of educated British non-combat soldiers and officers whose mission included providing engineering support for the army (fig. 6.7). Two of the portraits (bottom row, last two images) represent groups of newcomers (of eleven and thirty, Galton suggests) to the British Corps of Royal Engineers at the rank of "Private." Like the New England class of semi-aristocrats who were represented in *Composita*, these young men have "smooth," "slender," "pallid" faces with "regular" features, or those of "a certain delicacy" (Holmes, 1860: 92). Viewers also gain access to the majority of these soldiers' pupils, which are with "bright and quick" (Holmes, 1860: 92). As such, they conform to the "generic mental image" of the upper class that was described by Holmes and given tangible visual form in other composites by Lovell and Stoddard (Galton, 1883: 75, 77). Likewise, Galton's composites of the

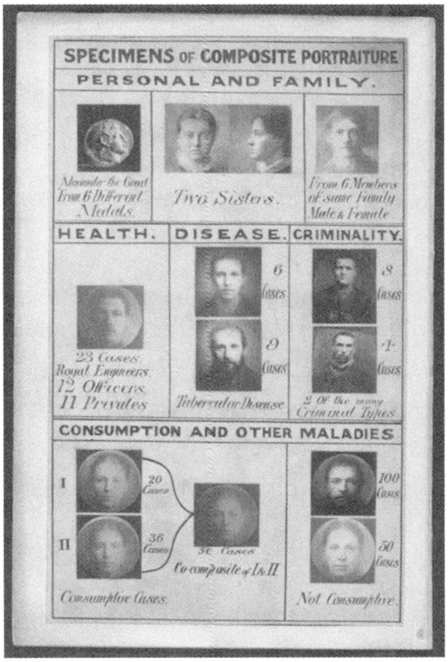


Fig. 6.6. Francis Galton, Frontispiece to *Inquiries into Human Faculty and Its Development*, 1883. (London, Macmillan: 1883). The Metropolitan Museum of Art. Joyce F. Menschel Photography Library Fund, 2002, transferred from the Joyce F. Menschel Photography Library.

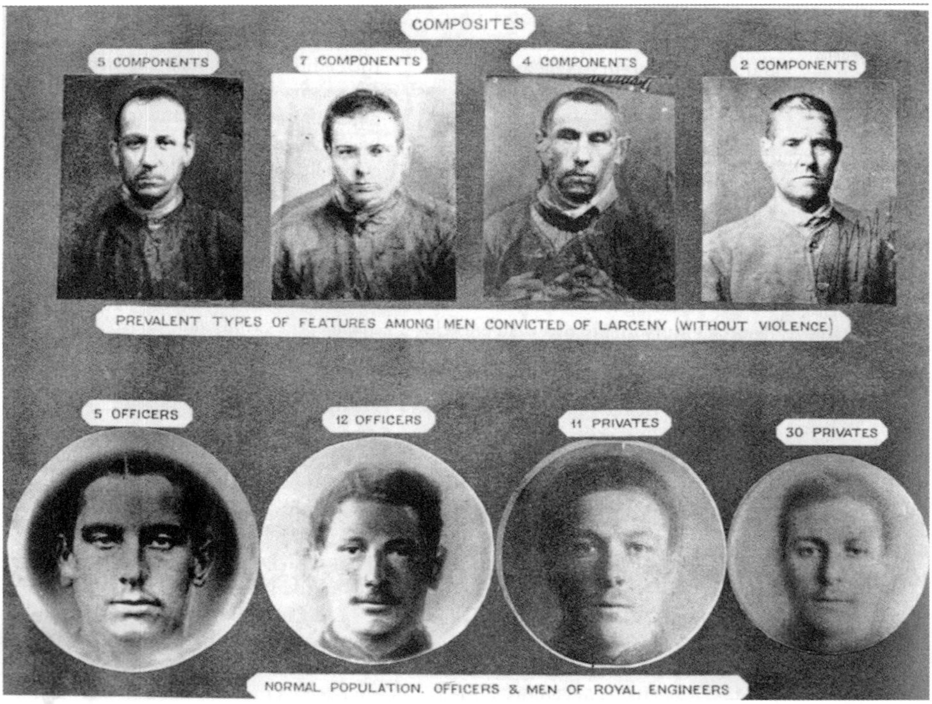


Fig. 6.7. Francis Galton, *Inquiries into Human Faculty and Its Development* (1883), 3rd Edition, Gavan Tredoux, ed. (London: Galton Archives, 2004), n.p. https://galton.org/books/human-faculty/text/galton-1883-human-faculty-v4.pdf (accessed December 24, 2020).

two officers (bottom row, first and second from the left) are shown in close-up facial view, with pupils fully revealed, smooth skin, and heroically squared jaws. By showing viewers composites of the Royal Engineers in close-up view, Galton invites them to access his subjects and to consider that they may possess what was of the utmost importance in society in the mid-to-late 19th century: "a perfect sincerity or 'transparency' of character," while also contrasting the valor of a life of service and patriotism to a life of crime (Halttunen, 1982: xvi).

In contrast to the Royal Engineers, the four aggregated criminals squint their eyes, likely in response to a frontal light source shining at them from above the photographer. Their gazes are obscured by the shadows of their brows and their distance from the camera. Two have undisciplined facial hair that stands in particular contrast to the well-trimmed mustache of the "12-Officers" composite (bottom row, second image from left). The criminals visually deviate from the "normal": the presumably "well-bred" men on the bottom row who represent the "ideal." Galton intended for these images to aid police in the identification of criminals and potential law-breakers by aggregating their appearances into a visual typology. But as these images engaged the discourse of Positive Eugenics (the identification of the "well-bred"), they also gave visual definition to the "ill-bred" in society. In doing so, Galton here inserts a eugenics-related message: that society could have been spared the presence of these criminals through the practice of good breeding.

The lessons of eugenics – and photographs such as Galton's that tangibly delineated the appearances of the "well-bred" and the "ill-bred" – helped upper-caste New England women identify potential husbands and eliminate "unfit" men from contention (Auger-Day, 2011: 11). This task was otherwise made increasingly difficult by the prolific presence of "'feeble-minded' men, especially high-functioning ones, [who] could much more easily pass as acceptable potential mates" (Auger-Day, 2011: 11). Upper-class New England women were taught to distrust "conscious social climbers" who might be "passing" for members of the upper-class bloodline for their own financial gain (Halttunen, 1982: xv). The women of Smith College and their families were incessantly reminded in mass-press articles that the young women's husband selections would directly impact the characters of their children: "A civilized person certainly inherits, by virtue of being born of civilized parents in a civilized country, a predisposition to certain modes of conception and feeling" (Holland, 1882: 43).

Torn between social/cultural expectations and their newfound freedom, almost all of the members of the Class of 1886, according to annual alumni letters, pursued careers in education as high school teachers and/or administrators. Five of the 49 women became college/university professors (Smith College, College Archives, 1909 and 1913). Three returned to Smith College as professors or administrators. According to an alumni letter written in 1888 by a member of the class, Sarah Dole, "the fact that any member of the class has turned pedagogue has ceased to be a novelty" (Dole, 1888: n.p.). Among those 41 women of the Class of 1886 who opted to become teachers, 29 of them (or every woman from the class who chose to get married) quit teaching and became full-time homemakers/socialites after marrying. Only about half of the women of the Class of 1886 had children (Various Authors, 1887–1948: n.p.).

The institution of marriage was a subject of frequent discussion among the members of the Class of 1886 and was the source of polarization within the group. Many of the women wrote of their beloved spouses and "engrossing" children in annual alumni update letters (Jones, 1901: n.p.). Margaretta (Duncan) Demarest echoed the sentiments of many classmates when she wrote that "[m]y interests are so merged in husband and daughters that a letter even to '86 must include my family" (Demarest, 1892: n.p.). In alumni letters, classmates shared news about engagements, their wedding plans, their spouses, their husbands' careers, their children, their children's marriages, and their grandchildren – in addition to sharing news about travel and illnesses, and extending open invitations to all classmates to drop by for a visit.

However, while just under 60 percent of the class married, twenty women from the class, or 40.8 percent of the group, never did. In a series of creative predictions about the ultimate life paths of her classmates written for graduation, Alice Waite recalled that Sarah Corns (who never married) spoke liberally against the expectation of matrimony (Waite, 1886: 69). More than a decade later, Corns lamented in an alumni letter from 1901 that her housekeepers would quit when they found husbands (Corns, 1901: n.p.). Edith Gaylord regularly voiced "strong personal feelings on the subject of Matrimony" (and never married), according to Waite (Waite, 1886: 67). Mary Eastman wrote in her alumni update letter of 1888 that "Marriage is a failure." Eastman never married (Eastman, 1888: n.p.).

Non-heteronormative sexuality was not overtly referenced in the women's correspondence, in keeping with Victorian-era social norms. Hints of it appear, however. In annual alumni reports, two classmates (who never married) separately mentioned having long-term, live-in "companions" of twenty or thirty years (Bradley and Hurlburt, 1932–1933: n.p.). Cisgender deviance was not only viewed with distain by the field of Eugenics, but also was seen as a willful subversion of the social/cultural expectations of the women of the Class of 1886, who were reminded of their missions to marry men, have children, manage the household staff, and maintain the family's social profile. References to LGBTQ desire were cleansed from the mass press. For instance, at the start of this essay, Adams quotes a "young man" who speaks eagerly of meeting the woman pictured in *Composita*. That "young man" actually was Elizabeth ("Bessie") Chandler, who wrote the poem "Her Photograph," which likely came to Adams's attention through its publication in *The Century Magazine* in April 1887 (fig. 6.8) (Chandler, 1887: 976). In this poem, Chandler begins with an expression of attraction: "My heart was captured by her face: / I loved her at first-sight." She refers to *Composita* as a "queen" who made her "pulses stir." After finding out that the photograph described a woman who never existed, she closes the poem as follows: "And this one thing I ask of you, – / Can you, with all your art, / Unite then forty-nine poor bits / And give me back my heart?" For readers of *The Boston Daily Globe*, to speak freely of homoerotic attraction as a flood of immigrants threatened the stability of the Brahmin-led social/political/economic order was potentially destabilizing.

The women of the Class of 1886 were split over fulfilling the expectations of their social caste, vis-à-vis marriage and children, or the antithesis: remaining single and pursuing their careers independently and/or living in accord with their non-heteronormative sexualities. *Composita*, an image of class unity and a New England social-caste typology, cloaked these divisions, while subtly underscoring the mission of Positive Eugenics. As a "data portrait" that vacillated between objectivity and subjectivity, *Composita* at once reified upper-class New England privilege while at the same time becoming an icon of liberation for Smith graduates hoping for a different future from that of their mothers. It was a complex image that perhaps was fitting as the unofficial "mascot" for a graduating class of women who came of age during a period of transformation not only of their social caste, but also of their gender.

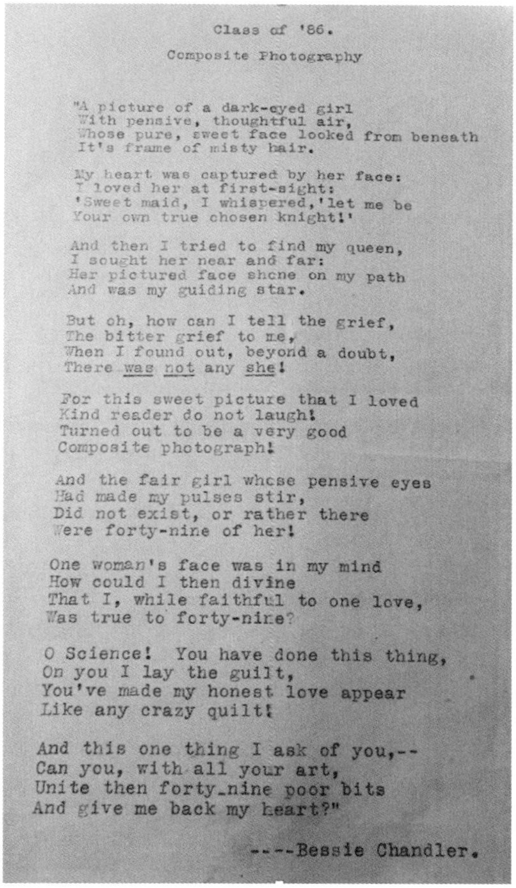

Class of '86.

Composite Photography

"A picture of a dark-eyed girl
With pensive, thoughtful air,
Whose pure, sweet face looked from beneath
It's frame of misty hair.

My heart was captured by her face:
I loved her at first-sight:
'Sweet maid, I whispered,'let me be
Your own true chosen knight!'

And then I tried to find my queen,
I sought her near and far:
Her pictured face shone on my path
And was my guiding star.

But oh, how can I tell the grief,
The bitter grief to me,
When I found out, beyond a doubt,
There was not any she!

For this sweet picture that I loved
Kind reader do not laugh!
Turned out to be a very good
Composite photograph!

And the fair girl whose pensive eyes
Had made my pulses stir,
Did not exist, or rather there
Were forty-nine of her!

One woman's face was in my mind
How could I then divine
That I, while faithful to one love,
Was true to forty-nine?

O Science! You have done this thing,
On you I lay the guilt,
You've made my honest love appear
Like any crazy quilt!

And this one thing I ask of you,--
Can you, with all your art,
Unite then forty-nine poor bits
And give me back my heart?"

----Bessie Chandler.

Fig. 6.8. Bessie Chandler, "Her Photograph," 1887. Retyped from original manuscript. Originally published in *The Century Magazine*, April 1887. Smith College, College Archives, Box 80, *Class of 1886: Records*, No. 1425. Public Domain.

## Notes

1 This is based on a Pictriev scan and comparison, made using this interface on Jan. 17, 2019: https://www.betafaceapi.com/demo_old.html.

## Bibliography

W. I. Lincoln Adams, "Composite Photography: Of Especial Interest to the Amateur," *The Boston Daily Globe* (June 2, 1890): 8.

Ceilidh Robin Auger-Day, "Six-Nippled Sheep and Other Eugenic Oddities: Exploring Voices of the American Eugenics Movement in the Northeast from 1883 to the Mid-1920s," *Theses, Dissertations, and Projects*, Paper 269, Smith College (2011).

Matthew Biro, *The Dada Cyborg: Visions of the New Human in Weimar Berlin* (Minneapolis: University of Minnesota Press, 2009).

Henry Pickering Bowditch, "The Physique of Women in Massachusetts," *21st Annual Report of the State Board of Health of Massachusetts* (Boston: Wright & Potter, 1890): 287–304.

Henry Pickering Bowditch, "Are Composite Photographs Typical Pictures?," *McClure's Magazine*, 3, 4 (Sept. 11, 1894): 331–42.

Emma Bradley and Katherine Hurlburt, "Letters of the Class of 1886," Unpublished. Smith College Archives, Class Records, Box 80.CLA.1426. (1932–1933).

Chloe S. Burke and Christopher J. Castaneda, "The Public and Private History of Eugenics: An Introduction," *The Public Historian,* 29, 3 (Summer 2007): 5–17.

Bessie Chandler, "Her Photograph," *The Century Magazine* (April 1887): 976.

Sarah Ann Corns, "Letters of the Class of 1886," Unpublished. Smith College Archives, Class Records, Box 80.CLA. (1901).

Kati Curts, "Shadowy Relations and Shades of Devotion: Production and Possession of the 1886 Smith College Composite Photograph," in *Sensational Religion*, ed. Sally Promey (New Haven: Yale University Press, 2014): 113–34.

Charles B. Davenport, *The Trait Book* (Cold Spring Harbor, N.Y.: Eugenics Society/United States Government, 1912).

Margaretta (Duncan) Demarest, "Letters of the Class of 1886," Unpublished. Smith College Archives, Class Records, Box 80.CLA.1426. Feb. (1892).

Sarah Dole, "Letters of the Class of 1886," Unpublished. Smith College Archives, Class Records, Box 80.CLA.1426. (1888).

Judith Donath, Alex Dragulescu, Aaron Zinman, et al., "Data Portraits," *Leonardo*, 43, 4 (2010): 375–83.

Mary Eastman, "Letters of the Class of 1886," Unpublished. Smith College Archives, Class Records, Box 80.CLA.1426. (1888).

James Emmott, "Parameters of Vibration, Technologies of Capture, and Layering of Voices and Faces in the Nineteenth Century," *Victorian Studies,* 53, 3 (Spring 2011): 468–78.

Francis Galton, "Composite Portraits, Made by Combining Those of Many Different Persons Into a Single Resultant Figure," *Journal of the Anthropological Institute of Great Britain and Ireland,* 8 (1879): 132–44.

Francis Galton, *Generic Images* (London: William Clowes and Sons, 1879).

Francis Galton, *Inquiries Intro Human Faculty and Its Development* (1883), Third Edition, ed. Gavan Tredoux (London: Galton Archives, 2004). https://galton.org/books/human-faculty/text/galton-1883-human-faculty-v4.pdf (accessed December 24, 2020).

Francis Galton, *Memories of My Life* (London: Methuen, 1908).

Mark H. Haller, *Eugenics: Hereditarian Attitudes in American Thought* (New Brunswick: Rutgers University Press, 1963).

Karen Halttunen, *Confidence Men and Painted Women: A Study of Middle-Class Culture in America, 1830–1870* (New Haven: Yale University Press, 1982).

Marouf Arif Hasian, Jr., *The Rhetoric of Eugenics in Anglo-American Thought* (Athens: University of Georgia Press, 1996).

F. M. Holland, "How Virtue and Vice Are Transmitted," *Index Newspaper* (July 27, 1882): 43.

Oliver Wendell Holmes, Sr., "The Professor's Story – Chapter 1: The Brahmin Caste of New England," *The Atlantic Monthly*, 5, 27 (1860): 91–92.

Jane H. Hunter, *How Young Ladies Became Girls: The Victorian Origins of American Girlhood* (New Haven: Yale University Press, 2002).

Katherine Hurlburt, "Letters of the Class of 1886," Unpublished. Smith College Archives, Class Records, Box 80.CLA.1426. (1888).

Joseph Jastrow, "Composite Portraiture," *Science*, 6, 134 (Aug. 28, 1885): 165.

Allen Johnson, ed., *The Chronicles of America*, 33 (New Haven: Yale University Press, 1921).

Margaret Clarke (Atwater) Jones, "Letters of the Class of 1886," Unpublished. Smith College Archives, Class Records, Box 80.CLA.1426. (1901).

Ingrid Kallick-Wakker, "Science Icons: The Visualization of Scientific Truths," *Leonardo*, 27, 4 (1994): 309–15.

*Our Famous Women: Comprising the Lives and Deeds of American Women* (Hartford, CT: A.D. Worthington and Co., 1883).

Charles Sanders Peirce, "Logic as Semiotic: The Theory of Signs," in *Semiotics: An Introductory Anthology*, ed. Robert E. Innis (Bloomington: Indiana University Press, 1985): 1–23.

Leona Peirce, "Letters of the Class of 1886," Unpublished. Smith College Archives, Class Records, Box 80.CLA.1426. (Feb. 1892).

Zulema A. Ruble, *Composita: A Drama in Three Acts* (Canton, IL: Canton Register Printing House, 1886).

Kate Sanborn, "Social Life at Smith College," *Demorest's Monthly Magazine* (1881): 539.

Allan Sekula, "The Body and the Archive," *October*, 39 (Winter 1986): 3–64.

Smith College, College Archives, Box 80, No. 1425, Class of 1886: Records/Alumni Letters.

Smith College, Class of 1886. *Bulletin and Alumnae Register, 1908–1909* (Northampton: Smith College, 1909).

Smith College, *Alumnae Catalog: 1875–1915* (Northampton: Smith College, 1916).

Smith College, *Academic Departments, Records*. Various Departments. CA-MS-01010 (Northampton: Smith College, c. 1886).

Elmer Ernest Southard, 1876–1920, "Concerning the Study of Eugenics in Massachusetts," Center for the History of Medicine, Harvard University. Papers of Elmer Ernest Southard, 1893–1940 (inclusive). GA 81, Box 7, Folder: Eugenics in Massachusetts (1910), http://collections.countway.harvard.edu/onview/items/show/6236 (accessed April 18, 2016).

Oren Baruch Stier, "Picture Imperfect: Photography and Eugenics, 1870–1940 (Review)," *Holocaust and Genocide Studies*, 24, 3 (Winter 2010): 476–79.

John T. Stoddard, "Composite Portraiture," *Science*, 8, 182 (July 30, 1886): frontispiece.

Unknown. "The Class of '86, Composita," (Poem) Verse 6, Line 1, *Smith College Commencement Exercises,* 1886 (Boston: South End Industrial School Press, 1886).

Various Authors, "Letters of the Class of 1886," Unpublished. Smith College Archives, Class Records, Box 80.CLA.1426.

Alice V. Waite, "Prophecy," Smith College Commencement Exercises, 1886 (Boston: South End Industrial School Press, 1886).

Richard Wright, "Computer Graphics as Allegorical Knowledge: Electronic Imagery in the Sciences," *Leonardo*, Supplemental Issue, 3 (1990): 65–73.

Nanci Young, "Composita of Smith," *Smith College Archives* (Blog), Feb. 14, 2011. Accessed May 10, 2016. Available online at: https://smitharchives.wordpress.com/2011/02/.

# "A Single Multiple Image": The Visual Rhetoric of *An Ethiopian Chief*

Geoff Bender

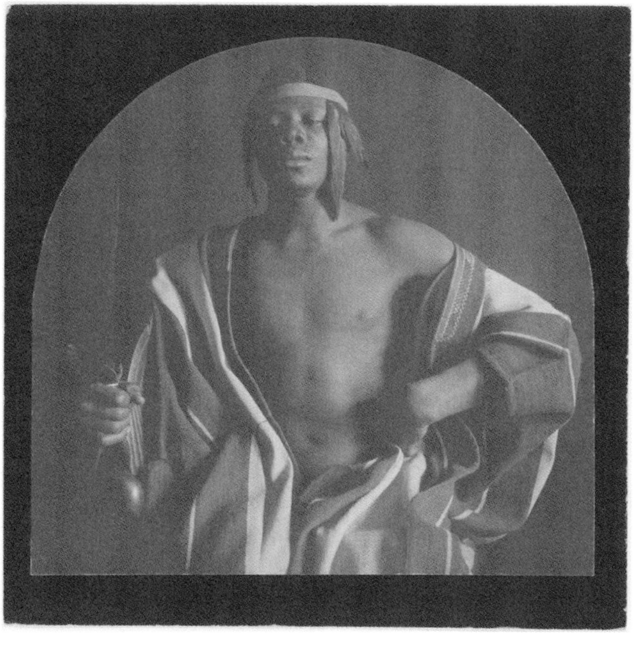

Fig. 7.1. F. Holland Day, *An Ethiopian Chief*, 1897. Alfred Stieglitz Collection, The Metropolitan Museum of Art, New York. Source: Art Resource, NY.

F. Holland Day's portrait of J. Alexandre Skeete, *An Ethiopian Chief* (fig. 7.1), is not the most famous of a suite of photographs later critics would call Day's "Nubian Series" (Crump, 199: 24; Jussim, 1983: 131), which comprised roughly fifteen art portraits of two African American models, Skeete and J. R. Carter, taken between 1896 and 1897.[1] Of these portraits, the most famous was, and likely still is, *Ebony & Ivory* (pl. 10), a full-length nude profile of Carter, crouched before a black background and lifting up, as if for contemplation, a white plaster satyr. During its time,

*Ebony & Ivory* was celebrated as "a novel and beautiful study of contrast," "perfect as a composition," and "exquisitely rendered" (White, 1897: 104). Today, recent critical appraisal still lauds the composition for its portrayal of an "exquisitely formed black body" amplified by "a starkly white antique statuette," which Carter "admiringly held" (Curtis, 2017: 147). And yet, if *An Ethiopian Chief* isn't Day's most striking portrait of African American male beauty, it might well be his most remarkable – for the relatively unremarkable detail of Skeete's closed eyes, refusing to engage the photographer, the viewer, and the world. These shut eyes become the convergence point for a striking clash of visual agencies: Day's, for one, working to fashion Skeete's body an exemplar of a distinctly queer form of male beauty; the agencies of dominant culture, racializing Skeete as the exotic and dangerous Other; and, lastly, Skeete's, working against this cacophony of aesthetic coding. This agential clashing endures as the photograph's irresolvable problem presented as a rhetorical conundrum.

What follows is an exploration of the portrait's irresolution, performed by a tracing out of its networks, visible and invisible, which make the picture work in such conflicting ways. As explained below, these networks will be theorized along the lines of Bruno Latour's Actor Network Theory, which has inspired exciting new work in visual analysis, particularly in the field of visual rhetorics. The ensuing analysis seeks to extend that work further into the field of photography studies, where Latourian theory has just begun to make inroads.

## Network Theory, Visual Rhetorics, and Material Agency

Perhaps because it is so adaptable to such a wide range of problems dealing with systems and structures, network theory now proliferates academic writing, spanning disciplines across the humanities, social sciences, and natural sciences. Indeed, the network itself is now considered a science, promoted by such writers as sociologist Duncan J. Watts, who describes the network as encompassing everything from "the world of people, friendships, [and] rumors" to "disease, fads, firms, and financial crises" (2003: 13). Although network theory has yet to deeply penetrate photography studies, it is crucial to related fields, including media studies, communication studies, and rhetoric and composition. Visual rhetoricians, in particular, such as Laurie Gries, Bradford Vivian, Cara A. Finnegan, and Jens E. Kjeldsen have meaningfully adapted network theory, especially Latourian network theory, to their respective projects, and for two important reasons: (1) it provides compelling accounts of how images metamorphose as they circulate; and (2), relatedly, it provides compelling accounts of how images acquire and use material agency, so they are not just passive receivers of human-imposed meaning, but are instead possessed of their own power to shape that meaning through an exchange with the things they are linked to, including the viewers. Such an exchange gives images rhetorical power that is partially the consequence of the work of images themselves rather than merely what spectators project onto them. As Laurie Gries notes, "Visual things are recognized" by rhetorical scholars "as co-constituting reality and having a rhetorical life of their own" (2015b: xviii) – a life that is integral to but also apart from human life. Thinking of photographs and, by extension, of all visual objects in this posthuman way necessitates a shift in understanding about what such objects do, and what they are, via paradigms that are, as Scot Barnett and Casey Boyle argue, "expansive enough to speculate about things ontologically" (2016: 2). Things, from this viewpoint, have lives independent of human creation and human systems, however much human creation might be integral to them.

As such, thing-centered network theory moves away from linguistically rooted interpretive models. Composed of assemblages of objects, networks are understood, frequently, as "nondiscursive" (Barnett and Boyle, 2016: 3), made of a concreteness that linguistic frameworks, such as semiotics, often lack. This is not to say that linguistic methodologies like semiotics must, of necessity, give way or that they lack profound explanatory power. Indeed, as a map of linguistic operations, semiotics is a form of network theory. However, because sign systems define uniquely human categories of meaning they are less useful to posthuman speculations about object relations, or what Timothy Morton calls relations of "interobjectivity" (2013: 82), which seek wider ecologies that inevitably decenter the human. In these ecologies, humans are but one subset of objects in dense, interlocking organizations dominated, in sheer numbers, by nonhuman things.

Some of the most compelling versions of network theory are founded on Bruno Latour's Actor-Network Theory, which will serve as the primary methodological driver of this study. In a Latourian network, each constituent is an actor, or, as Latour has frequently put it, an "actant," to remove the morphological distinction between subjects that initiate action and objects that receive it (1999: 180). Actants in a Latourian network both initiate and receive action from surrounding actants in a perpetual relay of network-structured influence. For Latour, action is necessary to a thing's very existence. "[T]here is no other way to define" an entity, he writes, "but through its action" (1999: 122). Thus things – people included – cannot exist in a state of isolation. Instead, they're in a constant state of dynamic interplay, unfolding through impact on and from other things they are webbed to. As Latour says: All actants "are modified, transformed, perturbed, or created by the character that is the focus of [a network's] attention" (1999: 122). Simultaneously receiving and performing action, a thing plays the double-role of an "actor-enacted" (Law and Mol, 2010: 72), working as "a mediator" in a Latourian network, "demanding its [own] share of reality" (Harman, 2009: 18).

Provocatively, such actants operate in both actual and virtual spaces; they include things as empirically verifiable as "single-malt scotch, Land Rovers, [and] lychee fruit" (Bogost, 2012: 12) and things far out of the purview of the empirical, such as "Harry Potter" and "hallucinations" (Bryant, Srnicek, and Harman, 2011: 5). For Latourians, the "incorporeal and corporeal realms are equally capable of having effect in the world" (Bryant, Srnicek, and Harman, 2011: 5), and "effect in the world" is an actant's *sine qua non*. Discerning *how* an image has effect in the world is, of course, a visual rhetorician's fundamental task.

In Latourian terms, the photograph is both a network and a node in a set of intersecting networks. These networks might be constructed entirely outside of human culture, as when a photograph is dropped in the woods and decomposes there. Conversely, they might be made of the things of human culture – actants organized by the categories of culture to serve as the conduits of meaning that make photographs rhetorical. Discerning the networks that inform a photograph is thus crucial to a rich understanding of that visual object. Gries articulates a visual rhetorician's methodology precisely: "[I]f we follow an actant, trace its collective activities, and embrace rich description to create symmetrical accounts, it *is* possible to learn, at least in part, how a single multiple image becomes rhetorical with time and space" (2015a: 301; emphasis original). This is precisely the work that will be performed here.

Digital photographs likely provide the readiest examples of photographs situated in networked environments, leading Alexandra Moschovi, Carol McKay, and Arabella Plouviez to call the digital photograph a 'networked image": an "adaptable, connected *process* of communication" (2013: 13; my emphasis). Thinking in Latourian terms, however, leads us to the inevitable conclusion that digital photographs are but one form of the networked image. As objects whose meanings are determined through complex relays of information entailing multiple networks to make and sustain them, analog photos, too, qualify as networked images.

Because of the dynamism that is a condition of networked engagement, the photograph remains in an ever-unsettled state, ever contingent on the work of actants to assert its presence. This is a matter that visual rhetoricians have dwelt on at some length, though not always within the parameters of network theory. For Barbie Zelizer, for example, the photograph's status as a linked, ever-changing object "introduc[es] chance and relativity into its appropriation by [human] spectators," as any variable linked to the photograph will, in ways both dramatic and subtle, change the picture the spectator beholds (2004: 161). For Kjeldsen, a photograph's "situational" and "embedded narrative" scenarios are imbricated in – or are networked to enable – the photograph's material form (2015: 201–202). Vivian elaborates on the capacity of such visual networks by suggesting that "the non-representational dimensions of images," dimensions that "resist saturation" by human-derived meaning, are especially instrumental to a photograph's rhetorical agency, prompting photographic images to "disseminate sense and value of their own accord" rather than "as instruments of conscious design or reasoned [human] interpretation" (2007: 474, 479). And if the photograph has the power to "disseminate," it also, as an actant, has the power to "sting" or "cut" the viewer, as in Roland Barthes's photographic theory (1980/2010: 27) – or, in Geoffrey Batchen's gentler version of a photograph's tactility, to "casually graz[e] the pores of our skin with [its] textured surfaces" (2001: 61). Either way, the photograph both receives our gaze and agentially "touch[es] back" (Batchen, 2001: 61) as an actant in the visual network that beholding a photograph constructs.

## Racializing *An Ethiopian Chief*: A Network Operation

While *An Ethiopian Chief* is technically an example of *fin-de-siècle* fine art portraiture, it assumed rhetorical power in American visual culture via the intersection of multiple, competing networks of images that made the picture generically complex. Two of the most important networks entailed in racializing Skeete entered the photograph from white supremacist culture to perform its nefarious work. These are the network of nineteenth-century anthropological photography, which might be considered an iteration of high-culture white supremacism, and the network organized by lynching photography, a low-culture counterpart that was peaking during the turn of the century, when *An Ethiopian Chief* was taken (Apel, 2004: 15). While these species of photography were intended for different audiences and purposes, their common derogatory aims linked them profoundly.

## Making *An Ethiopian Chief* Anthropological

From the outset, it's important to note that nineteenth-century anthropology was practiced very differently from today's versions of the discipline. "For much of that century," Christopher Pinney explains, "it was the human body" – not culture – "that constituted the proper terrain for study" (2011: 15). Anthropology was thus "little more than a form of comparative anatomy" (Pinney, 2011: 15). The discipline's body focus undoubtedly assisted anthropology's elite culture assertions about white superiority. Anthropology's formalized racialist discourse coexisted with that of related academic disciplines, ethnography and ethnology, which, over the nineteenth century, either competed with anthropology for dominance (Stocking, 1987: 247–248) or were incorporated into anthropology as sub-disciplines (Sibeud, 2008: 96). As anthropology remained the academic constant in dominant culture's scholarly inquiry into human populations during the *fin de siècle*, this will be the preferred term here.

Photography's role in 19th-century anthropology was not minor. As Pinney and others have persuasively argued, the two practices matured together (Pinney, 2011; Edwards, 1992). Photography was, after all, deeply involved in the scientific empirical enterprise of bringing what was otherwise invisible – either because of size or speed or geographical remoteness – to the mainstream eye. Photography was, as Tom Gunning notes, enlarging viewers' sense of the "finite and tangible world of material things" into a "limitless, expanding, and decentered space" (2008: 53). Anthropology, arguably, aimed for an analogous expansion, though its ethnocentric drives clearly sought to retain white culture's colonial center. Nevertheless, both photography and anthropology participated in a series of reorienting shifts, in parallel and collaborative ways, in a "quest to re-present areas of darkness under the revealing light of [empiricist] investigation" (Pinney, 1992: 78).

Such "areas of darkness" included, of course, those peoples of color whom anthropologists taxonomized as inferior in their obsessive development of racial hierarchies that located Anglo-American modernity and Greco-Roman antiquity at the cultural and physical pinnacles of human development. Anthropologist Samuel George Morton, for example, takes pains in his exhaustive study of human skulls to contrast the "fine oval...voluminous head" of the "perfect Grecian countenance" (1839: 12) possessed of an indisputable "intellectual character" (1844: 34) with the "long and narrow" head, "small" chin, "broad and flat" nose, and "thick" lips of the "joyous, flexible, and indolent" members of the "Ethiopian Race," who rank, in Morton's thinking, in "the lowest grade of humanity" (1839: 6–7).

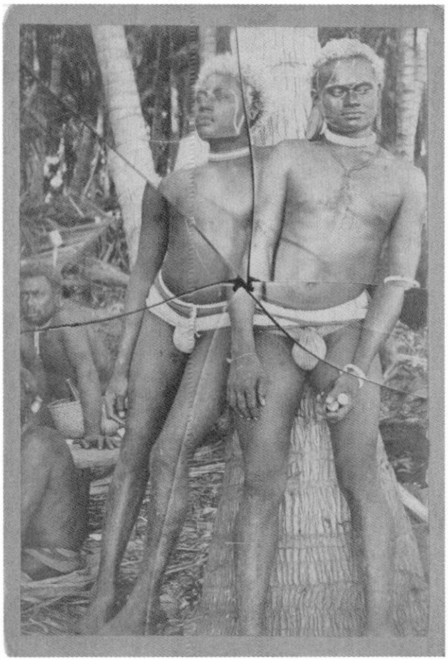

Fig. 7.2. H. T. B. Somerville, *Men of New Georgia Solomon Islands*, 1893-94. RAI 1773. The Royal Anthropological Institute of Great Britain and Ireland.

While Morton's phrenological and physiognomic studies are supported by line drawings rather than photographs, photographs appeared in anthropological works later in the century as proof positive of anthropological claims about race. The positivistic visual analysis buttressing these claims, in turn, shaped interpretations of future photographs in mutually reinforcing cycles (Baker, 1998: 3). Racist assertions thus became deeply embedded in the language of social scientific objectivity with the assistance of visual mechanisms. The ostensible disinterestedness of empiricism and the otherizing apparatus of anthropological investigation enabled nude or scantily dressed black bodies to circulate visually over transatlantic disciplinary networks, filling articles and books where white bodies would have been more likely to set off alarm bells triggering Victorian moral censure.

Anthropological photographs of nonwestern bodies that circulated and gained power in the discipline emerged from a variety of sources. Many were taken *in situ*, in the communities where "missionaries, traders or colonial administrators" took pictures that "theorists and synthesizers based in the colonial metropole" would later make sense of (Pinney, 2011: 15). The practice of fieldwork was only just emerging, and so visual material tended to move from the academically untrained to the trained for analysis. Lieutenant H. T. B. Somerville's photograph, *Men of New Georgia Solomon Islands* (fig. 7.2), taken while Somerville was conducting a hydrographic survey for the Royal Navy (Wright, 2013: 5), serves as a case in point. In the photograph, two young men stand contrapposto, their hair and faces accented with lime, their bodies on full frontal display. It's difficult not to see seduction in the combination of their far-off gazes and bodily availability, what looks like a feint of nonchalance as Somerville takes the shot. The picture nevertheless passed as something else: a clinical sample of an indigenous people doing what natives do when at home.

Such *in situ* photographs composed one version of the visual network in anthropology. It was joined by a second, organized around the science of anthropometry, which, in the 19th century, amounted to the measurement of body forms for racially diagnostic purposes. One example of such anthropometric pictures, prominent in recent photography scholarship (Pinney, 2011: 29; Smith, 2013: 45–47; Spencer, 1992: 102–103), is John Lamprey's frontal view of a Malayan male (fig. 7.3). Lamprey developed a grid of two-inch squares to assess the height, girth, and posture of his subjects, enabling easy comparison with, in his words, "the anatomical structure of a good academy figure or model of six feet" (Lamprey, 1869: 85). Like Morton, Lamprey invokes classical anatomy as an ostensibly objective standard against which to measure the nonwestern exotic. As with Somerville's *in situ* photograph, Lamprey's picture is formulated by an empiricist aesthetic that permits spectators to look long at the naked subject. The Malayan man's body is presented as a kind of absolute availability because it's understood, in this empiricist fiction, as incapable of arousing erotic response from Western viewers.

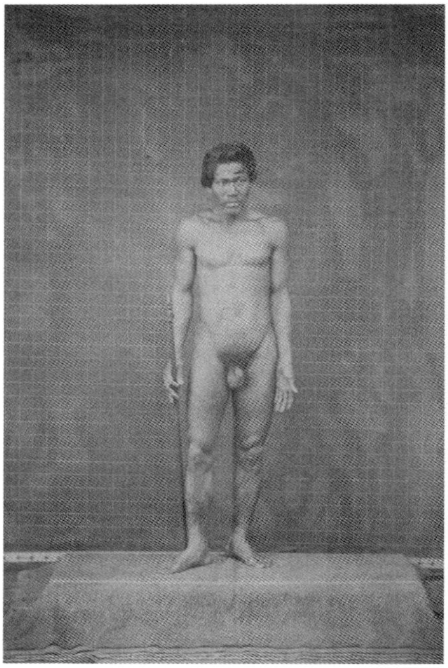

Fig. 7.3. John Lamprey, Front View of a Malayan Male, Ternate, Aged Twenty-five, c. 1868-69. RAI2116. The Royal Anthropological Institute of Great Britain and Ireland.

A crucial difference between Somerville's and Lamprey's photo, however, is the presence, in the latter, of an impromptu studio in place of native habitat. Such a site was not unique to Lamprey's work. The studio provided anthropologists with the means to focus a viewer's eye on the body-as-specimen in a decontextualized space, so that the exoticism could be constructed by the body alone, with minimal if any props. In the United States, Harvard professor of natural history Louis Agassiz made similar use of studio space to conduct studies of American slaves born in Africa – putatively pure representatives, Agassiz thought, of ethnological differences that could be categorized and ranked. As an exemplar of the Gullah people, Agassiz chose Jem (fig. 7.4), whose full-length nude portraits were taken in the studio of South Carolina photographer J. T. Zealy. Agassiz's underlying motivation here was to present African bodies as "ocular evidence" that the races emerged from different originary parents (Schneider, 2012: 214) – that, in other words, polygenesis was self-evidently real. The studio space in this photograph is striking both for its empty background – it lacks even the Lamprey grid – and for the ironic presence of the set pieces typical of bourgeois portraiture: a parquet floor and a posing stand used when middle-class clients sat for their portraits to ensure stillness. Once Zealy completed his commission for Agassiz, his studio likely reverted to this use.

Regardless of whatever socially neutral claims Agassiz's empiricism might have been aiming for, Jem's nakedness, like that of the Malayan male and of the New Georgian youths, is unmistakably erotic – a matter that has drawn sustained attention from scholars analyzing Agassiz's work. For Suzanne Schneider, Jem's nakedness signals a "troubling collapse of distinctions" between "empirics" and "erotics" (2012: 214). While this conclusion has merit, it could also be said that

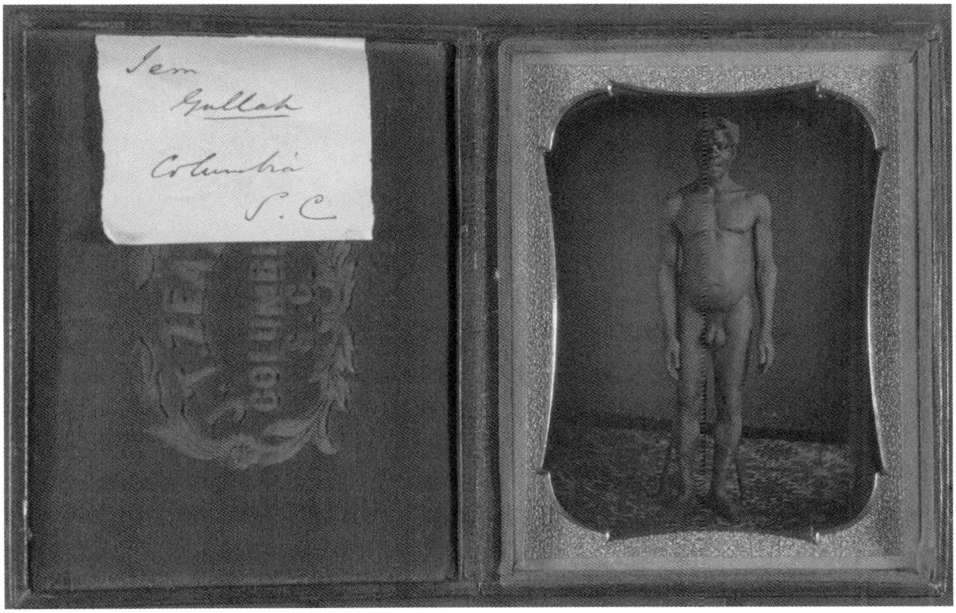


Fig. 7.4. J. T. Zealy, *Jem*, 1850. Courtesy of the Peabody Museum of Archaeology and Ethnology, Harvard University, PM 35-5-10/53046.

empiricism doesn't just collapse into eroticism but rather *becomes a means* to eroticism, to the end of making nonwestern bodies sexually immediate and simultaneously distant to spectators from dominant culture. Moreover, the collapse Schneider refers to could be seen, otherwise, as a strategic disjunction in which the unfamiliar (exoticized male nudity) is made to stand beside the familiar (the middle-class portrait studio) in a mélange that deepens the eroticization of Jem's body for a bourgeois viewer like Agassiz. Alan Trachtenberg addresses this point precisely when he argues that Agassiz's slave photographs are possessed of "a power to subvert the very conventions of portraiture" created by nineteenth-century studios (1989: 56). It is the subversion effected by visual disjunction that conduces to the portraits' erotic outcome. Such compositional disjunction puts the spectator, in the view of Brian Wallis, in the role of "unwavering...voyeuris[m]" – hardly the stance of a disinterested scientist – that moves this picture of Jem swiftly into the realm of pornography (1995: 54), however much anthropology has laid claim

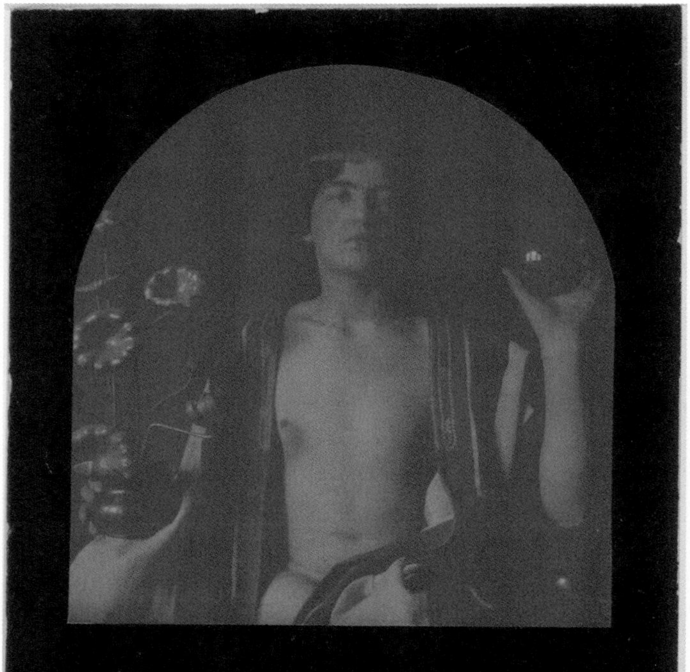

Fig. 7.5. F. Holland Day, *Beauty Is Truth, Truth Beauty*, 1896. The Louise Imogen Guiney Collection. Library of Congress, Prints and Photographs Division.

to loftier grounds. Much the same could be said about the portraits of the Malayan male and the New Georgian youths.

Though the degree of F. Holland Day's familiarity with the anthropological photography of his time remains uncertain, *An Ethiopian Chief* clearly draws on this genre's empiricist aesthetic in its rhetorical construction. To put the relationship between Day's photograph and this genre in more Latourian terms, *An Ethiopian Chief* could be said to a be a node where several anthropological networks converge, where the *in situ* and anthropometric strands of anthropological visual culture join with Agassiz's natural history to leave their agential presences in Day's portrait of Skeete. Imported with these presences are the viewing conventions that have been naturalized to anthropological photography, permitting a long look at Skeete. Anthropologizing props like the striped shawl Skeete is made to wear and the spear he is made to hold are especially important visual reinforcers of this aesthetic, casting Skeete as both exotically "Ethiopian" and diminutively safe.

The winged crown, however, poses a more complicated problem. On one hand, it could be seen as an inverted version of a American Indian headdress, further exoticizing Skeete without deepening the pseudo-African references. On the other hand, the headdress reproduces the crown said to be worn by the Greek god Hypnos, as Shawn Michelle Smith has noted (2013: 60). Indeed, this prop, and also the striped robe, are the very same items worn by a white model in Day's earlier portrait, *Beauty Is Truth, Truth Beauty* (fig. 7.5), which serves an additional antecedent of – and actant tracing its way through – *An Ethiopian Chief*'s visual construction, further complicating its rhetorical significance.

While these props create a degree of aesthetic indeterminacy for both white and black models, it is Skeete's black body alone that links to the anthropological photography explored above. The white model can be seen, in contrast, as more straightforwardly classicized. This is not to say, however, that Skeete's body has not also been classicized or in some way ennobled through Day's aesthetic design. Smith is not wrong to see *An Ethiopian Chief* as "celebrat[ing] African royalty as the pinnacle of classical values and the black male body as the height of beauty and truth" (2013: 60). The portrait is thus, in Latourian terms, a particularly fraught example of the "tangled objects" that "circulate in [Latour's] metaphorical flatland of distributed agency" (Herndl and Graham, 2015: 49). Both ennobled and degraded, Skeete's body is, in any case, constructed by Day's version of the white gaze – to be sure, an aesthete's gaze – for white spectators who can look long in "the pursuit of endless, if unspoken, pleasure" (Schneider, 2012: 232) derived from the visual conquest of Skeete's form.

Considered anthropologically, then, *An Ethiopian Chief* demonstrates one version of white fetishization of the black male body that renders it, as Homi K. Bhabha has argued, "at once an object of desire and derision" (2004: 96) before the gaze of dominant culture – a precise outcome of the agency of networked images working at cross purposes within and around Day's photographic practices. As such, *An Ethiopian Chief* becomes a *fin-de-siècle* version of what Maurice O. Wallace describes as "the most egregious problem for representations of the black man in American public life" (2002: 20). Which is to say that the empiricist aesthetic Day deployed did more than provide a means by which white spectators could look long at naked black bodies without moral censure. Indeed, this fetishization technique also effectively contained the double threat of black masculinity: its putative hypersexuality and its so-called "innate savagery," both of which cast black male bodies as deeply dangerous to white men's potency and white women's chastity in the paranoia of a white supremacist, heterosexual universe (Leiter, 2010: 31). In *An Ethiopian Chief*, Skeete's body was rendered safe for white viewers because of the "necessary anonymity" that his Ethiopianness, empirically constructed, produced (Wallace, 2002: 32). Such othering completed a process of objectification that has made black male bodies, then and now, fully ready "to be penetrated and possessed by [the] all-powerful desire" of the white gaze (Mercer, 1994: 177) – a rhetorical strategy that, in the 19th century, linked anthropological scientificity quite explicitly with lynching.

## The Lynching Photograph and Skeete's Refusal

In *An Ethiopian Chief*, the two hems of Skeete's robe join at his navel, pointing downwards towards his groin. For Hazel V. Carby, this juncture marks a point in the "erotic triangle of sexual promise" that centers Day's portrait of Skeete. Carby's allusion, however, is not to the empiricist erotics of anthropological photography, but instead to the lynch mob, which would frequently castrate its victims before hanging them (1998: 55). Castration, as Dora Apel notes, worked on symbolic and literal levels alike, "emasculat[ing] the African American male in both political and physical terms" (2004: 24) to render him doubly impotent. In the act of castration, white "fears and desires" were "acted out in ritual fervor" to ensure white men's power over the perceived black threat (Carby, 1998: 46).

At the time Day created his "Nubian" portraits, the practice of lynching was reaching a zenith (Apel, 2004: 15), and lynching photographs were proliferating white popular culture. Images of lynched black men, in particular, circulated widely. Inevitably, they coalesced into a discrete photographic genre, a visual network that channeled into and freighted Day's African American portraiture. The lynching photograph, Carby explains, "must be recognized as the ever-present underside of artistic or philosophical imaginings of black masculinity as tropes of utopian possibility" (1998: 47) – tropes that include *An Ethiopian Chief* as a *fin-de-siècle* exemplar. Smith argues as much when she asserts that "Day's African American male nudes openly valorize the black male body at a time when that body was literally torn apart by lynch mobs" (2013: 53). However, following Carby's logic, such valorization of the black male body was inseparable from the violence of white supremacy that made lynching the counter to, or strange twin of, such idealization. Put differently, it could be argued that rendering a black male body "utopian" in white supremacist culture could only take place against the background of lynched black men. The link between foreground and background, between white supremacist idealization and demonization of black bodies, was Jim Crow, which defined the white supremacist code of post-Reconstruction America, particularly in the South.

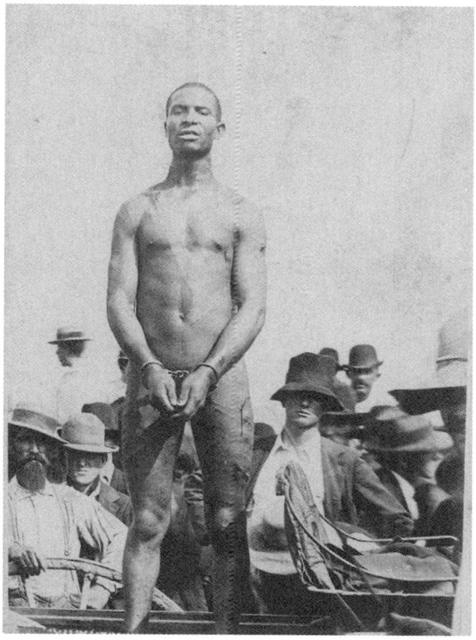

Fig. 7.6. Anonymous, *Frank Embree*, 1899. The Allen and Littlefield Collection. National Center for Civil and Human Rights, Atlanta, GA.

A crucial dimension of this code related to the rules for social looking, which determined who could look, who could look back, and who must look away. bell hooks explains:

> Reduced to the machinery of bodily physical labor, black people learned to appear before whites as though they were zombies, cultivating the habit of casting the gaze downward so as not to appear uppity. To look directly was an assertion of subjectivity, equality. Safety resided in the pretense of invisibility. (1992: 168)

Frank Embree refused such a “pretense of invisibility.” His picture (fig. 7.6), taken on July 22, 1899, in Fayette, Missouri, appeared in an exhibition of lynching photographs owned by James Allen and John Littlefield that toured several US cities at the turn of the 21st century. The exhibition was later made into a book, *Without Sanctuary: Lynching Photographs in America* (2000), which serves to remind present-day readers that the gruesome practice of lynching photography established a longstanding visual network composed of a range of media, from framed photographs to postcards. In the book’s center is Embree. Though stripped and scarred, and though surrounded by a smirking mob of white vigilantes who will soon hang him, Embree, undaunted, stares directly back at the cameraman who is seeking a final humiliation. In that stare, as Apel argues, Embree asserts “the right to return the ‘look’ of his white torturers for whom the cameraman is a surrogate” (2004: 34). It’s a look of defiance that continued to circulate with this photograph, long after Embree’s body was destroyed.

In some ways, the contrast between this portrait of Embree and Day’s of Skeete could not be more striking – Day, after all, was aiming for beauty, while Embree’s anonymous photographer was aiming for penultimate shame. Their looks, however, unite them in what Latour calls a chain of “*traceable associations*” that would otherwise appear “completely incommensurable” if that chain had not been carefully scrutinized (2005: 108, 142; emphasis original). However markedly different in appearance, Embree and Skeete cooperate to violate the code of Jim Crow. For while Embree stares directly at the camera to defy his white tormenters, Skeete also refuses the deferential downcast gaze, but differently. Skeete refuses by simply closing his eyes – an act that, like Embree’s, works to negate Jim Crow’s reach.

While it’s true that Skeete’s closed eyes might have been suggested by Day himself during the photo shoot, such a suggestion would have been uncharacteristic. In Day’s series of black male nudes, *An Ethiopian Chief* is the only example of a frontal portrait with closed eyes. In *Ebony* (fig. 7.7), for example, Skeete’s eyes are clearly open, looking off and away from the camera’s penetrating gaze, something between deference and outright resistance. However, in Skeete’s portrait published in Boston’s *Colored American Magazine* (fig. 7.8), where he worked as a member of the art staff four years after posing for Day, Skeete’s eyes are notably half-closed, adding evidence that the device of refusal was quite plausibly his own. And while Skeete would have had little reason to refuse *The Colored American Magazine*’s staff photographer in the way he likely refused Day, it’s plausible that what Skeete learned to do in Day’s studio entered his posing repertoire and transferred to future, less threatening contexts such as that of the magazine.

Thus, if Day belonged to the "colonialist exploiting class," as Allen Ellenzweig contends (1992: 64), then Skeete, as a colonized subject, could be said to be deploying what Tina M. Campt has called "the grammar of black fugitivity," whose end is a "refusal" that black portrait subjects "enact" in "reclamations of interiority" and "dignity" to the end of "their persistent striving for futurity" (2017: 11). Though Skeete submits to the exoticizing, primitivizing appropriation of his body, subject to the brutal code of Jim Crow, in *An Ethiopian Chief* he denies Day full and final cooperation by shutting his eyes in an act of will that Day, for whatever reason, did not contest, perhaps even enjoyed. Through a visual rhetoric of resistance, Skeete's agency entered the circuits of 19th-century visual culture to publicly revise, in a small but powerful way, the making – which is to say the fetishizing – of another black body pressed into white supremacist utopia.

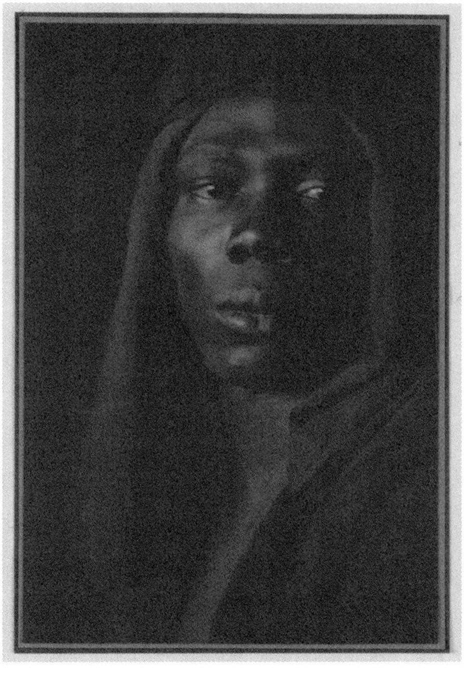

Fig. 7.7. F. Holland Day, *Ebony*, 1897. Royal Photographic Society Collection. Victoria and Albert Museum, London.

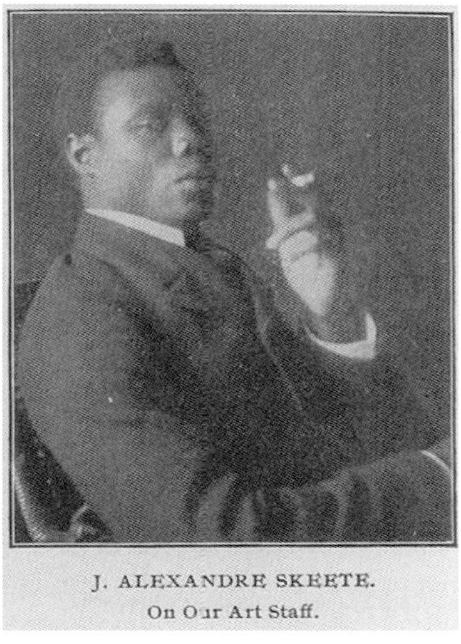


Fig. 7.8. Anonymous, *J. Alexandre Skeete*, 1901. *The Colored American Magazine* (May 1901): 50. Public Domain, via The Digital Colored American Magazine coloredamerican.org.

## Reimagining Antinous: F. Holland Day's Queer Portraiture

It would, however, be premature to cast *An Ethiopian Chief* solely as a racist image containing embedded refusal, though it is that. Such a characterization would neglect other, more progressive aspects of this portrait, aspects that don't contradict its racism, but yet move in more liberatory directions along different species of visual networks. Because the portrait is, semiotically speaking, polysemous (Barthes, 1977: 39), what it signals in terms of queer sexuality needs to be examined on terms that are conversant with, but also semi-independent of, issues of race. In positing sexuality and race as interrelated but mutually distinguishable forms of representation in Day's portrait, my aim is not to offer counterpoint to Aliyyah I. Rahman's important queer-of-color claim that "there is always already something queer about blackness" (2012: 158), a premise I substantively agree with. However, to conflate queerness with blackness entirely is to miss a different aspect of Day's photographic project, for which *An Ethiopian Chief* was just a part. Indeed, Day strove to queer the bodies of young men of great variety, and the ensuing visual performances spanned significant breadth. Day's range of models included, in addition to Skeete and Carter, the sons of his friend and fellow photographer Clarence H. White, who were firmly aligned with dominant culture; the Italian immigrant Nicola Giancola, who accompanied Day to his Maine retreat in Little Good Harbor, Maine, and was likely his lover; and the Lebanese-American poet, Kahlil Gibran, whom Day discovered in Boston.[2] Of course, the body of each young man Day photographed was queered differently depending on the racial or ethnic category he belonged to. But visual agency invested in this queering had its own rhetorical outcomes, which deserve a separate but related exploration.

With such photographers as Frederick Rolfe (Reed, 2011: 100), Guglielmo Plüschow (Cooper, 1995: 158), and Plüschow's cousin, Wilhelm von Gloeden – whom Thomas Waugh calls Day's "great transatlantic peer" (1996: 80) – Day participated in what could be called the first wave of queer photographic portraiture. The work of these photographers was aligned with the turn-of-the-century aestheticist movement and deeply imbued with Greco-Roman classicism as a means of articulating a queer vernacular that could yet pass – because of classicism's widespread appeal – relatively unnoticed. Different from Rolfe, Plüschow, and von Gloeden, who focused primarily on European models, Day was the first prominent photographer to feature African American male models as central to his work (Weiermair, 1988: 18). It is for this reason that scholars such as Curtis (2017: 147), Michaels (1994: 335), and

Smith (2013: 53) find a progressive politics in Day's African American portraiture, in spite of the evidence to the contrary presented above.

To add to these critical assessments, consider *An Ethiopian Chief* beside the *Antinous* bas-relief (figs. 7.9a & 7.9b), one of the foremost examples of classical masculinity promoted by 19th-century America. The original, found in the Villa Albani in Rome, was a pilgrimage spot for droves of English and American tourists undertaking the Grand Tour for their refinement. *Murray's Handbook*, the Grand Tourist's travel bible, bestows the highest cultural capital on the sculpture by quoting the venerated 18th-century German art historian, Johann Joachim Winckelmann, whose judgments were received as settled truths. Winckelmann, *Murray's* says, deems the Albani *Antinous*, "after the Apollo and the Laocoon,...perhaps the most beautiful monument of antiquity which time has transmitted to us" (in *A Handbook*, 1872: 294). Because it was so revered abroad, copies of the *Antinous* were also pervasive at home, contributing to the image's widespread recognition value in the U.S. (Haskell and Penny, 1981: 146).

For mainstream bourgeois America, the *Antinous* signaled a proper taste, which members of the middle class asserted to claim a measure of social power and distinction among their peers (Bender, 2019: 67). However, for queer communities that were just emerging in the American Northeast during the *fin de siècle* (Chauncey, 1994: 12), the bas-relief had particular rhetorical force. After all, Antinous was the legendary lover of Hadrian, reputedly drowning in the Nile to save his beloved emperor (Davis, 2010: 53). For savvy spectators, the bas-relief consequently emblematized same-sex desire. As Whitney Davis observes, the *Antinous* possessed the "seemingly immediate aesthetic charge" that "devolved from its erotic history" and, at the same time, served as an icon of "efforts to constitute a *new* human community of taste and sociability" (2010: 191; emphasis original). Antinous's visual agency helped to galvanize turn-of-the-century queer communities[3] – so much so that queer preoccupation with the sculpture gave rise to what David Greven has called the era's "Antinous cult" (2012: 187). In the contours of this young athlete were "a shared set of references and an index of representations" that queer spectators used to identify their own (Greven, 2012: 188).

Day's contribution to this cult was Skeete as *An Ethiopian Chief*. Although Day's portrait of Skeete is frontal and Antinous is in profile, their visual resemblance is, indeed, otherwise uncanny. Through their juxtaposition, Skeete's robe is clarified into a version of toga, loosely draped. His exposed left shoulder is the mirror image of Antinous's exposed right. He holds the toga's loose folds with his left hand poised against his torso in roughly the same casual manner as Antinous does with his right. And Antinous's lotus crown is reprised in Skeete's crown of feathers, whose otherwise equivocal meaning seems suddenly simplified and elevated. Finally, both figures share a blindness to their audience – Skeete with closed eyes and Antinous without distinct eyes – that translates into a disregard for the spectators who might ogle them admiringly. Thus while Day's artistic contemporary and sometime fellow Bostonian, John Singer Sargent, whitened the African American model Thomas McKellor in painting after painting (Tugend, 2020: 6), Day reversed the color trajectory. He took Antinous's white marble (or the white plaster copy of that marble) and blackened it to refashion ideal – and quietly but poignantly queer – masculine beauty.

Considering the queer visual network *An Ethiopian Chief* signals beside the networks of race already discussed helps make clear just how fraught this portrait is with irresolvable rhetorical tension. Day worked to make Skeete fit his purposes, so that Skeete, as *An Ethiopian Chief*, revised the *Antinous* to become an elevated form

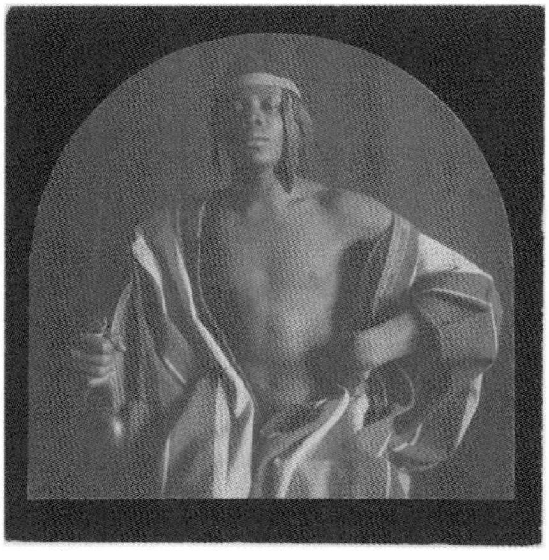

Fig. 7.9a. F. Holland Day, *An Ethiopian Chief*, 1897. Alfred Stieglitz Collection, The Metropolitan Museum of Art, New York. Source: Art Resource, NY.

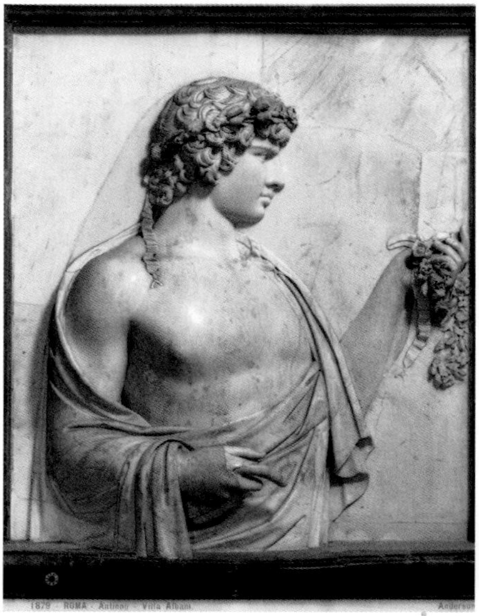

Fig 7.9b. *Antinous, Hadrian's Favorite*, c. 130 CE. Torlonia Collection. Source: Alinari / Art Resource, NY.

of a variant masculine beauty. And yet, as Day's paid model, Skeete was also his servant, objectified as the exotic Other to do the artist's bidding – a predicament Skeete likely registered with a subtle performative resistance that challenged but did not cancel out the codes of primitivization that were imposed upon him. Thus, even as Day reconceptualized a queer ideal to broaden its racial possibilities and in some way empower Skeete's body to signify uncommonly, Skeete closed his eyes to these forms of possibility and empowerment, which were not his own. His refusal stood as an act of independence that contributed to the photograph's state of suspended animation, where networks defined by queer visual culture, the high-culture white supremacy of anthropology, and the low-culture white supremacy of lynching, met with a fourth network motivated by a black diasporic will to futurity, all locked in a state of perpetual conflict, without any apparent hope of relief. It is here where *An Ethiopian Chief* resides, as "a single multiple image" (Gries, 2015a: 301) or a "continual multiplicity" (Vivian, 2007: 490) organized and reorganized by the material operations of agency that have kept the portrait alive and assured its existence, within and beyond the frame.

## Notes

1 It's important to note that these are not the only portraits Day took of African American subjects. Some of his most significant images followed later, during Day's 1905 visit to the Hampton Institute. What makes Day's "Nubian Series" cohere, beyond the portraits' historical co-emergence, is a unifying thematic approach that prioritizes the black male body, wholly or partially nude, attired in costume or street dress, to construct images of idealized and, I will argue, distinctly queer masculine beauty.

2 For more on Day's complex social circle, see Patricia Fanning's *Through an Uncommon Lens: The Life and Photography of F. Holland Day* (2008), the most complete biography of Day to date.

3 I rely here on Jenny Edbauer's model of rhetorical circulation as a sustained "ecology of effects, enactments, and events" that constitute a social identity within a visually organized network (2005: 9).

## Bibliography

Aliyyah I. Abdur-Rahman, *Against the Closet: Black Political Longing and the Erotics of Race* (Durham: Duke University Press, 2012).

Dora Apel, *Imagery of Lynching: Black Men, White Women, and the Mob* (New Brunswick, NJ: Rutgers University Press, 2004).

Lee D. Baker, *From Savage to Negro: Anthropology and the Construction of Race, 1896–1954* (Berkeley: University of California Press, 1998).

Scot Barnett and Casey Boyle, "Introduction: Rhetorical Ontology, or, How to Do Things with Things," in *Rhetoric, through Everyday Things*, eds. Barnett and Boyle (Tuscaloosa: The University of Alabama Press, 2016): 1–14.

Roland Barthes, "Rhetoric of the Image," in *Image, Music, Text*, trans. Stephen Heath (New York: Hill and Wang, 1977): 32–51.

Roland Barthes, *Camera Lucida: Reflections on Photography*, trans. Richard Howard (New York: Hill and Wang, 1980/2010).

Geoffrey Batchen, *Each Wild Idea: Writing, Photography, History* (Cambridge: MIT Press, 2001).

Geoff Bender, "Roderick's Body, Winckelmann, and the Screen of the Touristic Gaze," in *Henry James' Travel: Fiction and Non-Fiction*, ed. Mirosława Buchholtz (London: Routledge, 2019): 63–81.

Homi K. Bhabha, *The Location of Culture*, (Abingdon, UK: Routledge Classics, 2004).

Ian Bogost, *Alien Phenomenology, or What It's Like to Be a Thing* (Minneapolis: University of Minnesota Press, 2012).

Levi Bryant, Nick Srnicek, and Graham Harman, "Introduction," in *The Speculative Turn: Continental Materialism and Realism*, eds. Bryant, Srnicek, and Harman (Melbourne: re.press, 2011): 1–18.

Tina M. Campt, *Image Matters: Archive, Photography, and the African Diaspora in Europe* (Durham, NC: Duke University Press, 2012).

Tina M. Campt, *Listening to Images* (Durham, NC: Duke University Press, 2017).

Hazel V. Carby, *Race Men* (Cambridge, MA: Harvard University Press, 1998).

George Chauncey, *Gay New York: Gender, Urban Culture, and the Making of the Gay Male World, 1890–1940* (New York: Basic Books, 1994).

Emmanuel Cooper, *Fully Exposed: The Male Nude in Photography* (London: Routledge, 1990/1995).

James Crump, *F. Holland Day: Suffering the Ideal* (Santa Fe, NM: Twin Palms Publishers, 1995).

Verna Posever Curtis, "Clarence H. White in the Light of F. Holland Day," in *Clarence H. White and His World: The Art & Craft of Photography, 1895–1925*, ed. Anne McCauley (New Haven: Yale University Press, 2017): 145–159.

Whitney Davis, *Queer Beauty: Sexuality and Aesthetics from Winckelmann to Freud and Beyond* (New York: Columbia University Press, 2010).

Jenny Edbauer, "Unframing Models of Public Distribution: From Rhetorical Situation to Rhetorical Ecologies," *Rhetoric Society Quarterly*, 35, 4 (2005): 5–24.

Elizabeth Edwards, "Introduction," in *Anthropology and Photography, 1860–1920*, ed. Edwards (New Have: Yale University Press, 1992): 3–17.

Allen Ellenzweig, *The Homoerotic Photograph: Male Images from Durieu/Delacroix to Mapplethorpe* (New York: Columbia University Press, 1992).

Patricia J. Fanning, *Through an Uncommon Lens: The Life and Photography of F. Holland Day* (Amherst, MA: University of Massachusetts Press, 2008).

David Greven, *The Fragility of Manhood: Hawthorne, Freud, and the Politics of Gender* (Columbus, OH: The Ohio State University Press, 2012).

Laurie Gries, "Dingrhetoriks," in *Thinking with Bruno Latour in Rhetoric and Composition*, eds. Paul Lynch and Nathaniel Rivers (Carbondale, IL: Southern Illinois University Press, 2015a): 294–309.

Laurie E. Gries, *Still Life with Rhetoric: A New Materialist Approach for Visual Rhetorics* (Logan: Utah State UP, 2015b).

Tom Gunning, "Invisible Worlds, Visible Media," in *Brought to Light: Photography and the Invisible, 1840–1900*, ed. Corey Keller (New Haven: Yale University Press, 2008): 51–63.

*A Handbook of Rome and its Environs*, 11th ed. (London: John Murray, 1872).

Graham Harman, *Prince of Networks: Bruno Latour and Metaphysics* (Melbourne: re.press, 2009).

Francis Haskell and Nicholas Penny, *Taste and the Antique: The Lure of Classical Sculpture 1500–1900* (New Haven: Yale University Press, 1981).

Carl G. Herndl and S. Scott Graham, "Getting Over Incommensurability: Latour, New Materialisms, and the Rhetoric of Diplomacy," in *Thinking with Bruno Latour in Rhetoric and Composition*, eds. Paul Lynch and Nathaniel Rivers (Carbondale, IL: Southern Illinois University Press, 2015): 40–58.

bell hooks, *Black Looks: Race and Representation* (Boston, MA: South End Press, 1992).

Estelle Jussim, "F. Holland Hay's 'Nubians,'" *History of Photography*, 7, 2 (1983): 131–142.

Jens E. Kjeldsen, "The Rhetoric of Thick Representation: How Pictures Render the Importance and Strength of an Argument Salient," *Argumentation*, 29 (2015): 197–215.

J[ohn] H. Lamprey, "Ethnological Notes and Queries," *The Journal of the Ethnological Society of London (1869–1870)*, 1, 1 (1869): 84–85.

Bruno Latour, *Pandora's Hope: Essays on the Reality of Science Studies* (Cambridge, MA: Harvard University Press, 1999).

Bruno Latour, *Reassembling the Social: An Introduction to Actor-Network Theory* (New York: Oxford University Press, 2005).

John Law and Annemarie Mol, "The Actor-Enacted: Cumbrian Sheep in 2001," in *Material Agency: Towards a Non-Anthropocentric Approach*, eds. Carl Knappett and Lambros Malafouris (New York: Springer, 2010): 57–77.

Andrew B. Leiter, *In the Shadow of the Black Beast: African American Masculinity in the Harlem and Southern Renaissances* (Baton Rouge, LA: Louisiana State University Press, 2010).

Kobena Mercer, *Welcome to the Jungle: New Positions in Black Cultural Studies* (New York: Routledge, 1994).

Barbara L. Michaels, "New Light on F. Holland Day's Photographs of African Americans," *History of Photography*, 18, 4 (1994): 334–347.

Samuel George Morton, *Crania Americana; or, a Comparative View of the Skulls of Various Aboriginal Nations of North and South America* (Philadelphia: J. Dobson, 1839).

Samuel George Morton, *Crania Aegyptiaca; or, Observations on Egyptian Ethnography, Derived from Anatomy, History and the Monuments* (Philadelphia: John Penington, 1844).

Timothy Morton, *Hyperobjects: Philosophy and Ecology after the End of the World* (Minneapolis: University of Minnesota Press, 2013).

Alexandra Moschovi, Carol McKay, and Arabella Plouviez, "Introduction," in *The Versatile Image: Photography, Digital Technologies and the Internet*, eds. Moschovi, McKay, and Plouviez (Leuven: Leuven University Press, 2013): 11–32.

Christopher Pinney, "The Parallel Histories of Anthropology and Photography," in *Anthropology and Photography, 1860–1920*, ed. Elizabeth Edwards (New Haven: Yale University Press, 1992): 74–95.

Christopher Pinney, *Photography and Anthropology* (London: Reaktion Books, 2011).

Christopher Reed, *Art and Homosexuality: A History of Ideas* (Oxford: Oxford University Press, 2011).

Suzanne Schneider, "Louis Agassiz and the American School of Ethnoeroticism: Polygenesis, Pornography, and Other 'Perfidious Influences,'" in *Pictures and Progress: Early Photography and the Making of African American Identity*, eds. Maurice O. Wallace and Shawn Michelle Smith (Durham: Duke University Press, 2012): 211–243.

Emmanuelle Sibeud, "The Metamorphosis of Ethnology in France, 1839–1930," in *New History of Anthropology*, ed. Henrika Kuklick (Malden, MA: Blackwell, 2008): 96–110.

Shawn Michelle Smith, *At the Edge of Sight* (Durham: Duke University Press, 2013).

Frank Spencer, "Some Notes on the Attempt to Apply Photography to Anthropometry during the Second Half of the Nineteenth Century," in *Anthropology and Photography, 1860–1920*, ed. Elizabeth Edwards (New Haven: Yale University Press, 1992): 99–107.

George W. Stocking, Jr., *Victorian Anthropology* (New York: The Free Press, 1987).

Alan Trachtenberg, *Reading American Photographs: Images as History, Mathew Brady to Walker Evans* (New York: Hill and Wang, 1989).

Alina Tugend, "His Secret Muse," *The New York Times* (13 March 2020): 6.

Maurice O. Wallace, *Constructing the Black Masculine: Identity and Ideality in African American Men's Literature and Culture, 1775–1995* (Durham, NC: Duke University Press, 2002).

Brian Wallis, "Black Bodies, White Science: Louis Agassiz's Slave Daguerreotypes," *American Art*, 9, 2 (1995): 38–61.

Duncan J. Watts, *Six Degrees: The Science of a Connected Age* (New York: W. W. Norton, 2003).

Thomas Waugh, *Hard to Imagine: Gay Male Eroticism in Photography and Film from Their Beginnings to Stonewall* (New York: Columbia University Press, 1996).

Peter Weiermair, *The Hidden Image: Photographs of the Male Nude in the Nineteenth and Twentieth Centuries*, trans. Claus Nielander (Cambridge, MA: MIT Press, 1988).

Gleeson White, "The Two Great Exhibitions: II. The Photographic Salon," *Photograms of '97* (London: Dawbarn & Ward, 1897): 93–114.

Christopher Wright, *The Echo of Things: The Lives of Photographs in the Solomon Islands* (Duke University Press, 2013).

# Spirit Photography & Rogue Objects

Zachary Tavlin

Spirit photography is not always revelatory. Take this 1913 photographic sequence of a woman reabsorbing "ectoplasm," the fluid or viscous plasma that supposedly provides the physical medium for the appearance of spirits (fig. 8.1). Formally, it is an uninteresting sequence. There are more flashes of epistemic insight in stop-motion arrays of horses trotting. What holds our attention is not normally unperceivable change beneath surface flow but the event of the happening itself. We do not learn anything new about ectoplasm as our eyes move from frame to frame. Rather, we encounter an impossible substance anew each time. Until it disappears, wherein the sequence lingers on the medium's tortured face, and the motion picture becomes a portrait. Those last still images reflect the camera as much as its subject, and we take on *its* function as *our* spiritual medium, seeing in the space opened by the shutter as it offers to receive another vision that might not come.

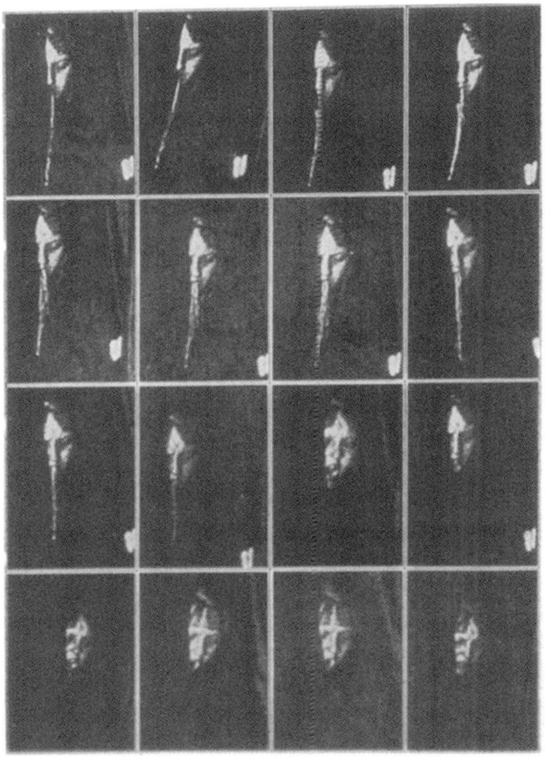

Fig. 8.1. Albert von Schreck-Notzing, *Selected Cinematograph Pictures of 13 July, 1913, Showing Widening and Narrowing of the Substance, and Its Recession Into the* Mouth, 1913. Albert von Schrenck-Notzing, *The Phenomena of Materialisation: A Contribution to the Investigation of Mediumistic Teleplastics* (London: K. Paul, Trench, and Trubner, 1923): 258.

This chapter aims to consider spirit photography as an epistemic phenomenon rather than a successful body of artforms. It asks what kinds of objects were thought to be involved in both their production and within their representational fields, and how rethinking objecthood and objectivity through spiritualist practices specifically informed the aesthetic impulses of photography in general. Throughout, I test the affordances of a vocabulary otherwise new to studies of the phenomenon. In *Onto-Cartography: An Ontology of Machines and Media*, Levi Bryant distinguishes between several types of objects on the basis of the way they "gravitationally" structure encompassing ecologies. The difference between a "bright object" and a "dim object," for instance, has less to do with their essential, individual characteristics than the magnitude by which they impact surrounding objects and systems. A rather mysterious category, "rogue objects," describes those elements of an ecology that seem to appear out of nowhere, untethered to any existing visible network yet containing the power to modify or even irrevocably alter those networks as they appear. In what follows, I will consider the late 19th-century phenomenon of spirit photography from the perspective of Bryant's object-oriented approach to technologies and machines that, despite appearances of utter strangeness and singularity, "structure the spatio-temporal paths along which other entities move, become, and develop" (Bryant, 2014: 10).

While the most common contemporary explanations for the production of spirit photographs fell into diametrically opposed camps – along either spiritualist or skeptical lines (though not necessarily religious and secular lines) – many practitioners kept the hoax alive by producing visual traces of triangulating materials like ectoplasm. While this material practice produced several pseudo-scientific tracts, including many famous writings by William Stainton Moses, it also operated as a stand-in for developing scientific and ontological worldviews that did not appeal to transcendent forces. Spirit photographs did not reveal a supernatural plane of existence that impinged upon our world from the outside, nor were they simply cases of chemically produced illusion that left one's humanist intuitions undisturbed. They reveal the camera as itself a rogue object that was challenging traditional ontological divisions between (human) subject and (inhuman) object. Beginning by accompanying a brief account of 19th-century analytic photography – broadly referring to photography used for investigative and empirical purposes – with a few particular responses by the Victorian scientific community to spirit photography, I will ultimately claim that the peculiar junctures between materialism and spiritualism that appear in these texts and performances illustrate a developing ontological standpoint within late 19th-century visual culture more generally: one increasingly mechanical, post-humanist, and cognizant of the abject remainder that blurs conventional epistemic categories. Spirit photographs are not merely curiosities; they capture more than a temporary moment of historical insanity, susceptibility, or duplicity. We are still learning how to look at them, which also means understanding how they look back at us, a century later.

## Spirit Photography's Gnostic Impulse

> *The time wasted on [spirit] photography, the money thrown away and the violent emotions that have been engendered render the subject of more than passing interest to the student of human stupidity, credulity and superstition.*
> **–Eric Dingwall**[1]

Take Eric Dingwall's condemnation of spirit photography and the history of its many adherents to be the epigraph to this essay as a whole. Presumably the "student of human stupidity" is not the person, like myself, who gladly chooses to waste his precious time writing on spirit photography, though nor can it be Dingwall given how much time *he* spent on it, annotating a massive collection of spirit photographs for the British Library in 1960. In any case, looking at the range of responses to spirit photographs in their earliest days – originating almost exactly a century before Dingwall's efforts with spirit photographer William Mumler's self-portrait – stupidity is not the most apt designation for the wide range of believers, which included scientists like Alfred Russel Wallace and William Crookes and several men of letters, most famously Arthur Conan Doyle. A century on, after numerous advances in scientific discourse and corresponding developments in the "proper" use of photography as scientific illustration, it seems all too obvious that spirit photography never had any scientific value. But in its 19th-century context, the practice "not only took on the mantle of the miraculous image but also accomplished a rapprochement between science and the supernatural" (Harvey, 2007: 26), attaining prominence at a time when the new technology was being adapted for use in several eventually dismissed but nonetheless influential fields of mainstream inquiry.

One of spiritualism's distinguishing features is its conviction that "the proof of the spirit was in the seeing," as John Harvey explains: "Unlike earlier manifestations of spirit communication such as raps, remote or disembodied voices and poltergeist activity, which were ephemeral and authenticable only by the witnesses present, spirit photographs were an enduring and reviewable expression of disembodied consciousness" (2007: 27). Indeed, spirit photographs seem to fulfill Lorraine Daston and Peter Galison's definition of 19th-century scientific objectivity. Whereas 18th-century naturalistic image-making required the scientist's willful, "idealized intervention" – so that "human mediation between nature and representation" was what guaranteed empirical integrity in the first place – new regimes of "mechanical objectivity" required abstention from human manipulation, grounded in a "moral comportment that aimed to quiet the observer so nature could be heard" (Daston and Galison, 2007: 120). Along with 19th-century scientific methods came an "insistent drive to repress the willful intervention of the artist-author, to put in its stead a set of procedures that would, as it were, move nature to the page through a strict protocol" or algorithm (Daston and Galison, 2007: 121). The criterion of mechanical objectivity meant relying heavily upon supplementary recording instruments, with photography "the emblem for all aspects of noninterventionist objectivity...because the camera apparently eliminated human agency" altogether (Daston and Galison, 2007: 187). One can see parallels between the general move to the valuation of mechanical objectivity in the scientific community (as well as in the fine arts) and the budding distinction in the spiritualist community between traditional forms of occult communication (requiring an expertly trained medium) and the practice of spirit photography, whose supposed epistemic strength derived from the seemingly objective mechanism of the camera, whose products could be subsequently verified and reviewed by anyone in possession of the developed photograph.

Spirit photography thus became the ultimate test for empirically minded spiritualists like Wallace (a man otherwise known as one of the period's leading "naturalists"), supposedly answering objections that even sincere otherworldly experiences were more likely hallucinations than perceptions. Taking the position of a skeptic for rhetorical purposes, he poses a "crucial test,"

> which would quite settle the question of the possibility of [the spirits'] being due to a coincident delusion of several senses of several persons at the same time; and, if satisfactory, would demonstrate their objective reality in a way nothing else can do. If they really reflect or emit light which makes them visible to human eyes, *they can be photographed*. Photograph them, and you will have an unanswerable proof that your human witnesses are trustworthy. (Wallace, 1875: 185; emphasis original)

Wallace's adamant emphasis reveals, more than anything else, the mystification of the photographic process prevalent as late as 1875, ignorant as many scientific minds still were about the possibility of (literal) false positives. He admits a page later that "'ghost-pictures'...can be made to order by any photographer," but argues that "a little consideration will show [skeptics] that the means by which sham ghosts can be manufactured being so well known to all photographers, it becomes easy to apply tests or arrange conditions so as to prevent imposition" (Wallace, 1875: 186). Thus, as if in an unknowing demonstration of Derridean *différance*, Wallace supplements the "unanswerable proof" of the "crucial test" of the photograph (open to anyone with working eyes) with a series of *post facto* verification tests applied only by experts.

Wallace's teetering position aside, spiritualist photography was nested neatly in the trajectory of 19th-century analytic visual culture (as strange as that claim might at first seem). Tom Gunning labels the general epistemic presupposition that the "proof is in the seeing" as the "gnostic impulse" that motivated scientific – or pseudo-scientific – photographic experiments preceding and leading into early cinema (1997: 2). Contemporary with the rise of spiritualist photography were G. B. Duchenne de Boulogne's photographic catalogues of facial muscular phenomena (stimulated by electrodes), Hugh Diamond's portraits of the committed at various stages of onset and cure in the Surrey County Lunatic Asylum, Jean-Martin Charcot's arrays of diagnosed hysterics' gestures, Etienne-Jules Marey and Eadweard Muybridge's human and animal motion studies, and Francis Galton's composite portraits used to isolate features and classes of criminal physiognomies. In all these cases, the assumption that the camera achieves mechanical objectivity turns it into a gnostic apparatus, though as Chiara Ambrosio writes in her analysis of Galton, chronophotography, and the semiotics of C. S. Peirce, it is ultimately still the "*control* exercised in the critical use of the medium (as well as the critical interpretations of its products) that renders it a reliable and yet fallible source of knowledge" (2016: 576; emphasis original). Reliability and fallibility are always linked – reliability depends upon the possibility of error, the possibility that results can always be challenged – even in the era of supposed mechanical objectivity. Hence the very real dialectic between science and pseudo-science throughout the rise of photographic experiments and their archives: the "proof is in the seeing," yes, but there is always an operator determining and manipulating the field of the seen.

Such an acknowledgement does not, however, diminish the power of the camera's (and its analytic operator's) constant *claim* to objectivity. It is in such a cultural *episteme*, one also still beholden to the novelty and freshness of the camera that produces fixed images, that something like spirit photography could rattle so many cages. The grandfather of the practice, the aforementioned Mumler, was taken to trial for fraud in 1869, a case fascinating for the presuppositions contained in the New York City Special Sessions's acquittal. The most compelling evidence for and against Mumler could only be described as *materialist*: while P.T. Barnum – whose sideshow business interests could not abide the threat of spiritualism in excess of the usual humbuggery – testified against him by presenting similar examples of mere prestidigitation and forgery, respected judge John Worth Edmonds's testimony supported Mumler, whose studio he had visited, by arguing that his images "could only be spirits because everything had some form of materiality, even spirits, so there was no reason why they could not be photographed" (Jolly, 2006: 14).

Without getting into theories of the photograph, at least not explicitly, the court essentially deliberated on the issue of the camera's objectivity – whether it is essentially a magic trick or a machine for producing indices of reality – but never seriously questioned or even considered the tenets of spiritualism as such. The movement's metaphysical belief in discarnation, the soul's gradual liberation from its physical body into an afterlife accessible by trained mediums, thus remained unchallenged. Mumler was acquitted for lack of evidence, though reports suggest that the prosecutor irreparably harmed the state's case by "directly attacking Spiritualism as a belief, as well as the Spiritualists themselves," arguing that it was "antagonistic of Christianity, the very basis of United States law," and that believers show "evidence of a transition from reason to insanity proceeding from a heat-oppressed brain and a derangement of the nervous and circulatory systems" (Jolly, 2006: 15). Several other related fraud cases from the period lived and died upon the epistemic question of belief and intent to deceive rather than evaluations of materialist or spiritualist ontology. For instance, the trial of the American medium Henry Slade, whose opponents argued that "in the absence of positive proof, the ability to mechanically replicate the phenomena according to the generally accepted laws of nature was enough to demonstrate the intent of the medium to deceive" (Mitchell, 2014: 16). The latter was not up for debate; the question was whether a practiced photographer or medium, given all the necessary knowledge of his *material and technological* medium, could legitimately believe in the spirits as he said he did. In photographic terms, could Mumler have really operated his camera without knowing that the specters produced were of his own manipulative hand (and thus without knowingly perpetrating fraud on his patrons and customers)?

That the court's understanding of how the camera works and what it ultimately presents in the final positive image required, as a matter of law, actual eyewitnesses to the scene of the practitioner's blatant manipulation of the exposure in order to pass a judgment of fraud was a significant moment in photographic reception. It seemed to vacate the possibility that even a trained eye could trace the layout of a scene, through the translucent "medium" of a practitioner's method or techne, back from a finished photograph. If one is not in the room or *en plein air* with the photographer, if one leaves the photographer and his apparatus alone for even a minute, an abyssal distance opens between the sites of production and reception, between the scenes corresponding to each. The camera is hardly Henry Fox Talbot's "pencil of nature" at this point, but not because the camera was the pencil of the supernatural either (at least not for the court). The photograph was no longer obviously an index of nature different in kind from a painting, or at least it had to *prove* itself as such all over again, a battle Talbot, Daguerre, and other early practitioners had supposedly already won.

More than the result of a groundswell in metaphysical spiritualism, spiritualist photography coincided most directly with what Jonathan Crary calls a "repositioning of the observer" beyond the locked relations of interior and exterior "presupposed by the camera obscura and into an undemarcated terrain on which the distinction between internal sensation and external signs is irrevocably blurred" (1990: 24). The claim that the camera was the "pencil of nature," writing the world directly onto plate or paper through the transparent medium of light, still kept the daguerreotype, calotype, and succeeding media within the orbit of the *camera obscura* and a corresponding epistemological model grounded in classical optics, premised upon the "virtual instantaneity of optical transmission" and a Euclidean-Cartesian geometry of light reflection and refraction (Crary, 1990: 98).

By contrast, developments in physiological optics lent hard credence to the idea that no visual system – whether as part of a human body or a mechanical camera – constructs its field in one-to-one correspondence with a field of objects "out there." Xavier Bichat decentralized and scattered the body's living systems, beginning the process of piecing back together the interlocking mechanism of sensory and motor nerves. Augustin-Jean Fresnel found that light waves were transverse rather than longitudinal, calling into question the independent identity of light itself relative to the human sensory apparatus. Johannes Müller posited a seeing subject analogous to the photographic camera, with a physiological apparatus susceptible to external procedures of manipulation that continuously produce new experiences for a subject suspended within a circuit of circulating energy. Finally, Hermann von Helmholtz asserted that as perception begins with "effects" of reality rather than complete images, the eye's truths were ultimately "practical truths" depending upon the interests of the perceiver who, never able to overcome the physical distortions of the bodily eye, is able to manage them the way a person who looks "through a prism and executes movements of his body and hands as they appear in his field of view soon learns to see through the prism correctly" (Helmholtz, 1962: 537).

I have now mentioned two truncated genealogies, both analytic with claims to objectivity and the status of science: practitioners of the "gnostic impulse" that used the camera to transcend the limits of the human sensorium and thus reveal phenomena deeper in the texture of nature than previously available to the eye, and a developing physiological literature that challenged the very notion that an eye could ever de-mediate a visual field without producing a new (embodied) structure of mediation. I do not think one can understand the rise of spiritualist photography without understanding both of these discourses. That Muybridge's *The Horse in Motion* settled a legitimate controversy – whether a galloping horse's feet are ever all off the ground at the same time – seems peculiar over a century later, while the confusion derived from the difference between the speeds of a camera's shutter and glance of a human eye remains enduringly noteworthy. This juxtaposition of problems entailing the camera's encounters with physical world well illustrates how the nature/machine distinction never congealed into a clear, unproblematic opposition. On the one hand, if it appears in the camera's visual field, it is real, even if never available to the human eye. This was the position of the spiritualists as well. But on the other hand, it is also true that a visual field is always mediated by the bodily-mechanical structure of the eye, and so a crafty hand and well-prepared plates and lenses – the "tricks" of the trade – can in principle produce the appearance of spirits. Such a counter-position nevertheless kept many non-believing materialists agnostic on the matter of epistemic justification, in something akin to the position of a killjoy audience member at a magic show. And yet disbelief was serious business, for it meant denying the immortality of the human soul at a time when Darwinism and other scientific materialisms were calling human exceptionalism *tout court* into radical question. For skeptics armed with optical knowledge, the truth was still in the seeing, but the question simply became: "whose truth?"

Not necessarily nature's, if by nature one means a stable, eternal, and law-abiding mega-object in principle discoverable by the (technologically augmented) senses. From Kierkegaard's *Concluding Unscientific Postscript* (1846, exactly contemporaneous with the Fox sisters' experience with spirit "rappings" in New York state) through Nietzsche's writings on appearance and reality, such a concept of nature or world was thoroughly under attack. And in visual culture more broadly, in the exhibitions of Charcot's demonstrations as much as in spiritualist photographic "evidence," a presupposition about the world on display – reality justified by its display, its exhibition, the *sine qua non* of its capacity to be consumed – grounded social experience. As Timothy Mitchell writes in his study of mid to late 19th-century fairs and exhibitions, everyone was

> beginning to live as tourists or anthropologists, addressing an object-world as the endless representation of some further meaning or reality...but *reality*, as it turns out, means that which can be represented, that which presents itself as an exhibit before an observer. The so-called real world outside is something experienced and grasped only as a series of further representations, an extended exhibition. (1989: 232–3; emphasis original)

Spiritualist photography, far from being a private mystical revelation to the initiated believer from the beyond, was the practice of spirit's *exhibition*. The camera resituated spirit in a new socio-aesthetic landscape, one not necessarily characterized by hard (theretofore commonsense) distinctions between appearance and reality, subject and object, or even the spiritual and the material.

## Rogue Abjects

In *Camera Lucida*, Roland Barthes narrates his straining attempt to resuscitate the presence of his deceased mother through her photographic portrait. He writes in spiritualist terms about an otherwise standard photograph, registering the ghostly haunting of any photograph whatsoever: "Every photograph is a certificate of presence...the *ectoplasm* of 'what-had-been': neither image nor reality, a new being, really: a reality one can no longer touch" (Barthes, 2010: 87; emphasis mine). Though ectoplasm is supposedly excreted by the medium in order to draw a spirit into the physical realm, Barthes uses the term to describe the excretion of the camera, the finished photograph as a chemical residue of light that mediates present and past. In both cases, though, there are ghosts, drawn back by a chemical trick that mediates the physical and spiritual worlds. Barthes undergoes an experience of conjuring and transport when simply looking at the portrait, and writes of photography as neither art nor science but as dark magic. The camera turns a subject into a specter of his or herself, as Barthes describes: "I have become Total-Image, which is to say, Death in person [...]. Ultimately, what I am seeking in the photograph taken of me (the 'intention' according to which I look at it) is Death: Death is the *eidos* of that photograph" (2010: 15).

Barthes is not saying much that is new here. The association between photography and death – the death of those exposed, the camera as soul-stealer – was not uncommonly made in the 19th century. In a deeply affective sense, many people appear to have had spiritualist intuitions when in the daguerreotypist's studio.[2] There are few atheists in foxholes, as it's often said, and for a long time, there were fewer physicalists in front of cameras. Still, I believe Barthes, by writing in the specific way he did, was making a point about photography he did not necessarily know he was making. By synecdochically raising spirit photography to the level of the whole – by rhetorically collapsing genre species and media genus and thereby universalizing the ectoplasmic character of the photograph – he literalizes an analogy that always bubbled below the surface of 19th-century spiritualist practice. Thanks to the work of Levi Bryant, we can concentrate Barthes's influential (but not always precise) semiotic account – including what he calls the photograph's "punctum" – in an object-oriented concept: "rogue objects" that operate like ectoplasm supposedly does, "appearing as if from nowhere...suddenly erupt[ing] into worlds, transforming relations between the machines that compose an assemblage" (Bryant, 2014: 208). In the structure of many spirit photographs and in the underlying ontological economy of spiritualist practice and metaphysics, ectoplasm functioned as a rogue object.

Bryant models rogue objects on "rogue planets in astronomy...moving throughout the galaxy, unattached to any particular solar system" (2014: 208). Prior to conceptualizing rogue objects (as well as the other categories), Bryant posits "gravity" as the element that "holds worlds together" according to his onto-cartographical approach, replacing more popular concepts like "force" and "power" because the former is "too occult to be of much analytic use in the analysis of worlds" (2014: 187) while the latter "tend[s] to be deployed in an occult fashion to explain social phenomena, [and] also suffers from the drawback of being overly anthropocentric in its connotations" (2014: 188). Bryant's gravity is not simply the phenomena studied by physicists, but more generally captures "the way in which one machine influences the movement and becoming of other machines, as well as the interactions possible between machines." Gravity gathers things together into assemblages, including social fabrics, the elements of an individual life, organizational structures, and systems of belief. Bryant's general onto-cartographical project "seeks to map the gravitational relations between machines...to determine why assemblages take on the patterned organization they possess" (2014: 197). He takes a machine to be an object, and specifically a certain *type* of object, "whenever it is mediated by another object or mediates other objects" (2014: 197–8). Objects are gravitational systems.

Bryant writes of conceptual terms – especially "force" – too "occult" for a rigorous materialist ontology. But nothing prevents Bryant's onto-cartographical approach from encountering objects designated within a social assemblage *as* occult. Meanwhile, his claim that "no one has gone further in thinking rogue objects than Alain Badiou" – specifically in the French philosopher's theory of the unpredictable revolutionary Event that erupts in(to) the world in an untimely fashion – courts at least the *appearance* of occult activity in the rogue, in the wholly unforeseen and immediate epistemic shock of the rogue object's eventual character (2014: 209). The difference between an object like ectoplasm and Bryant's main examples – a rogue planet like Lars von Trier's Melancholia (within the diegetic space of his 2011 film), Occupy Wall Street, Hurricane Katrina, the Internet – is that the latter, having been identified and named as objects or object-assemblages, produce dramatic and hard to miss empirical effects, clearly "reconfigur[ing] gravitational relations between entities within the world in which they appear" (2014: 209). Ectoplasm's effects are far easier to disbelieve, despite fulfilling the first feature of rogue objects ("they seem to appear out of nowhere," in the context of a photograph and/or a session). Ectoplasm does not, moreover, resolutely force the skeptic to acknowledge its wide-ranging gravitational pull, even though its role in a spiritualist economy is great indeed, mediating physical and spiritual worlds, collapsing their abyssal difference.

Harvey notes that, even well before photography could claim an indexical relationship between a representation and the real appearance of spirits, "[o]ne of the corollaries of a spirit's visibility and tangibleness was solidity. In a tradition that goes back at least to the Middle Ages, ghosts were believed to be corporeal and to assume several forms" (2007: 13). Spirit histories from at least the early modern period "record that ghosts assumed temporary bodily semblance sufficient to enable them to handle and move objects," a popular trope from the 19th century through contemporary cinema and television as the final proof to the skeptic that a ghost was real, and truly among them (Harvey, 2007: 17).[3] Imagining objects gone rogue (even if not quite in the non-occult way Bryant conceives it) means imagining epistemic doubts overcome, and new ontological constellations formed, in an immediate act of seeing. It means (or *would* mean) the breakdown of post-Kantian assumptions about the relation between a transcendental subject – applying logical categories like causation and modality to a sensory manifold, shaping it completely and consistently through apperception – and the world of appearances. The many famous, highly problematic, and much debated ectoplasmic portraits posit a visible and epistemically available phenomenal link to the world of supposedly inaccessible noumena.

The most disturbing photographs, like Baron Albert von Schrenk-Notzing's flashlight photographs (fig. 8.2), early 20th-century examples that culminate a longer history of ectoplasmic representation, play up the threshold crossing pain that make spiritual visitations a true limit experience. In *Author's Flashlight Photograph of 16 May, 1913* one cannot easily un-see the violence contained in the expulsion of ectoplasm from the subject's mouth, revealed as much by her fastened grip on the surrounding curtain as in the contortions of her face. The most effective ectoplasm pictures take advantage of their black and white format, producing a luminous, viscous energy set in relief against a mostly undifferentiated dark background. In this particular case, the plasma's luminosity matches the subject's clenched right hand, a partial object seemingly disconnected from the rest of her body, draped as the latter is in a camouflaging dark cloak. Photographs like Schrenk-Notzing's are in some sense a departure from the origins of the practice. By largely anonymizing the visited subjects, they differ from Mumler's sensational pictures of celebrity spirits,

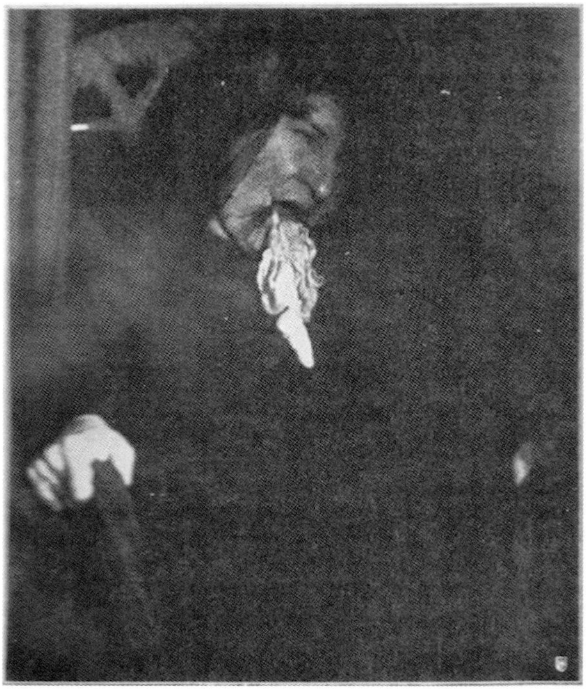

Fig. 8.2. Albert von Schreck-Notzing, *Author's Flashlight Photograph of 16 May*, 1913, 1913. Albert von Schrenck-Notzing, *The Phenomena of Materialisation: A Contribution to the Investigation of Mediumistic Teleplastics* (London: K. Paul, Trench, and Trubner, 1923): 234.

like his famous *Mrs. Lincoln, with spirit of Abraham Lincoln* (1865) (fig. 8.3) and *Emma Britten with Beethoven's Spirit* (1871). Composed in far more benevolent patriarchal fashion, these great men posed with their arms draped over the shoulders of their female counterparts. The abject spirit photographs, those that produced affects of transformative horror rather than protective calm, are the more believable, productive as they are at presenting an event visually and compositionally attuned to the violence of crossing over worlds that Western culture and thought had labored for centuries to keep resolutely apart.

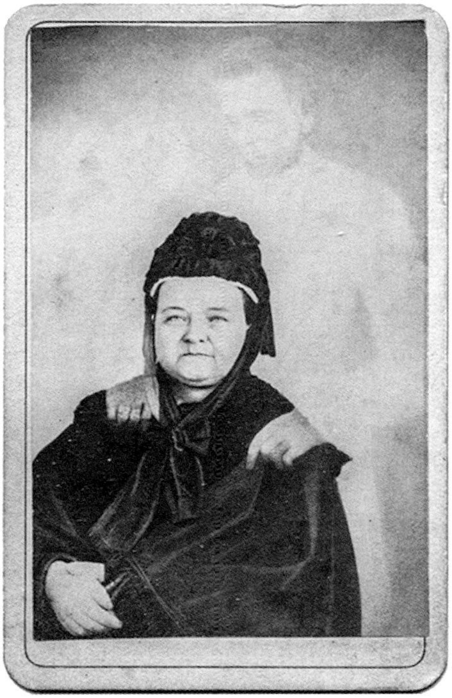

Fig. 8.3. William H. Mumler, *Mary Todd Lincoln with Abraham Lincoln's "Spirit,"* c. 1872. Lincoln Financial Foundation Collection, Allen County Public Library, Fort Wayne, IN.

Bryant's examples of rogue objects are both liberatory and destructive; they are all dangerous, though in good or bad ways depending upon the context. His examples are all quite *large*: mass social movements, technological revolutions, natural disasters, celestial bodies. But there is nothing in his definition that makes such scales necessary for analysis. At a small enough level of bodies and machines, in the context of lesser magnitudes of assemblage, a bullet could be a rogue object, its impact no less startling for the person by chance standing in its way than a mass catastrophe on the other side of the globe. And as one considers object ecologies at the level of the subject, rogue objects can come to be defined – though not by Bryant, exactly – as abject.

In Julia Kristeva's definition, established in her influential *Powers of Horror* (1980), the abject is neither subject nor object but both and neither:

> The abject is not an ob-ject facing me, which I name or imagine. Nor is it an ob-ject, an otherness ceaselessly fleeing in a systematic quest of desire. What is ab-ject is not my correlative, which, providing me with someone or something else

> as support, would allow me to be more or less detached and autonomous. The abject has only one quality of the object – that of being opposed to *I*. (1997: 230)

In Kristeva's psychoanalytic analysis, the abject is a "jettisoned object," both a cultural and biological residue of subject formation, that which must be disavowed in order to attain coherent subjective form. Associated especially with "all those bodily wastes – excrement, pus, menstrual blood, mucus, vomit – that anticipate the culminating moment when the total body becomes waste through its transformation into a corpse," the abject returns to the subject-ego as a violent (both horrifying and fascinating) return of its repressed primordial substance (Jay, 1998: 146).

Bryant discusses waste in the context of large assemblages (like cities) containing their own propensity for entropy, where "the transformation of energy into work and material bodies is never without its remainder, a sort of Lacanian *objet a* or surplus" that unsettles the assemblage (2014: 102). Though waste is not exactly a rogue object in this example (a city, for instance, produces waste as "unsettl[ing]" byproduct, but it can in turn manage that waste as part of its continued regular operation), Bryant's regular psychoanalytic references – like Lacan's *objet a*, the non-object that is also abject, a stand-in for the desiring subject's renunciation of primordial attachments – suggest some underlying affinity between his object-oriented analysis and abject theory. The Kristevan abject is also a rogue object, as its affective power derives from a lack of place, its refusal to stay in an allotted place. "The abject confronts us...with those fragile states where man strays on the territories of *animal*," across fundamental species divides integral to our sense of place in a consistent and well-arranged natural world (Kristeva, 1997: 239; emphasis original). For Kristeva, the abject recalls a renounced primal fusion with the maternal body before Oedipalization, confronting us "with our earliest attempts to release the hold of *maternal* entity even before ex-sisting outside of her, thanks to the autonomy of language" (1997: 239). In other words, the abject recalls us to the primal (maternal) site before egoic self-sufficiency and symbolic communicational separation and distance.

To return to Schrenk-Notzing's photograph, we would be remiss not to acknowledge the dominance of female subjects in late 19th- and early 20th-century spirit photographs, many of which appear to be producing ectoplasm from the mouth (though occasionally from other even more sexualized orifices). The medium's violent transport takes away the effectiveness of differential speech, the oozing leak of the ectoplasm a stand-in for Kristeva's "semiotic" register, tied to the undifferentiated (feminine) prosodic flow of pre-Oedipal language. At the same time, this return to the primal scene – the primal "pulsation" of the drives in the breakthrough space Kristeva names "*chora*" in reference to Plato's *Timaeus* (1997: 240) – involves a deathly encounter. The subject takes on a corpselike masque, her dark shroud now doubling as sartorial preparation for an ultimate transition.

In the representational economy of the photograph, with its ectoplasmic *objet a* neither fully real nor false but something in between, the "extra" is the symptom of repression, including of the camera's structure of repression, its inherently selective bias, its indexical umbilical cord connecting image to reality through light masking the "reality" of staged manipulation. The ectoplasm becomes photography's abjective symptom, "a language that gives up, a structure within the body, a nonassimilable alien, a monster, a tumor" (Kristeva, 1997: 238). It is a rogue element in the photographic index, a stain that self-reflexively marks the camera itself as a rogue operator from the perspective of vulgar materialism. Hence Barthes' intuition about the photographed object as (like an) ectoplasm: it is a "certificate of presence" that verifies both the medium's *and* the media's experience of the real (2010: 87). The ectoplasm is monstrous because it collapses the difference between the materialist presuppositions that identify the camera as an index-producer, channeling the neutral medium of light, and the spiritualist credit advanced to the (feminized) medium that births a new being unassimilable to prior material cause.

Skeptics content on exposing spirit photography as a fraud often enumerated the technical methods by which the practitioner could produce "extras," as in the following list by conjuror William Marriott in a 1922 issue of the *Journal for the Society of Psychical Research*:

> The substitution of a dark slide containing prepared plates for the one loaded by the sitter with his own plates.
> The substitution of prepared plates for unprepared ones before these are loaded in the dark slide.
> The use of a pocket flash light apparatus for impressing an unprepared plate after it has been placed in the dark slide.
> The addition of extraneous chemical during the process of development
> The use of pinholes in the fabric covering the dark-room lamp.
> The use of similar pinholes on the cloth used for focussing the camera.
> The placing of a negative or a positive in the camera in front of the plate in such a position that the light passing through it will produce an image more or less blurred. (Harvey, 2007: 83–4)

That it was so common for (usually male) magicians to break their art's prohibition on revealing technical secrets suggests, first, a sense of mimetic rivalry with spirit photographers. But the photographer is, of course, not the one claiming access to the supernatural world; he acts as a passive recorder, often with a separate conjuror-subject-sitter whose powers are put on display. So empiricist rhetoric like Marriott's can be seen as an attempt to contain the powers of the (typically female) medium and give control back to the (typically male) photographer, cleansing the photograph of its abjective remainder and recuperating its most disturbing qualities in the aseptic assemblage of the numbered list. It fights visual semiosis with linguistic order.

And yet while the spirit photograph shows us that reality produces images of itself, it also demonstrates that objects – mediated by light and chemicals – do not project singularities:

> These "physical objects" do not have a single "image" – "their image" – but, rather, the camera can manipulate the reflected light to create an infinite number of images. An image is simply not a property which things naturally possess in addition to possessing size and weight. The image is a crafted, not a natural, thing. (Snyder, 1975: 151)

The image is crafted despite maintaining its indexical relation to natural laws; the camera re-presents objects according to their fundamentally systematic character (objects as systems that alternatively conceal and reveal their sensuous profiles and powers in their interaction with other objects and systems, including the photographic apparatus). Even without replicating the ontological debates rousted by spiritualism, we might humbly note that spirit photography's obsession with rogue specters, abject substance, gender difference, and physiological extremes was as much a product of its historical moment as Gunning's "gnostic impulse" that bridged enemy camps.

Spirit photography collapsed distinctions between immanent and transcendent phenomena at the very moment when, according to Michel Foucault, "life becomes a fundamental force...posited as the most general law of beings...function[ing] as an untamed ontology, one trying to express the indissociable being and non-being of all beings" (1970: 278). No matter how its extras were produced – by cheesecloth, by chemical cocktail, by plate preparation – the practice presented analytic visual culture with a problem, in part because of the era's photographic dogmas. Late 19th-century vitalisms and *Lebensphilosophie* were tuning in to the flow of "life" beneath our cognitive and socially produced categories and reifications, beginning to vilify all manner of mechanistic thinking and industry for abstracting our attention from the lifeworld's colorful plenitude of intensities.

In this context, images were no longer being conceived fundamentally as representations, as Henri Bergson writes in *Matter and Memory*: "by 'image' we mean a certain existence which is more than that which the idealist calls a *representation*, but less than that which the realist calls a *thing*, – an existence placed half-way between the 'thing' and the 'representation'" (1912: vii–viii; emphasis original). As photographers came to accept (and play with) the function of the camera as a tool for mediating worldly relations rather than transparently reflecting reality, the "problem" of spirit photography became productive rather than negative, an example not just of deceit but of the desire for art to glimpse the very things we have been trained to disavow, whether in the process of socialization or in our ascent to aesthetic maturity. "[W]hat we call life," David Wills explains in his recent book *Inanimation*, "has from the beginning left something we would normally call dead behind it," something inanimate (2016: 91). Wills describes this operation – this paradoxical *process* of "inanimation" – as "the structural inclusion or incursion, within life, of inanimate remains," these "remains" making up a sort of "thing theory" of death and survival where objects cannot be easily divided along the lines of animate and inanimate, organic and inorganic (2016: 97). Spirit photography, no matter what its aims or intentions, always tarried with the vitality of inanimate life, of death in life. It also revealed the camera itself – as many modernists would come to acknowledge – as a rogue object piercing pinholes in the lines separating the conceptual domains of subject and object, object and abject, appearance and reality, the real and the ideal.

## Notes

1 See Jolly, 2006: 8.

2 Honoré de Balzac presents an archetypal case, cited extensively as neurotic but nevertheless typical in his response to the advent of the daguerreotype. He believed that every body contains several layers of spectral images, one of which is stolen by the camera with every exposure. Walter Benjamin cites a passage from Cousin Pons as exemplary of such 19th-century anxieties: "[A]ll existing objects have there a kind of specter which can be captured and perceived...that is what Daguerre's discovery proved...[P]hysical objects in fact project themselves onto the atmosphere, so that it retains the specter which the daguerreotype can fix and capture" (in Benjamin, 1999: 688).

## Bibliography

Chiara Ambrosio, "Composite Photographs and the Quest for Generality: Themes from Peirce and Galton," *Critical Inquiry*, 42, 3 (2016): 547–579.

Roland Barthes, *Camera Lucida: Reflections on Photography* (1980), trans. Richard Howard (New York: Hill and Wang, 2010).

Walter Benjamin, *The Arcades Project* (1927–1940), trans. Howard Eiland and Kevin McLaughlin (Cambridge, MA: The Belknap Press of Harvard University Press, 1999).

Henri Bergson, *Matter and Memory* (1896), trans. Nancy Margaret Paul and W. Scott Palmer (London: George Allen & Co., 1912).

Levi R. Bryant, *Onto-Cartography: An Ontology of Machines and Media* (Edinburgh: Edinburgh University Press, 2014).

Jonathan Crary, *Techniques of the Observer: On Vision and Modernity in the Nineteenth Century* (Cambridge, MA: MIT Press, 1990).

Lorraine Daston and Peter Galison, *Objectivity* (Cambridge, MA: MIT Press, 2007).

Michel Foucault, *The Order of Things: An Archaeology of the Human Sciences* (1966) (New York: Vintage Books, 1970).

Tom Gunning, "In Your Face: Physiognomy, Photography, and the Gnostic Mission of Early Film," *Modernism/modernity*, 4, 1 (1997): 1–29.

John Harvey, *Photography and Spirit* (London: Reaktion Books, 2007).

Hermann von Helmholtz, *Treatise on Physiological Optics* (1925), 3 vols, ed. James P.C. Southall (New York: Dover Publications, 1962).

Martin Jay, *Cultural Semantics: Keywords of Our Time* (Amherst: University of Massachusetts Press, 1998).

Martyn Jolly, *Faces of the Living Dead: The Belief in Spirit Photography* (London: The British Library, 2006).

Julia Kristeva, "Powers of Horror" (1980), in *The Portable Kristeva*, ed. Kelly Oliver (New York: Columbia University Press, 1997).

Benjamin David Mitchell, "Capturing the Will: Imposture, Delusion, and Exposure in Alfred Russel Wallace's Defence of Spirit Photography," *Studies in History and Philosophy of Biological and Biomedical Sciences*, 46 (2014): 15–24.

Timothy Mitchell, "The World as Exhibition," *Comparative Studies in Society and History*, 31, 2 (1989): 217–236.

Joel Snyder and Neil Walsh Allen, "Photography, Vision, and Representation," *Critical Inquiry*, 2, 1 (1975): 143–169.

Alfred Russel Wallace, *On Miracles and Modern Spiritualism: Three Essays* (London: James Burns, 1875).

David Wills, *Inanimation: Theories of Inorganic Life* (Minneapolis: University of Minnesota Press, 2016).

Barbie Zelizer, "The Voice of the Visual in Memory," in *Framing Public Memory*, ed. Kendall R. Phillips (Tuscaloosa, AL: University of Alabama Press, 2004): 157–186.

# Object Lessons: What Cyanotypes Teach Us About Digital Media

David LaRocca

Not long ago, Michael Fried gave reasons why photography matters as art as never before (in his book of that title, 2008). He is perhaps more famous for having a half-century earlier addressed the relationship between art and objecthood (in his essay of that title, 1967). Pulling these two lines of thought together and drawing from research in object-oriented ontology (OOO) – especially in the visual aesthetics of the material basis of photography – I wish to pursue why photography matters as an *object* as we have perhaps seldom theorized before.[1] The locus of my attention is the distinctive qualities of the cyanotype, a technology of imagemaking that emerged in its modern form during the 19th century and that contests the familiar, formalist distinction between referent and representation, between object and image.

I wish to consider the traits of intimacy and immediacy that we find in the cyanotype, what some might think of as the real material stuff and substance of the image – not merely its objecthood but its objectness. To borrow from Rita Felski's conceptual locution, we have reason to consider the "messy and multidimensional entanglement" of material with the depiction it appears to send forth (Felski, 1995: 209); indeed, the admixture feels promiscuous and productively so. With a contact print (even of a photochemical sort), for example, we are not speaking of an image made "through a lens" – thus involving optics, framing, filters, apertures, and the like – but instead a kind of "death mask" of the scene, whether it be the weeds and plants of Anna Atkins (in the 1840s and 50s) or the cyanotype studies of Buffalo-based artist John Opera in the 21st century. Even the phrase "contact print" does a great deal of work for us – for it emphasizes the radical proximity, the adjacency, indeed, the *entanglements* that have attracted our attention. Our habitual confidence in seeing "through" an image to its referent is abruptly countered by evidence that suggests we are looking *at* an object of its own kind, where the recording medium and the after-effects of the referent have joined in a curious cohabitation.

If my initial reflections unpack the significance of Atkins's and Opera's work for our thinking about the objecthood (and objectness) of cyanotypes, in my second movement, I aim to push observations (about the ontological nature of the cyanotype) in the direction of Lev Manovich's remarks on the "painterly" status of digital media. The look at cyanotypes – and their particular, peculiar object-qualities – pair handsomely and productively with Manovich's incisive claim that digital media is (or are) better considered as a party to the history of painting (and indeed, logically so, also animation). We may have been insufficiently critical in the rapid shift from celluloid film to digital media – missing, in the process, the way in which the newest media, in fact, throw us back to pre-digital categories, especially the qualities pertaining to painting. Indeed, as with François Laruelle's *The Concept of Non-Photography* (2011), photochemical photography seems an interstitial point in the history of imagemaking, caught between archaic modes and digital options. It is time, Laruelle suggests, to challenge anew our "onto-photo-logical" presumptions (2011: 56–58).

Since we are – with the 19th-century technology of the cyanotype and cutting-edge 21st-century digital media – in the realm of painting, then we are also, necessarily, in the realm of discrete objects.[2] The image is no longer an "index" (of a profilmic event); the movie has ceased being a "print" of an historical happening; rather, the artwork is constituted graphically, materially, as a unique inhabitant of the world. If the century-plus dominance of photochemical photography lured us into separating referent from representation, the coincidence of the pre-silver-halide-based processes (among them, cyanotypes) and the current innovations of digital imaging, serves as an arresting rebuttal to that entrenched perspective and its distinct conceptualization of mimesis. In the digital age, it turns out that a 19th-century technology provides the terms and conditions for thinking anew about the objecthood of images, offering a chance to reassess our accounts of how art is related to the world it is said to "reflect."

Reaching back a half-century, consider a provocative, early instigation for thinking beyond the subject in *Negative Dialectics* (1966), where Theodor Adorno castigated the still-prevailing "jargon of authenticity" that infected the theorizing of Husserl, Heidegger, and Sartre, among others – and, according to Adorno, compromised their insights. On the constructive side, when Adorno speaks of "the primacy of the object," there may be reason to regard Adorno as an unintentional but nevertheless bona fide spiritual and intellectual godfather of OOO (Adorno, 1973: 188).[3] Adorno offers just the sort of re-orientation that OOO carries as a hallmark: namely, questioning, that is, displacing human centrality – and thus subjectivity – in the order of things. Indeed, since most "things" are not human, we are quietly prompted to ask an unfamiliar question: "What are *they* thinking?" Repurposing an account Hannah Arendt has given in a political context, it would be misleading (and defeatist) to say that OOO is a "revolution," for the metaphor suggests that one ends where one begins – a full 360. Rather, in what follows, we want to consider how OOO gets us halfway: gets us to flip or invert our relationship to things, to objects (and doubtless to our thinking about and relation to objects – perhaps in the process, ourselves among them). Our goal is, therefore, a 180-degree reversal. Following Arendt, the point is not "revolution" but "restoration" (Arendt, 1963: 43). We are trying to get back to where we began.

What is at hand, then, is an attempt at conducting, in the open, a project of discernment: in particular, trying to get clear (or at least clearer) about *the kind of thing cyanotypes are*; in large measure, this involves exploring what cyanotypes *do*. As any inquiry into the ontology and phenomenology of images must hold dear – and as this collection takes as a signature trait of its methodologies – I begin by paying scrupulous attention to the surface features that inform visual representations, then move on to the second-order (but by no means secondary) consideration of "thingness" (or again, if you prefer, objectness) – what many now call quite comfortably, even intuitively (after Fried, and after Graham Harman), objecthood.

As Harman has underscored: "For Fried, 'object' means a physical obstacle literally present in our path, as he famously complains in the case of minimalist sculpture. For OOO, by contrast, objects are always absent rather than present" (Harman, 2020: 1). Harman's conceptual and terminological inversion sustains Adorno's well-established critique of the subject-centered, providing in the process new traction for addressing both the nature of objects and the character of aesthetic critique. If a photograph is an object (not a "window" onto an object), yet its objecthood is not derived from human subjectivity, what exactly are we speaking of? Cyanotypes may illuminate the way in which photographs afford humans a presence in a mode of absence.

## Metaphorism

As Ian Bogost writes in *Alien Phenomenology*: "The way a film emulsion or a CCD perceives an object is not merely an accident of the photographer's agency. It is a material process that deserves attention for its own sake before questions of agency, reference, meaning, or criticism enter into the picture" (2012: 68).[4] When

Bogost analyzes a specific brand of digital camera, he notes that what we may instinctively treat as a technological fault of image rendition (e.g., a miscalibrated hue) is, in fact, "the way the Sigma DP *itself* perceives the world," which he emphasizes is "the subject of interest for the alien phenomenologist" (Bogost, 2012: 70). Thus, the human perception that the Foveon sensor has "failed" depends on our sense of the image's deviation from what we expect (i.e., what we expect our own eyes to see). There is an implied preference for the rectitude of "matching" – yet another sign of the human/subjective desire for images to imitate the private experiences of the observer. In the context of photographing wildfires, for instance, Bogast has declared, "Your phone wasn't built for the Apocalypse" (Bogost, 2020). The way smartphones diminished the orange intensity of California skies, for instance, is "a reminder that even as cameras have become a way to document every aspect of our lives, they aren't windows on the world, but simply machines that turn views of that world into images" (Bogost, 2020). As Bogost encourages, years earlier in *Alien Phenomenology*: "[T]he photographer must wrap his brain around the idea that the dimness of the Sigma DP is relative to the sensor, not the human eye" (2012: 72). The human (eye/I/subject-position) has been displaced. Referring to the de-dramatizing smartphone images of catastrophe, he notes: "The un-oranged images were caused by one of the most basic features of digital cameras, their ability to infer what color is in an image based on the lighting conditions in which it is taken. Like the people looking up at it, the software never expected the sky to be bathed in orange" (Bogost, 2020). When Bogost speaks of the shift away from the subject(ive) as involving "metaphorism" – that we can appreciate "what it's *like* to be a Foveon digital image sensor, even if this isn't what it *is* to be one" – we are trading in analogies, albeit important ones. If this moment when "object relations become metaphorized" is not a terminal or comprehensive reply, it at least helps those who are not yet "object-oriented" to appreciate the reversals and shifts underway (Bogost, 2012: 67, 72).

As Bogost's notion of metaphorism implies, any reader or interpreter of nonhuman objects should be on guard to avoid slipping into literalism – e.g., treating the analogy or relationship or "unit operation" (Bogost's preferred syntagma for "object-oriented") as a thing (Bogost, 2012: 72). The habit of literalizing is familiar and entrenched, since we see how commonly the natural sciences allow a trope to define (or constrain) its researches. Ludwig Wittgenstein spoke of how a "picture held us captive," and Thomas Kuhn described the process by which "paradigms" are suddenly displaced through a process of feverish rupture and replacement. Likewise, in this more limited and proximate example of the Foveon image sensor and the images it makes, we could practice our resistance to the compulsion for literalism. It is a compliment to Bogost's awareness of the apparatus he is creating that he notes matter-of-factly how "[m]etaphorism is necessarily anthropomorphic" (Bogost, 2012: 74). Displacing the subject, we might have expected, is not easy; then again, neither is it necessary. The point, instead, appears to be a coming-to-awareness of certain habits of mind: ones that preference the subject and diminish the object.

In order to get a sense of "what it's like to be a Fovean digital image sensor," we have to push beyond metaphorism to what Bogost – somewhat inevitably – must call *metametaphorism*. That is to say, how we, as humans, can deliberate on "the vantage point of the sensor itself" (Bogost, 2012: 80). Can we? This move – this invitation – returns us to the basic terms of Bogost's alien phenomenology where we are prompted to ask, "What sort of being do objects have?" The metaphysical question is set at an epistemological distance, since we (as humans) are no longer asking "how do I know what it's like to perceive this object," but "how do I know what it's like for the object to 'perceive' this object." The second instance of "perceive" is placed in scare quotes to underscore the anthropocentrism/anthropomorphism that has slipped into the alien phenomenology of the image sensor; in short, we count another instance of metaphorism. Bogost provides some counseling on the matter:

> [M]etaphorisms are always self-centered. The photographer's metaphorism of the sensor can't help but draw its notes into the event horizon of human experience. Anthropocentrism is thus both a torment and a foregone conclusion for us humans, but we need not feel alone in suffering under it. If anticorrelationism amounts to a rejection of one correlation and an embrace of multiple correlations, then centrism is inevitable [...]. (Bogost, 2012: 80)

Bogost makes an incisive clarification in noting that centrism remains part of alien phenomenology – even as it has always already been a hallmark of both dominant forms of correlationism (namely, scientific naturalism and social relativism). The proposal of a world of polycentrisms at once liberates our proceedings here and motivates them, for we are given ground on which to postulate the life (or being) of specific kinds of processes and the things they come to constitute. To this end, and in what follows, I wish to speak more specifically and concretely about the imagemaking process of cyanotyping and the kinds of objects that that process yields. To apply Bogost's metaphorism, then, let us call the following reflections part of a study of cyanocentrism. As Bogost did for the Foveon digital image sensor, let us do for the 19th-century art of the cyanotype: consider "what it's like" to be immersed in the chemical, material life of this process, to inhabit "the vantage point" of the cyanotype itself.

## Nature Writing

One of the more remarkable facts of the celluloid arts emerges with the way naturally occurring materials – chemicals, minerals, water – are placed in relationship to another very dominant, natural resource: electromagnetic radiation, otherwise known by its common name, sunlight. In parallel, as if operating on a different register of representation, we find the architectural form known as the *camera obscura* – a "dark room" that relies on the uncanny reversal of live, unmediated imagery through a small aperture (or "pinhole"); add a lens, of course, and you can adjust focus and the passage of light; add a fixative emulsion (the result of the chemical side of the art), and you get a photographic picture. I rehearse in miniature this well-known history in order to find our place in the development of the cyanotype as a technology of imagemaking. A search for origins and early experimentation will find us squarely in the midst of mid-19th-century Victorian England.

In the swirl of animated scientific experimentation between William Henry Fox Talbot (1800–77) and John F. W. Herschel (1792–1871) – and including, at a distance, Louis Daguerre (1787–1851) in France – it was Herschel who argued for the name "photography," circa 1839. (Fox Talbot advocated for "photogenic," which of course we now use as a compliment for those appearing *in* photographs.) In 1842, Herschel also provided the name for one of several photographic processes he was innovating, the "cyanotype" among them. Though not the first technique that "fixed" an image permanently, what distinguished the cyanotype from other approaches was the simplicity of the materials and processes involved: as Beaumont Newell summarizes the process, it requires merely "developing" (specifically, oxidizing) ferric (i.e., iron) salts with water (Newhall, 1967: 61–62).

As with many arts, there are those who innovate its functioning and those who become innovative functionaries – the artists. If Herschel was the signature discoverer of the cyanotype, then Anna Atkins (1799–1871), who died less than a month after her British compatriot, was the first artistic agent of the process. She and her father, John George Children, were friends with Talbot and Herschel, both of whom instructed her personally on their photographic inventions. Atkins coupled her already well-developed and avid study of botany with the photographic – especially cyanotographic – processes she was learning to master. The coupling itself is uncanny since her work becomes a testament of one set of natural phenomena (iron salts, for example) upon another set of natural phenomena (plants) (fig. 9.1). Nature was being used to represent Nature. The reflexivity is arresting as is the incumbent sense of isomorphic representation being achieved *acheiropoieton*, "without hands."

Atkins is now best known for her cyanotype photograms (the latter being a photograph made when an object is placed directly on emulsion). The objects of Atkins's photograms were botanical specimens. Her first book, *Photographs of British Algae: Cyanotype Impressions* was self-published in 1843; two further volumes appeared in the next decade.[5] If we are familiar with Gutenberg as the inventor of the printing press, we ought to take note of Atkins's book – made four centuries later – as the

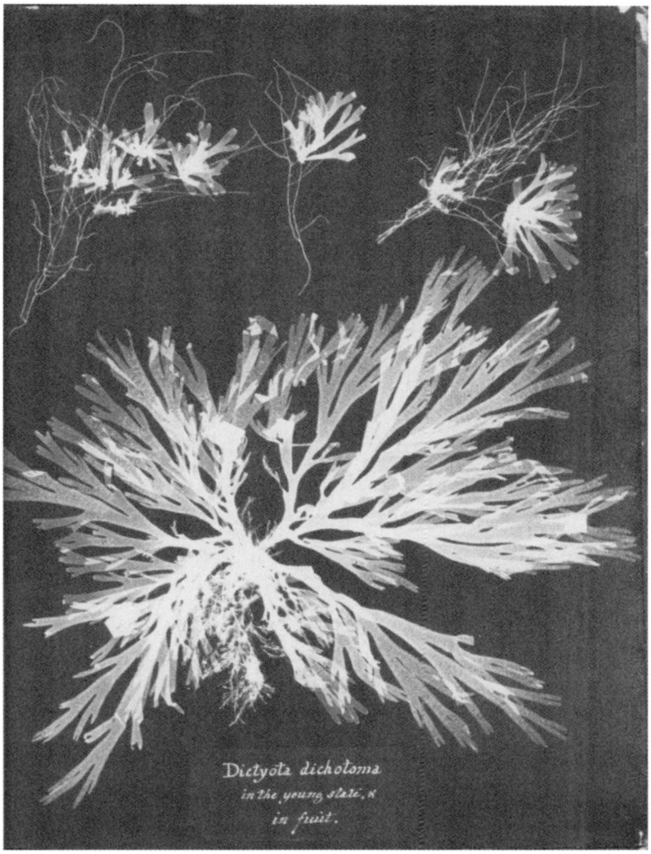


Fig. 9.1. Anna Atkins, *Dictyota Dichotoma in the Young State, and in Fruit*, c.1843. Cyanotype, 26 × 20 cm (10.2 × 7.9 in). Courtesy of the British Library Board, London.

first in human history to feature photographic images. (Perhaps it is not surprising that the more famous, and male, Talbot usually gets credit for being first, with his *The Pencil of Nature* [1844–46]).

Acknowledging but also bracketing gender politics in the history of photography, let us return to the elements and their effects. As Christopher James explains in *The Book of Alternative Photographic Processes*, the cyanotype is "an ultraviolet (UV) sensitive contact printing process that requires, as do all of the non-silver processes, a negative the same size as the final print" (2002: 107). While this description helps us sort procedural aspects of the cyanotype, the following note by James pushes the kind of information we learned in the Newhall account above into distinctively new ontological and phenomenological territory:

> The cyanotype is highly stable but can be degraded by something alkaline, such as sodium carbonate or perspiration. It will also fade, like most things, if exposed to strong direct sunlight over a period of time. Should you experience fading, your image can be restored to its original blue intensity by storing it in a dark environment for a short time. (James, 2002: 107)

Let us pause to take stock of our familiar silver-based photographic technologies, for example, the 35mm negative and the Polaroid. Those who have worked in darkrooms are familiar with a negative being scratched by mishandling; many have come across a box of Polaroids that have faded – some to near white, as if the image had been washed away or bleached out. (In a like manner, but in a non-silver-based technology, most have been faced with a troubling error message that states a digital file – for example, a jpg – is "corrupted" or "cannot be opened.") In all of these cases, silver and otherwise, *there is no going back*; there is no restoration. Part of the value of these photographic records, we are tempted to think, is caught up in their fragility – we may even be tempted to say their mortality. Like their users, we humans, these representations – silver halide negative, silver bromide Polaroid, and digital bits of swirling electrons – seem distinctly in peril and destined to perish.

And then there is the cyanotype, which, in a word seems to be not just *alive* but *regenerative*. Drawing from Bogost's title and ur-concept, it seems apt to dwell on the "alien phenomenology" of ferric salts and the UV radiation that animates and re-animates them. Unlike the photographic negative and Polaroid and digital file, which feel so distinctly and definitively "fixed," the cyanotype is never quite finite. Cyanotypes do not possess the same stability as conventional silver-oxide prints; cyanotypes are "corruptible" by light, that is, by the very energies that generate them. Though the photo-sensitive emulsion registers the "impression" (in Atkins's lexicon) of the object that has lain upon its surface, that impression evolves *over time* in relationship to the presence (or absence) of UV radiation. The UV light, in effect, diminishes the expression of the potassium ferrocyanide: so, after having given birth to the project, it can also obliterate it, as if we needed yet another example of the parental – indeed, divining – attributes of the sun. While an anthotype continues to fade into oblivion (without any hope of restoration or regeneration), the cyanotype can fade (*does* fade), yet can also regenerate (in an almost Frankensteinian way – inert matter seemingly coaxed to life via an elemental, natural life force). As such, the cyanotype and its potential for ever-shifting characteristics check our presumptions about the "fixity" of photographic representations.

## Flat Ontology, Liquid Intelligence, and Cyanotypes

To bring theory and practice into conversation, a few years ago, I began interviewing John Opera (b. 1975), raised in Buffalo, working in Chicago for more than the last decade (since graduating with an M.F.A. from the School of the Art Institute [SAIC]), and as of Fall 2017, Assistant Professor in the Department of Art at the State University of New York at Buffalo. In the record of our conversation in *Afterimage*, there is a discernable line of inquiry: I am trying to understand how Opera seems to be leaving photography for painting (LaRocca, 2015).[6] (Or is it finding a mode of photography that is a species of painting?) In the interview, I approach this notion – this question – from several vantages: the materials he uses, his results, and how the art-objects exist after he has "completed" them. The quotation marks are here meant to set off the suspicion that the works are somehow *not* completed but independent, living lives (and experiencing deaths) of their own; recall, again, anthotypes fade beyond recuperation. We want to acknowledge the "existence of substances," as Levi R. Bryant has said, and at the same time appreciate their "autonomy from relations" (Bryant, 2011: x). Fittingly for a discussion of photographs and cyanotypes (that resemble paintings), Bryant deems this paired existence and autonomy as indicative of a "flat ontology."[7] The homology, of course, between the literal *flatness* of Opera's artworks and a flat ontology is more than clever – signaling instead a genuine invitation to think out what is happening *in* the (objecthood of the) representation itself.

Since Opera's work has increasingly become dominated by cyanotypes, I followed up the *Afterimage* interview with a visit to his Chicago studio. Our dialogue continued when Opera returned to Buffalo and established a new studio there.

Opera's cyanotypes are representations (yes, flat ones), but the bolt of insight comes in sussing out the way(s) they are representing *themselves* (e.g., in the terms of Bryant's flat ontology). For instance, we cannot discern the difference between a raw egg and a hard-boiled egg. Despite its transformation, the egg, so to speak, still represents itself, leaving its "internal" state an outward mystery. Meanwhile, when we take a discernable chemical or compound – say, potassium ferrocyanide – and apply it to a canvas, then subject it to UV radiation, we (again, intuitively) believe we see an image or representation or, in time, a work of art. But what happened to the *material*? We have lost touch with it (as we did not lose touch with the materiality of the egg, however much some of its attributes remain veiled). With an indication of pattering, for instance, we no longer see the object – or its material origins – but its new status as a work of art, as it were, in the service of representation. Jackson Pollock's paint can hovering over a horizontal perimeter of cloth reminds us of the difference between what is in the can and what is on the canvas.

Familiar with Opera's earlier body of lens-based work, I was intrigued, in the *Afterimage* interview, by the way his practice was becoming dominated by cyanotypes (and the related process of anthotypes), thereby returning us to the mysteries at the heart of this bio-chemical event and also to the objecthood of the cyanotype. What I am identifying here as "mysteries" are not related to the *science* of cyanotyping – again, that has been well-known since the 1840s – but to the *ontology* and *phenomenology* of cyanotyping. The ontological-phenomenological mystery directs our attention to the nature of painting on the one hand and to the nature of digital media on the other hand. How this is so may link up profitably with an invocation of – and a comparison with – the "generative photography" of Gottfried Jäger. An artist and educator, Jäger speaks of a "generative photography" as one in which the medium 'no longer merely reproduces objects, but actually produces new forms" – and consequently "generates new images" (Jäger, 1986: 19).[8] *Acheiropoieta* by another name. In this way, images are not of things *in* the world, but are the very materials *of* the world; the work is not reproductive but productive; it is not reliant on the human recognition of mimesis, but is instead strangely endogenous, representative of itself.

Like Jäger's constructivist experiments, Opera's work undermines, or at least questions, the way we speak of the "objecthood" of images. Such a query is, as it must be, already *in media res*. For example, Bogost has leveled a critique of the phrase "object-oriented" because it latently contains an opposition to "subject-oriented," "since an *object* implies a *subject*, and the marriage of subject and object sits at the heart of correlationism" – viz., the antagonist to alien phenomenology (Bogost, 2012: 23; emphasis original). Bogost has countered with the idea of "unit operations" that can now, in a different context, serve our understanding of what Opera creates when he creates a cyanotype (Bogost, 2012: 25–26). In fact, there is uncanny – and certainly unexpected – pertinence to Bogost's terminological shift. While he says that "unit operations" are "sufficient to describe any system whatsoever," he tells us that he "absconded with 'unit operation' from chemical engineering, a field in which the name refers to the steps in a process (extraction, homogenization, distillation, refrigeration, etc.)" (Bogost, 2012: 26). Why does this confession resonate so intensely and productively in the context of Opera's operation? Precisely because he is intimately *involved in a form of chemical engineering*. When the homology – between "unit operations" and Opera's cyanotypes – is pointed out, nothing less than a Gestalt shift may occur in the viewer. Suddenly these "artworks" – in sizes familiar to large-scale photography and stretched upon canvases that bind the results to the history of painting – do not seem like artworks at all but something more like the residues of "unit operations" made by a special network of chemicals that have been applied artfully (one is tempted to swap the euphemism, after Bogost, to "engineered") to maximize their inherent potential. This is to say that from our (necessarily) anthropocentric position – and given our familiarity with the history of art, of painting, of photography – we are primed to see Opera's creations *as* artworks; in this habit, we participate in the mores of reception (and perception).

At this point in the proceedings, and given what I have said – and seen firsthand of Opera's labors in his studios – it feels odd, incorrect even, to speak of the individual cyanotypes as *objects*. The customary art-world designation is "works" (as in "artworks") and this seems just as misleading and potentially wrong-headed. So "unit operations," just as Bogost had intimated, may make for a better, more accurate, fit. After all, when we address one of Opera's pieces, we are not beholding a representation that points to an external or separate referent so much as materials that were "touched" – indexed – by the light that activated them; Opera's artistic contribution, to be sure, is evident in the particular and accomplished constellation of designs and arrangements he affords the media. Yet, dwelling on the ontology and phenomenology of the media, Christopher James's description of a kind of *re-animation* gets us some distance toward thinking about the cyanotype as *an interaction* between the materials that constitute the work of art and the environment that affects it (James, 2012: 107). For example, once a cyanotype is created, depending on the lighting conditions, it can become a space of fugitive impressions – those that emerge and those that flee. (See pl. 11.)

For one thing, it may be worth avoiding a panic about the wrongfulness or errancy of Graham Harman's familiar "object-oriented," since one could as easily describe Bogost's "unit" *as an object*. Whether we call the "unit" an atom or electron, bit or particle, mitochondrion or grain of sand, it may yet feel legitimate to speak of these "things" as "objects," no? In the case at hand, we are drawing up close to the "units" that comprise the chemical processes involved in cyanotyping – and at whatever level you look (e.g., at the microscopic or at the everyday of human visual perception), we may identify "objects" *and* "unit relations." Tempering any terminological friction is not for nothing, since, once again, we may appreciate how all of these words – object, unit, bit, thing, et al. – are metaphors. Indeed, Harman has underscored that "the OOO program emphasizes objects considered apart from their relations" and thus seizes "on the non-relational autonomy or closure of objects from their contexts" (Harman, 2020: 3). As Bogost says: "[a] metaphor is just a trope, not a copy" (Bogost, 2012: 72).[9] Thus, to speak of or refer to an object – e.g., this "batch" of ferrocyanide – is not to *duplicate* its reality (as if by some sort of linguistic legerdemain), but instead, and merely, to make *analogical reference* to something.

My visit to Opera's Chicago studio-laboratory bore the welcome elements of many other big-city visits with artists: the old factory building converted to studio space, and the entry into a workshop that also functioned as a make-shift gallery (with pieces hanging on walls but also standing in single-file, card-catalogue-style along the wall). I mention the first impression mostly to take note of how much Opera's space felt like a *painter's* studio; the same arrangement was replicated in Buffalo (albeit in a larger space afforded, as it were, by the smaller city). Opera's artworks, for the most part, are large, beginning at about sixteen inches high and reaching into the sixties. Moreover, the works are made in the fashion familiar to any painter who uses oil and acrylic: Opera builds frames and stretches cloth canvas over them. It is only at this point, with stacks of soldier-like stretched canvases awaiting their assignments, that one gets a first inkling of embarking on a photographic or photochemical process.

Opera applies a mixture of potassium ferrocyanide to the surface of the raw canvas. So, in a very literal sense, he is painting. But not to create a representational work, rather to apply the substance that will become – in Kantian language – the condition for the possibility of such a thing. As the potassium ferrocyanide dries, it oxidizes (turns yellow with a tint of green – like an unripe lemon – and, later, shifts darker to the green of split pea soup), but more importantly, in the process of drying, it becomes light-sensitive. When I reach back to Christopher James' description noted above – that we encounter "an ultraviolet (UV) sensitive contact printing process that requires...a negative the same size as the final print" – it hits me: when Opera holds up his canvas on a stretcher, now coated in potassium ferrocyanide, he is showing me an unexposed photo-sensitive emulsion (James, 2002: 107). The negative (since this is an original and a one-off) doesn't just look like a painting, it is one.

The next step in Opera's process is the use of UV lights, a technique for which he has built an array of custom instruments, including turntables, darkroom easels, light fixtures, and even light bulbs themselves. (See pls. 12 & 13.) As the photo-illustrations of his apparatuses show, Opera must create the conditions of his art, in some sense invent them; he does so by drawing on a knack for carpentry, electrical wiring, and elemental engineering. Precisely *how* Opera employs the lights to generate his artwork is not profitably described here; what is salient, however, is the photochemical process that underwrites the effects produced by the conjunction of UV radiation and a potassium ferrocyanide-covered canvas. Watching the work get made, one wants to know "What is happening?" And it is this kind of question that prompts a series of notes, references, and reflections by Opera himself that I hope to accurately recount and engage now.

I asked Opera about a 2016 exhibition in Cleveland that featured his cyanotypes (and anthotypes) entitled *Unfixed: The Fugitive Image*.[10] He found a catalogue from the show where the curators describe their purpose, with my emphasis added: to "consider the *physicality* of the photographic object as it changes and fades" over time (including the time of the exhibition, about three months). Opera told me about another, earlier exhibition – this one in 2015 at The Hole (in New York's Bowery) – entitled *Not a Photo*. As the director of the gallery, Raymond Bulman, puts it:

> The Hole is proud to announce a group show of photography in the expanded realm; a group photo show where no photos will be exhibited! 'Not a Photo' looks at the way artists are using photography today, not as a final product but rather as a tool or step in a multi-media process.... Many artists in this show have a step in their process that includes photography, but they don't stop there. (Bulman, 2015)

(Not incidentally, a show held earlier in the same year was entitled *Not a Painting*, which in turn was preceded by *Post-Analog Painting*.) Philosophers have always been susceptible to asking after essences (a Platonic residuum, no doubt), but even after Wittgenstein tried to disabuse us of such fruitless inquires, they persist. Yet on this occasion, in the light of Opera's remarks on how the "boundaries between photography and painting are breaking down, have broken down," pursuing any essentialism seemed misguided. So instead of the knee-jerk follow-up, "What is a photograph?," a question that *did* seem worth chasing made itself known: "*When* is a photograph?"[11]

It is easy to notice that the shift from "what" to "when" trades out essentialism (and to some extent spatiality) for a spectrum of temporality. For example, to ask "when is a photograph?" presumes an earlier, or at least ancillary question: "When does a photograph *begin*?" And this is precisely what seemed to be happening in front of me in Opera's studio, however slowly (the exposures for cyanotypes are often very long – "slow" – in comparison with the extremely light-sensitive – "fast" – emulsions of silver halide film); for reference, Opera describes his lab work as "darkroom photography in super-slow motion." Consider attention to this process as forming a conjecture for *when* a cyanotype *begins*: the light-sensitive potassium ferrocyanide emulsion is ready, Opera shines his UV lights upon its surface and...it begins. Or, to draw in a related metaphor from above: it is born, it begins its life as a cyanotype. These tropes need not be taken anthropocentrically, since there is much life that is nonhuman, and yet it may still sound odd – if not an outright category mistake – to attribute *life* to a cyanotype. Here is how Opera spoke of the interaction between the UV light itself (in this case radiating from a long, fluorescent tube) and the blank, just-activated canvas awaiting inscription: "The chemical reaction is visible before the work is even developed; this is different than, say, the typical latency in a gelatin silver darkroom print that *cannot* be seen during the process of accumulated exposure [but] only *after* [it's] developed. With cyanotypes, by contrast, I'm able to see the indexical impressions of the light as they make contact with the photosensitive surface. The chemical reaction becomes visually apparent; the appearance of the materials change *before* the canvases are fixed. The delay allows me to track the composition as it's being made."

Opera draws his studio practice into conversation with the uncanny world of natural phenomena: "I'm reminded of Jeff Wall's well-known text 'Photography and Liquid Intelligence' in which he describes water's essential role in photography, that it symbolically 'represents an archaism'" (Wall, 1989: 109–10). Opera continues: "When Wall speaks to the 'prehistorical' image of photography he suggests how we face 'a speculative image in which the apparatus itself can be thought of as not yet having emerged from the mineral and vegetable worlds.' This in turn, as Wall says, 'can help us understand the "dry" part of photography differently'" (Wall,

1989: 109). Sustaining a citation from Wall's visionary statement, Opera makes a summative connection to the logic of the cyanotype with its distinct assemblage of dry and wet, light and liquid, wave and particle, the analog and the digital, the painterly and the photographic; as Wall writes: "This 'dry' part I identify with optics and mechanics.... This kind of modern vision has been separated to a great extent from the sense of immersion in the incalculable which I associate with 'liquid intelligence'" (Wall, 1989: 109–110).[12] Perhaps it is this moment of Opera's engagement with Wall's iconic statement that most draws out resonances with OOO – as we find it in Ian Bogost, Levi R. Bryant, Peter Gratton, Graham Harman, and others[13] – and, as Wall remarks, as "a reflection on the meaning of Andrei Tarkovsky's *Solaris* (1972)," where "[s]ome scientists are studying an oceanic planet. Their techniques are typically scientific. But the ocean is itself an intelligence which is studying them in turn" (Wall, 1989: 110). Opera finds in Wall's remarks a recognition that the oceanic planet displays sentient behaviors.

## Cyanotypes and Digital Media

In this last movement of the essay, I wish to propel some lessons of the cyanotype beyond a phase of mere curiosity (such as one may have upon encountering a novel or forgotten technology) and into something more like an undeniable, even necessary, shift in our perception of media as we increasingly know them through the ubiquity of digital technologies. Let me draw upon a series of claims made by media theorists, among them Lev Manovich, author of the epochal, controversial article-cum-manifesto "What is Cinema?" With Manovich's well-articulated and boldly defended thesis in hand, the implications of cyanotypes for our contemporary sense of the ontological and phenomenological status of digital media should become readily apparent.

Manovich claims that "cinema can no longer be clearly distinguished from animation. It is no longer an indexical media technology but, rather, a sub-genre of painting" (1995: 1061).[14] That is to say, cinema used to be "the art of the index," "an attempt to make art out of a footprint" (Manovich, 1995: 1060). The latter claims are intimately tied to any observations about what Stanley Cavell, among others, has identified as the "photographic basis of cinema" (Cavell, 2017). As Manovich somewhat caustically puts it: "[B]ehind even the most stylized cinematic images we can discern the bluntness, the sterility, the banality of early 19th-century photographs" (1995: 1060). Let's not take that remark personally, as a judgment on the aesthetical qualities of photographs (from whatever era), and instead dwell on its *metaphysical* implications.

I am not the only one, after Cavell or Manovich, to notice potential and existing complications for the use and understanding of inherited ontological categories and, indeed, the very senses we have of, or definitions we use for, representations – namely, what they *are* and what they are *of*. For instance, Kris Paulsen has contributed essential work aimed to "challenge the rhetoric of the 'death of the index'" debate/crisis that has emerged in cinema and media theory.[15] She contends that the "loss of the index" in the digital present, if true, would rightly cultivate a "crisis of belief"; however, such accounts are "reductive and narrow, if not entirely inaccurate" (Paulsen, 2013: 85). To broaden and clarify the matter, then, and with Manovich's proposals in her sights – along with those proffered by other canonical theorists such as Anne-Marie Willis and W. J. T. Mitchell – she says the "index is not (and never has been) a sign based simply in materiality; it does not necessarily serve as a record of the past or testify to clear evidentiary truth" (Paulsen, 2013: 85, 87–88). Paulsen undertakes her corrective by returning to the source of the concept – C. S. Peirce – and a careful re-reading of his descriptions and definitions. Her analysis of abductive inference, among other neologisms of the Peircean lexicon, lends compelling weight to her critique.

I suppose, then, for present purposes – especially given that Manovich, Cavell, and other media theorists do not attend to Peirce's formulations with such care – we are forced to address what may come to be called "popular" (or even debased) definitions of the index, instead of, say, those that remain loyal to nuanced philosophical formulations. Still, we can glean from Paulsen the core recommendation yielded from her return to Peirce: "the index establishes a forceful present-tense connection to its receiver." For this reason, the "suppressed identity" of this temporality should be revealed anew so that the index can "emerge as the operative sign for mediated and digital images" (Paulsen, 2013: 85). And happily, Opera's cyanotypes may provide a path for testing (and confirming) Paulsen's claims, as for example, when Opera says above "with cyanotypes...I'm able to see the indexical impressions of the light as they make contact with the photosensitive surface." While cyanotypes are not themselves digital, they illuminate something distinctive about the materiality *and* temporality of the index (both central concerns of Paulsen's); hence, they offer conditions for assessing the objecthood of images and/or what constitutes them.

In Opera's process of creating cyanotypes, for example, we have a chance to notice that while the light-markings (made possible via classical photographic means of exposure) align with the active materiality of the index, the canvas itself – the space of or surface for those inscriptions – is, we could say, designed: the final look of the work of art is a function of Opera's intention to have these effects appear in just this way (admittedly, an intention that it met with much discovery of the unplanned and aleatory). A close study of the Opera works discussed in this chapter, but especially when encountered at-scale in person, provokes in the viewer a double sensation, or better, recognition: that the constituent elements of the image operate on a separate channel from the composition-as-a-whole. In other words, while a given figure confirms its photo-chemical origins, the total image is not a representation of anything other than, as it were, itself: just these constitutive light-markings made in this particular way. Without being coy, we could say that his chosen media and methods make literal the "light writing" that lives etymologically in the notion of the *photo-graphic*. Observing the cyanotype, we have quite gratifyingly, then, found ourselves in proximity to the productive frisson that obtains between painting, analog photograph, digital image, and object-as-such. Returning to these and similar observations by Opera, the cyanotype emerges as a veritable topography for Paulsen's Peircean recovery and recalibration of the index in the age of digital production and reproduction.

Such terminological articulation, and even in some cases, rapprochement between competing theories, is nicely achieved by Manovich himself when he surveys the contestations familiar to theoretical quarrels: "From the perspective of a future historian of visual culture, the differences between classical Hollywood films, European art films and avant-garde films (apart from abstract ones) may appear to have less significance than this common feature: that they relied on lens-based recordings of reality" (1995/2011: 1060). Parsing this last syntagma – "lens-based recordings of reality" – Manovich means to emphasize the *profilmic* nature of analog technology, namely that whatever appears on film had to "be there" at the time of recording; no doubt this is related to our designation of such works as "live action." In this way, we are always sure that this specific bit of celluloid was "on the scene" at the time of recording, when the events appearing before the camera in fact happened. No wonder, then, that "computer media redefines the very identity of cinema" (Manovich, 1995/2011: 1060).[16]

What then of cyanotypes? Are they not, then, simply part of the blunt, banal, moribund photographic arts of the 19th century? What can they possibly tell us or teach us about digital media in the 21st century? For a reply, I return to where I began with Manovich: digital cinema is a form of animation, and therefore, "a sub-genre of painting." When we think of the *uses* of computer-generated imagery (CGI), for example, in mainstream Hollywood films, we naturally think of photorealistic scenes generated "entirely in a computer using 3D computer animation," scenes that have "perfect photographic credibility though it was 'never actually filmed'" (Manovich, 1995/2011: 1061). But the resemblance of the photorealistic CGI scenes presents something of a red herring: it invites us to think of CGI in terms of its pronounced *indexical* powers. Yet, thinking of CGI in the wake of Manovich, we must remember that its indexical powers amount to zero. In a helpful distinction proposed by Gregory Currie (2017), with CGI and digital media, we are no longer in the realm of the "trace," but that of "testimony." If *digital media* is an art of testimony, what else is? Not lens-based photography or cinema, but painting. Currie makes the contrast plain: "a photograph is a trace of its subject, while a painting is a testimony of it" (Currie, 2017: 96). A trace, on Currie's account, involves a specific kind of material marking from or by one entity onto another (thus a silver oxide print as akin to a death mask or a footprint), whereas a painting is an *interpretation* of reality, independent of such material causation but not mental intention (Currie, 2017: 96). As Currie puts it: "A camera records what is in front of it, and not what the photographer thinks is in front of it, if there is a difference between them. But the painter paints what he or she thinks is there" (Currie, 2017: 96–97). Here cyanotypes – especially and emphatically in Opera's approach to cyanotypes – lend a first clue to their remarkable hybrid status as trace *and* testimony. Much has already been said above about the cyanotype's participation in the tradition of analog photography; what remains to be articulated is its credentials as a mode of painterly mark-making.

To be clear, while Manovich has argued persuasively for digital media's identity as a sub-genre of painting, I aim to extend the thesis so that cyanotypes are included in the same categorical or taxonomic designation. When we return to Opera's studio – closely attending to his process (the stretchers, the canvas, the instruments, the application of chemical compounds), studying how the cyanotype comes into being (the desiccation of the light-sensitive canvas, the application of UV radiation, the water rinse) – we see anew how the finished work can be understood as a painting (as well as a photograph). The cyanotype embodies a *blend* of painting and photographic processes: for example, without any controversy, Opera can be said to apply radiation (via UV light) to the sensitized surface of the canvas akin to the way a painter applies paint to the canvas (indeed, the base layer of cotton canvas is common to both pedigrees). Thus, honing the analogy, the "paint" is ultraviolet radiation as it affects potassium ferrocyanide; we might even say this reaction is a form of "mixing" (as one would describe the combination of paint colors on a palette). However, if we draw down the metaphor, we can also (more literally) describe cyanotyping as a form of mark-making; this description has the advantage of retaining *some* connection to the (photographic) realm of indexing, albeit from objects that exist beyond the capacity of human vision. The cyanotype possesses indices of micro-particular objects.

This last distinction – between the visible (level) and the invisible (realm) – may prove fruitful for accounting for the dual or hybrid (or simply paradoxical) status of the cyanotype's powers and capacities. For example, it may be advantageous to think of Opera's cyanotyping as a species of *painting* when it is regarded at the level of human perception, while ratifying its status as a form of *photography* (literally, as the etymology tells, us – *light-writing*) when we explore (or merely imagine) the atomic level.

Thus, just as we may have been intrigued by – and perhaps even grown comfortable with – cyanotypes as a species of-painting, we have been confronted with the persistence of *trace impacts of light* upon a photo-sensitive emulsion – and what, after all, at its fundamental level, is a photograph but precisely that? Let us hold in mind, then, that the cyanotype should be treated – in part – as a species of photograph. It is at this junction that OOO can help us navigate into new, relatively unexplored terrain – namely, in assessing the other portion of attributes, those that are not photographic in nature. For the sake of testing a thesis, then, let us begin to regard the familiar traits of photography as still intact (within the cyanotype), and yet augmented – or complemented – by the presence of other kinds of mark-making activity (bleaching, toning, tinting, and the application of subsequent selectively masking layers of acrylic or vinyl paint). For example, in *Double Lens (yellow with lines)* (pl. 14), the foreground solid portions are paint, whereas the background gradient areas reveal the cyanotype. The paint, in effect, *obscures* the cyanotype but also *frames* it.

What we are trying to identify in the cyanotype are the "unit operations" of the ultraviolet radiation as they interact with the potassium ferrocyanide emulsion. When Opera holds the UV light above the canvas, he does not occupy a profilmic space – at least on the *human* level; standing in front of the canvas, he does not subsequently appear on the canvas (as he would in a scenario of lens-based, photo-cinematic, analog technologies). Instead, Opera paints – and here we can use the term without quotation marks, for it is a process of applying material, in this case UV radiation. How the light/potassium ferrocyanide interaction reveals itself is a matter of their *material* conjugation, and has nothing whatsoever to do with the human world "in front of" the canvas (again, as it does necessarily in the profilmic scene). To re-orient ourselves, then, we must *shift scale* and come to appreciate that the profilmic space exists, just not for our eyes. The electrons are the objects that make their impact known; it is their index that the potassium ferrocyanide registers. Likewise, the electrons projected onto the digital camera sensor make their impact known through the process of translating light signals into binary code.

When asked to describe what is happening *in* a cyanotype, given what has been said about its mechanics and organics, we may come up with this equivalency: *the image is object*. Such a description should sound familiar, as it might be said of a painting. With Opera's cyanotypes, then, we are in a very good position to speak of the "thingness" of the work, and also perhaps in an allied way, the "thisness" (or haecticity) of the image-object. I am tempted to say that the cyanotype is differently expressive from a painting, in part, because of its more apparent transformations in relation to the presence and absence of light-as-medium: thus, radiation must be spoken of in analogy with pigmentation.

If we have noted that the entire canvas (prepped with potassium ferrocyanide) is akin to a giant negative, we must stop short of a full overlap, since the cyanotype (in the species presented to us by Opera) is unique in the way a painting is unique. While, for instance, one can use a photographic negative (as an original) to make an endless series of enlargements ("prints"), one *cannot* use a cyanotype in this way. It is a negative and yet it is singular (not the basis for further copies or editions of itself). Making a copy of a cyanotype one would have to employ methods of copying a painting (e.g., photographing it! – but then this is not a painting, of course). Mutatis mutandis, there is no such thing as a copy of a cyanotype in the same way as there is no such thing as a copy of a painting; rather, we are conscribed to speak only of "reproductions" (e.g., as photographs, or as re-painted works familiar to the forger). Like the painting, the cyanotype is an image-as-object, and therefore – at the level of surface, *and* we suspect, materially – a unique, independent inhabitant of the world.

Opera's cyanotyping process can be said to *partially* participate in representational art as we know it from photography (and photo-based, lens-based cinema), while also bearing demonstrable lines of affiliation with the heritage of painting, drawing, and animation – the hand-based arts involving the application of materials to vellum, canvas, or paper. If I were to lay my hand on a gessoed canvas and use a paint brush (equipped with a dollop of paint) to trace its outline, I would not remove my hand and declare what I see to be a *photographic* image of my hand; likewise, if I put my hand on a canvas coated with potassium ferrocyanide, apply UV radiation, and remove my hand, I would not – should not – regard the light patch surrounded by darkness as the same. The cyanotype image *is* a trace (or an index) of the hand, but it is *also* a testimony.

When we couple Manovich's re-orienting remarks on the status of digital media (as a species of painting) with Bogost's metaphorism and anticorrelationism, we seem capable of identifying precisely where cyanotypes should fit in the matrix of medium types. To clarify, a pictograph (fig. 9.2):

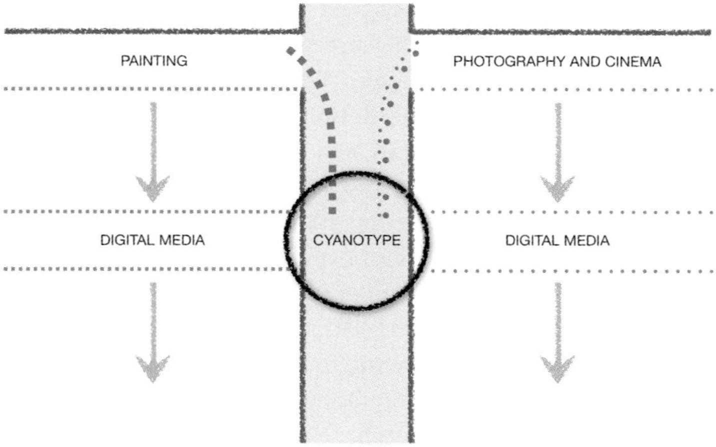


Fig. 9.2. Schematizing the cyanotype's affiliations with other media.

Notice the bottom of the pictograph where I suggest we have found – in Opera's cyanotype – what Rita Felski has termed a "messy and multidimensional entanglement" (Felski, 1995: 209). In other words, it is not that a cyanotype has been miscategorized (as photographic when it should have been a species of painting), but that – adjacent to and inclusive of certain characteristics of lens-based photographic processes – cyanotyping reveals an active blending of traits from both fields, from both ontological registers. Thus, the dashed lines (of painting and hence "testimony") and the dotted lines (of photography and thus "trace") come together in one process, or space of overlapping and interpenetrating relationships, marked out here as the encircled cyanotype. Call this a scene of promiscuous entanglements.

Instead of trying to *undo* the entanglements (as if the separation would yield some sort of special achievement – clarity, purity, etc.), I think that it is precisely the cyanotype's revelation of uncanny imbrication – of the painterly and the photographic – that offers the most fecund lessons for our contemporary (and future) thinking about digital media. Taking the cyanotype's promiscuous entanglements into consideration, digital media may have not identical but *analogical entanglements* of their own – ones not yet fully admitted, or even discerned. The cyanotype instigates, or better invites, the reevaluation of both our empirical and theoretical orientations to and definitions of digital media.

In a solo exhibition of his work in Chicago entitled *Technical Images* (after Vilém Flusser), Opera offered some remarks on a new body of cyanotypes that appears to bear out my observations.[17] Pushing us past the familiar domain of photography's representational alliances (e.g., as they are entrenched with respect to the index), I find this claim in the exhibit catalogue: "The original cyanotype is already something of an abstraction, and becomes doubly so when organized into a hybrid of painting and photography" (Opera, 2017). What I have identified as an "analogical entanglement" between photography and painting, Opera describes profitably as a "dialogue" between the forms (a trope that aligns agreeably with the dashed and dotted converging lines of the illustration above, fig. 9.2). A further resonance appears when Opera links his work – for example, *Double Slit (blue-blue)* (2017, pl. 15) – to Thomas Young's two-slit experiment (1801), which was said to "illustrate the wave/particle duality of light," one that we might adopt as yet another model, or metaphor, for thinking of the duality or simultaneity of photography and painting as they coexist or cohabitate in a given cyanotype. Not for nothing, Opera reminds us that the two-slit experiment is regularly "cited as one of the most puzzling observable phenomena ever discovered" (Opera, 2017). Perhaps we can forgive ourselves, then, if the dual status of the cyanotype remains a physicalist's conundrum and at the same time presents itself as a useful and illuminating metaphysical allegory.

As we draw down the present investigation, keeping in mind its relation to the ever-expanding universe of remarks from OOO theorists – Bogost, Bryant, Harman, and others – we can return again to digital media to ask after its (or their) "unit operations" in the wake of the cyanotype. If the unit operations of the cyanotype are bound up with UV radiation and potassium ferrocyanide, then the unit operations of digital media occur at the level of the electro-magnetic. This is where the "material life" of the digital image exists and persists; think, for example, of the digital file as it lives on one's computer. Digital data does exist as mass, so what is the *weight* of digital data? (Cass, 2007: np). Is a hard drive heavier when it is loaded with data than when it is empty? To ask such questions (even aside from precise mathematical answers) draws us back to the nature of the medium itself – media as such. The questions, moreover, point to the particular – *particle* – nature of such objects; Bogost's notion of "unit operations," then, seems to offer a useful picture of what we (might) mean when making reference to the (independent) "lives" of objects at any level, on any plane of existence (though, in this context, we are prepared to see it as a flat ontology). After Manovich, with OOO postulations in hand, and taking into account the cyanotype's promiscuous entanglements, we can assess – and perhaps confirm – the ways in which digital media (as painting) shares material life with the photocentric (as photography, as cinema).

How is this a discovery? And if it is, what is its import? First, with Paulsen's objections and corrections in mind, I still think Manovich's thesis stands; it may be usefully augmented by Paulsen's critique, but I don't think it is defeated. Indeed, in these proceedings, I have not tried to unseat it, but rather, for its apparent strength, aimed to deploy it as an ally for articulating how we ought to regard the cyanotype *in relation to* digital media and photography and painting. Indeed, isn't the cyanotype a canny figure of "mixed media" of the ultimate sort? Secondly, through a study of John Opera's specific practice of cyanotyping – and what his works of art, in turn, reveal – I am suggesting that digital media should earn some affiliation with the material life OOO takes seriously as composed of objects.

The descriptions above about the "living," "re-animating" powers of the cyanotype are so affecting, in part, because we can perceive them. But we must know that this same process happens (though most often imperceptibly) all the time to paintings...and digital media...and photographs...and celluloid cinema at a comparatively less perceptible degree. The latter modes or media are, of course, decaying and transforming, their colors fading, their embodied life degenerating and re-arranging in innumerable ways. This is to say that though we cannot always perceive these changes – bear witness to them – they persistently occur. And that evolutionary convulsion of matter is part of the shared life of objects beyond our embodied perception, yet not beyond our cognitive comprehension. We believe in things all the time – scientifically proven things, and to be sure, many things that are not at all scientifically vetted – that we cannot see with the unaided eye. The microscope and telescope expand our realms of reference, and reassure us in certain faiths, but we seldom take the next step to fathom the *objecthood* of material life on its own terms, beyond instruments and instrumental reason. The cyanotype may be a salient specimen for which that postulate feels at once intuitive and evident.

## Notes

I am happily indebted to Geoff Bender, Rasmus Rahbek Simonsen, and anonymous referees, for their crucial editorial input and support during composition and production. As with early publications devoted to his work, I remain grateful to John Opera for his expertise, his generosity in sharing it, and at each step of revision, his candor.

1 The 21st-century development of object-oriented ontology (OOO) may find a (partial) origin story in the final months of the twentieth century when Graham Harman, on September 11, 1999, used the syntagma "Object-Oriented Philosophy" for the title of a talk he gave at Brunel University (Uxbridge, England). Harman tells us that he met Bruno Latour for the first time the day before the lecture. See Harman (2010: 93). As Harman says in his Introduction to Levi R. Bryant's *Onto-Cartography: An Ontology of Machines and Media* (2014), Bryant coined the phrase "object-oriented ontology" in 2009.

2 For more on photography and painting, see Cavell (1971/1979: 23–25) and LaRocca, ed. (2020: 43–7, 63–5, 68–70, 237–9).

3 See Freeman (2017: 64), which includes an analysis of Peter Gordon's *Adorno and Existence* (2016). See also J. M. Bernstein (2001: 245, 287).

4 While the conversation of "new materialism(s)" is close in mind throughout this chapter – given its relation to, reliance on, and development of OOO theories – details of its special pertinence must remain at the level of implication and allusion to allow for a more pronounced engagement with Bogost. See for example Bennett (2010a; 2010b), Dolphijn and van der Tuin (2012), Hickey-Moody and Tara Page (2016), and Kelley and Rubenstein (2017).

5 See also more recent editions and collections, such as Atkins (1985) and Ankele and Ankele (2014).

6 For related investigations, see LaRocca (2003; 2011; 2014; 2017a; 2017b).

7 See Bryant (2011), especially chapter 6.

8 See also Jäger (2005).

9 Related research on this distinction is expertly expressed by Kaja Silverman (2015), and, not incidentally, cyanotypes are of principal interest to her. For Silverman's notes on cyanotypes, see especially chapter 6.

10 John Opera, *Unfixed: The Fugitive Image* (Cleveland: Transformer Station, 2016).

11 The structure of the question, including its spirit, is certainly influenced by my awareness of Dirk Eitzen's "When Is a Documentary?: Documentary as a Mode of Reception" (1995).

12 See also Michael Fried (2007).

13 See Bryant (2008; 2011; 2014); Gratton (2014); and Harman (2002; 2005; 2010; 2011).

14 See also LaRocca (2017a).

15 For more on the "crisis of the index," see LaRocca (2021).

16 In other versions of Manovich's essay, "digital media" appears in place of "computer media," therefore suggesting their native overlaps and shared attributes. Contrast, for example, the version in *The Digital Dialectic: New Essays on New Media*, ed. Peter Lunenfield (Cambridge: MIT Press, 1999), which is retitled "Digital Cinema and the History of a Moving Image," in

*Film Theory and Criticism*, 7th edition, ed. Leo Braudy and Marshall Cohen (New York: Oxford University Press, 2009): 794–96. See also LaRocca (2017a, 34).

17 John Opera, *Technical Images* (Chicago: Document Gallery, 2017), http://documentspace.com/exhibitions/john-opera (accessed June 3, 2020).

## Bibliography

Theodor W. Adorno, *Negative Dialectics*, trans. E. B. Ashton (Continuum: New York, 1973).

Daniel Ankele and Denise Ankele, eds., *Anna Atkins: Cyanotypes, The First Woman Photographer* (Ankele Publishing, 2014).

Hannah Arendt, *On Revolution* (New York: Penguin, 1963).

Anna Atkins, *Victorian Photograms* (New York: Aperture, 1985).

Jane Bennett, *Vibrant Matter: A Political Ecology of Things* (Durham: Duke University Press, 2010a).

Jane Bennett, "The Vitalist Stopover on the Way to a New Materialism," in *New Materialisms: Ontology, Agency, and Politics*, eds. Diana Coole and Samantha Frost (Durham: Duke University Press, 2010b): 47–69.

J. M. Bernstein, *Adorno: Disenchantment and Ethics* (Cambridge: Cambridge University Press, 2001).

Ian Bogost, *Alien Phenomenology, Or, What It's Like to Be a Thing* (Minneapolis: University of Minnesota Press, 2012).

Ian Bogost, "Your Phone Wasn't Built for the Apocalypse," *The Atlantic*, September 11, 2020, https://www.theatlantic.com/technology/archive/2020/09/camera-phone-wildfire-sky/616279/ (accessed December 9, 2020).

Levi R. Bryant, *Difference and Givenness: Deleuze's Transcendental Empiricism and the Ontology of Immanence* (Evanston: Northwestern University Press, 2008).

Levi R. Bryant, *The Democracy of Objects* (Ann Harbor: Open Humanities Press, 2011).

Levi R. Bryant, *Onto-Cartography: An Ontology of Machines and Media* (Edinburgh: Edinburgh University Press, 2014).

Raymond Bulman, *Not a Photo*, The Hole (New York City, 2015). http://theholenyc.com/2015/10/29/not-a-photo (accessed June 3, 2020).

Stephen Cass, "How Much Does the Internet Weigh?" *Discover*, May 29, 2007, http://discover-magazine.com (accessed June 3, 2020).

Stanley Cavell, "Photograph and Screen," *The World Viewed: Reflections on the Ontology of Film* (Cambridge: Harvard University Press, 1971/1979).

Stanley Cavell, "What Photography Calls Thinking: Theoretical Considerations on the Power of the Photographic Basis of Cinema," in *The Philosophy of Documentary Film: Image, Sound, Fiction, Truth*, ed. David LaRocca (Lanham: Lexington Books of Rowman & Littlefield, 2017)

Gregory Currie, "Documentary Traces: Film and the Content of Photographs," in *The Philosophy of Documentary Film: Image, Sound, Fiction, Truth*, ed. David LaRocca (Lanham: Lexington Books of Rowman & Littlefield, 2017).

Rick Dolphijn and Iris van der Tuin, eds., *New Materialism: Interviews and Cartographies* (Ann Arbor: Open Humanities Press, 2012).

Dirk Eitzen's "When Is a Documentary?: Documentary as a Mode of Reception," *Cinema Journal*, 35, 1 (Autumn 1995): 81–102.

Rita Felski, *The Gender of Modernity* (Cambridge: Harvard University Press, 1995).

Vilém Flusser, *Into the Universe of Technical Images*, trans. Nancy Ann Roth (Minneapolis: University of Minnesota Press, 2011).

Samuel Freeman, "The Headquarters of Neo-Marxism," *The New York Review of Books*, March 23, 2017, https://www.nybooks.com/articles/2017/03/23/frankfurt-school-headquarters-neo-marxism (accessed December 9, 2020).

Michael Fried, "Art and Objecthood" (1967), *Art and Objecthood: Essays and Reviews* (Chicago: The University of Chicago Press, 1998): 148–72.

Michael Fried, "Jeff Wall, Wittgenstein, and the Everyday," *Critical Inquiry*, 33, 3 (Spring 2007): 495–526.

Michael Fried, *Why Photography Matters as Art as Never Before* (New Haven: Yale University Press, 2008).

Peter Gratton, *Speculative Realism: Problems and Prospects* (New York: Bloomsbury, 2014).

Graham Harman, *Tool-Being: Heidegger and the Metaphysics of Objects* (Chicago: Open Court, 2002).

Graham Harman, *Guerrilla Metaphysics: Phenomenology and the Carpentry of Things* (Chicago: Open Court, 2005).

Graham Harman, *Towards Speculative Realism: Essays and Lectures* (Winchester, UK: Zero Books, 2010).

Graham Harman, *The Quadruple Object* (Alresford, UK: Zero Books, 2011).

Graham Harman, *Art and Objects* (Cambridge, UK: Polity, 2020).

Anna Hickey-Moody and Tara Page, eds., *Arts, Pedagogy, and Cultural Resistance: New Materialisms* (Lanham, MD: Rowman & Littlefield, 2016).

Gottfried Jäger, "Generative Photography: A Systematic, Constructive Approach," *Leonardo*, 19, 1 (1986): 19–25.

Gottfried Jäger, Rolf H. Krauss, Beate Reese, *Concrete Photography / Konkrete Fotografie* (Bielefeld: Kerber Verlag, 2005).

Christopher James, *The Book of Alternative Photographic Processes* (Albany: Delmar, 2002).

Catherine Keller and Mary-Jane Rubenstein, eds., *Entangled Worlds: Religion, Science, and New Materialisms* (New York: Fordham University Press, 2017).

David LaRocca, "The Grammar of Origin," in *John Opera: SOUP*, exh. cat. (Buffalo: Burchfield Penney Art Center, 2003): 2–4.

David LaRocca, "The False Pretender: Deleuze, Sherman, and the Status of Simulacra," *The Journal of Aesthetics and Art Criticism*, 69, 3 (Summer 2011): 321–29.

David LaRocca, "War Films and the Ineffability of War," in *The Philosophy of War Films*, ed. David LaRocca (Lexington: University Press of Kentucky, 2014): 1–77.

David LaRocca, "Equivalent Simulation: An Interview with John Opera," *Afterimage: The Journal of Media Arts and Cultural Criticism*, 42, 6 (May/June 2015): 16–21.

David LaRocca, "Representative Qualities and Questions of Documentary Film" in *The Philosophy of Documentary Film: Image, Sound, Fiction, Truth*, ed. David LaRocca (Lanham: Lexington Books of Rowman & Littlefield, 2017a): 1–54.

David LaRocca, "Shooting for the Truth: Amateur Documentary Filmmaking, Affective Optics, and the Ethical Impulse," *Post Script: Essays in Film and the Humanities*, 36, 2 & 3 (2017b): 33–37.

David LaRocca, ed., *The Thought of Stanley Cavell and Cinema: Turning Anew to the Ontology of Film a Half-Century after* The World Viewed (New York: Bloomsbury, 2020).

David LaRocca, "Memory Translation: Rithy Panh's Provocations to the Primacy and Virtues of the Documentary Sound/Image Index," in *Everything Has a Soul: The Cinema of Rithy Panh*, eds. Leslie Barnes and Joseph Mai (New Brunswick: Rutgers University Press, 2021): 188-201.

François Laruelle, *The Concept of Non-Photography*, trans. Robin Mackay (Cambridge: MIT Press, 2011).

Lev Manovich, "What is Digital Cinema?" (1995) in *Critical Visions in Film Theory*, eds. Timothy Corrigan, Patricia White, and Meta Mazaj (New York: Bedford/St. Martin's, 2011): 1058–70. See also versions in *The Digital Dialectic: New Essays on New Media*, ed. Peter Lunenfield (Cambridge: MIT Press, 1999) and (appearing as) "Digital Cinema and the History of a Moving Image," in *Film Theory and Criticism*, 7th edition, eds. Leo Braudy and Marshall Cohen (New York: Oxford University Press, 2009): 794–96.

Beaumont Newhall, *Latent Image: The Discovery of Photography* (Garden City, NY: Anchor Books, 1967).

John Opera, *Technical Images* (Chicago: Document Gallery, 2017), http://documentspace.com/exhibitions/john-opera (accessed June 3, 2020).

Kris Paulsen, "The Index and the Interface," *Representations*, 122, 1 (Spring 2013): 83–109.

Kaja Silverman, *The Miracle of Analogy: Or, The History of Photography, Part 1* (Stanford: Stanford University Press, 2015).

Jeff Wall, "Photography and Liquid Intelligence" (1989) in *Selected Essays and Interviews* (New York: The Museum of Modern Art, 2007): 109–110.

# Afterword

Rasmus R. Simonsen and Geoff Bender

Early in *Within a Budding Grove*, the second volume of *In Search of Lost Time*, Marcel Proust pronounces that "it is essential that the artist..., if he wishes his work to be free to follow its own course, shall launch it, wherever he may find sufficient depth, confidently outward bound towards the future" (Proust, 2006: 492). In a way, the entirety of Proust's *oeuvre* is about the aesthetics of distance measured by time. In his comparative piece on Proust and Valéry, Theodor Adorno refers to "the nimbus of distance" to explain the former's preference for things, not as they appear in the present, but rather in the fading bloom of their posterity. Although Proust was invested in photography primarily for its metaphorical value,[1] his attunement to what Adorno calls "the physiognomy of decomposing things" (1967: 182) nevertheless offers an occasion to address the material plurality of photography in these the closing pages of the present collection.

Proust's entire aesthetics of distance is based on the separation of sign and referent. But, as our collection has demonstrated, we should be wary of pronouncements that seek to cleave an image from the reality it depicts. Even if we must quarrel with Proust on this point – and Adorno, indeed, takes the author to task for his "unfettered subjectivism" (1967: 183), which "looks to art for the ideal, the salvation of the living" (1967: 183) – his notion of posterity is useful as a critical aesthetic category, since works of art can only be "free" "when they have been uprooted from their native soil and have set out along the path to their own destruction" (1967: 185). However, even when something dies or disappears into art, the concept of multiple materialities might still embrace its presence: a thing remembered is still a thing in itself, at least according to the posthuman conception of objectivity that has appeared, at various points, throughout this collection. For instance, in his careful consideration of the ontology of cyanotypes, David LaRocca suggests that we use this contact-print medium to challenge "[o]ur habitual confidence in seeing 'through' an image to its referent," since, as a kind of "death mask," each cyanotype is "an object of its own kind, where the recording medium and the after-effects of the referent have joined in a curious cohabitation." LaRocca's meditation on the power of the cyanotype's presence leads us to the crucial conclusion that a photograph, in the posthuman world we occupy, can no longer be seen as merely representing the thing itself, but instead assumes a material life of its own, becoming a thing *in itself*, both within and across time. In this way, a single photograph could be said to have many lives.

In this collection, we have been stressing the plurality of a photograph's materialities not just to elaborate its own embodiment, but also to reflect the many different approaches and contexts our contributors have enlisted in exploring the creation, practice, and enduring significance of photography. Common to all the material explorations found in the preceding pages is that photography is not about preserving the real in an imagistic frame to be hung in a museum. Instead, photographs, as visual works, confront us inherently as "something objective, something which makes demands in terms of its own inner structure and its own logic" (Adorno, 1967: 184).[2] Of course, as several authors in our volume have argued, the logic of photographs most strongly appears in connection with other media – when we locate them in intermedial conversation with objects beyond their own inner structure. This is how photographs are preserved: not as objects to be reified, but as intermediaries that push the viewer's capacity to understand the social, aesthetic, historical, and technological complications that prevent us from seeing photography as a self-contained medium.

We would like to end by returning to the concept of "cohabitation" that LaRocca introduces in his contribution. Reaching beyond the critical conversations collected in our volume, the risographic collages of Danish photographer and multimedia artist Stine Behrendtzen offer us an opportunity to reflect on how photography can cohabitate with other media to further investigate the borders between different temporalities and ontologies (pl. 16). In her current series of works, Behrendtzen uses a risograph copying machine to produce layered, cut-up images that seek to disrupt the distance between different timeframes and locations. A risograph prints in layers, utilizing a process similar to, but more efficient than, screen printing. "Risograph" is both the name given to the machine and to the kind of print it produces; like q-tip or xerox, it is an eponym. As with screen prints, the layers of a risograph can shift slightly, so that they overlap at the edge. The printing process itself, thus, might produce small "errors," or irregularities, but the coincidental nature of risographs are part of their appeal; no two prints are ever quite alike.

To create the image pictured in this collection (pl. 16), Behrendtzen cut up by hand a number of her own photos, which were then turned into a collage. The collage was then photographed and processed digitally. Afterwards, the digitally rendered collage was remediated as a risograph to materially emphasize and reinforce the layers and offsets of the collage itself. Finally, to enhance the visual bricolage, Behrendtzen cut up all five risographs in the series, creating a new surface of displaced visual objects. Some of the works in the series contain fragments of the other four "original" risographs, and, in this way, the boundaries between them are tenuous at best. Each time a layer is processed anew, it decomposes more, and Behrendtzen can thus be seen to complicate Proust's aesthetics of distance by a vertiginous measure. In this image, the viewer is unable to get a firm handle on the representational value of the composition (it is unclear, for instance, if the door that frames the right side of the image opens to anywhere). Resisting coherent framing, the viewer's eye flits from what appears to be a washed-out mountain range through what could be a shelving unit containing various electronic equipment to a cloaked, disembodied figure in the foreground that recalls the menacing cover art of 1980s punk bands.

Although much more fragmentary and playful in scope, Behrendtzen's risographic practice shares some affinity with Hippolyte Fizeau's experimental combination of daguerreotyping with electrotyping, where he would, as Jacob Lewis outlines in his contribution to our collection, submerge an exposed plate into a galvanic bath (see pl. 5). The deposited metallic layer that resulted from this process made the image look like an engraving plate. By thus fusing innovation with an older aesthetic, Fizeau succeeded in creating an ornamental object as well as a new, precise printing matrix. Aesthetics and innovation are constant companions in the history of photography. As it never quite captures the "real," photography lends itself to experimentation and the layering of different techniques; this is perhaps also why, as we've noted in our introduction, Raphaël Pirenne and Alexander Streitberger have called photography "the very heart of intermediality" (2013: xvii). In this way, the destruction of the original photos in Behrendtzen's series of collages is the beginning of a new productive process, which develops from the almost chaotic exchanges between several media and technologies to completely lay waste to Barthes's "*ça-a-été*" [that-has-been] (1980: 176).[3] Her practice builds on how Thomas P. Brockelman conceives of collage in *The Frame and the Mirror: On Collage and the Postmodern*, where he writes that, as an art form, "Collage intends to represent the intersection of multiple discourses" (2001: 2). Therefore, even if collages are generally non-referential, in that their effect relies on the juxtaposition and contiguity of different visual objects and forms, like many visual objects they may still point to and participate in cultural, political, and aesthetic conversations external to their own composition.

In a sense, our entire collection functions as a collage, a heterogenous image that attempts to capture and bring into cohabitation layers of materiality, expressed conceptually and also in practice. Like our analytical work, Behrendtzen's photograph has a long history of materially layered antecedents, some of which have been engaged in this collection. If the photographs in the preceding pages represent a "physiognomy of decomposing things," then, it is physiognomy that has been reconstituted, again and again, from lost time to the present moment, renewed in ever-proliferating networks that have taught Behrendtzen her craft and us our analytical vocations. And if the act of reading is the act of engaging in such networks, then it follows that *you*, too, have contributed to the new life of the photographic objects that have concerned us here, ensuring their vitality for at least a little while to come.

## Notes

1 At the time of its original publication in 1919, Proust's volume entered a world of mechanical reproduction, and it is not surprising that he should use photography as a trope to make sense of the relationship between the material world and subjective pleasure. In his private life, photographs mattered to him, and when he was writing the *Search*, he would keep his collection of portraits (including one of his beloved mother) close by, so that he could study the people he was "translating" into fictional composites on the pages of his great novel (White, 1999/2009: 90).

2 As LaRocca points out in his chapter, to the extent that he prioritizes the object, we are right to regard Adorno as the "spiritual and intellectual godfather" of object-oriented ontology.

3 See Zhang (2012: 107).

## Bibliography

Theodor Adorno, "Valéry Proust Museum," in *Prisms*, trans. Samuel and Shierry Weber (London: Neville Spearman, 1967): 173–185.

Roland Barthes, *La Chambre Claire: Note sur la Photographie* (Paris: Gallimard, 1980).

Thomas P. Brockelman, *The Frame and the Mirror: On Collage and the Postmodern* (Evanston: Northwestern University Press, 2001).

Raphaël Pirenne and Alexander Streitberger, eds., *Heterogeneous Objects: Intermedia and Photography after Modernism* (Leuven: Leuven University Press, 2013).

Marcel Proust, *Remembrance of Things Past, Vol. 1 (Swann's Way, Within a Budding Grove,* and *The Guermantes Way*), trans. C. K. Scott Moncrieff (London: Wordsworth Editions, 2006).

Edmund White, *Marcel Proust: A Life* (New York: Penguin, 1999/2009).

Dora Zhang, "A Lens for an Eye: Proust and Photography," *Representations* 118, 1 (Spring 2012): 103–125.

# Gallery with Color Plates

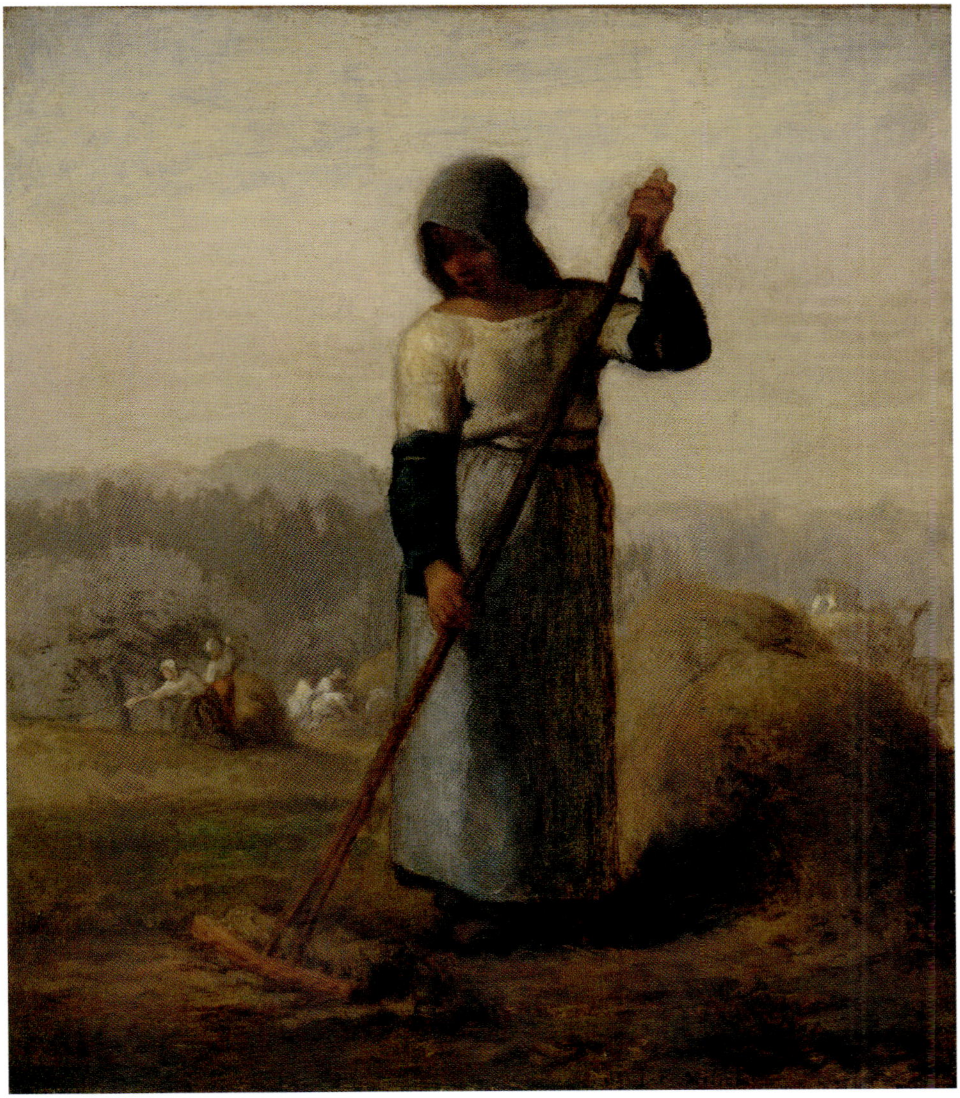

Pl. 1. Jean-François Millet, *Woman with a Rake*, 1856–57. Oil on canvas, 39.7 x 34.3 cm (15.6 x 13.5 in). Metropolitan Museum, New York. Public Domain. https://www.metmuseum.org/art/collection/search/437099.

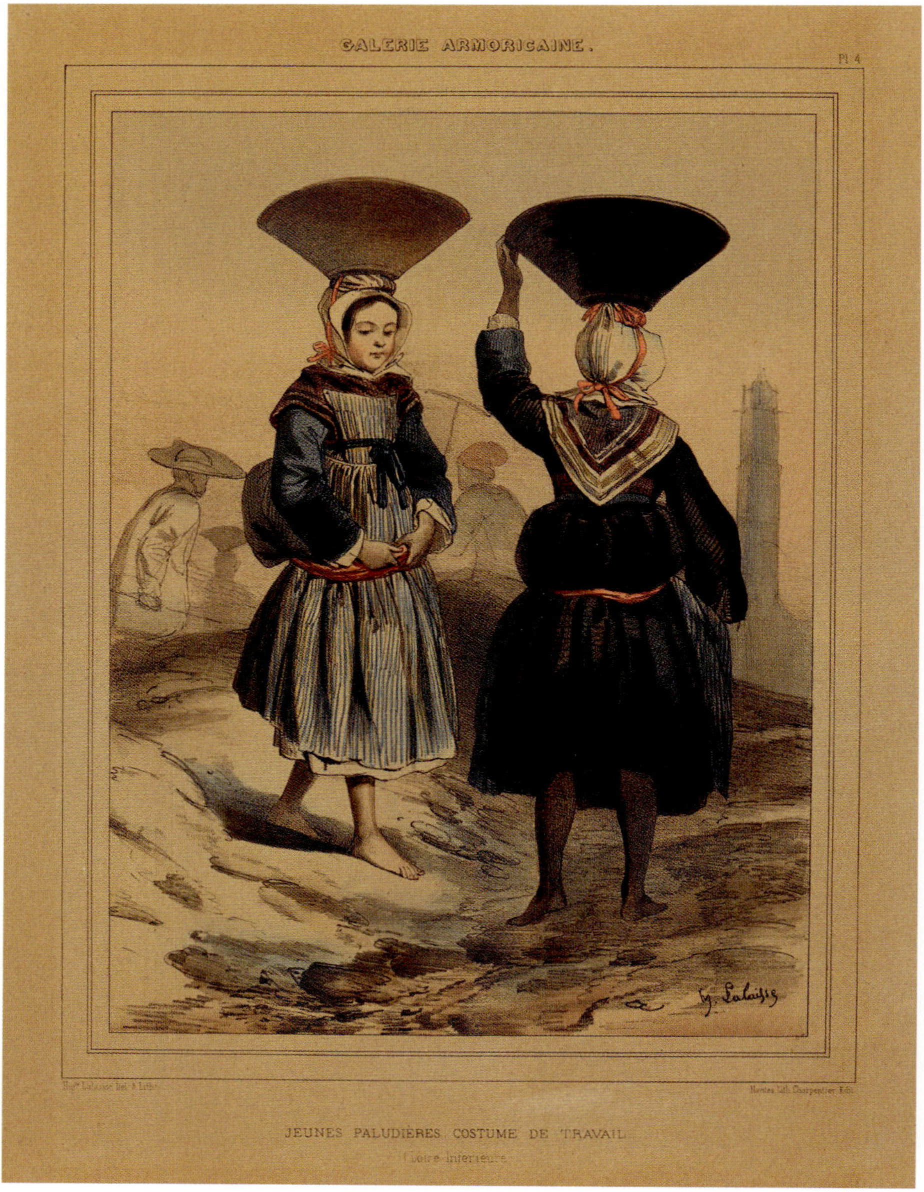


Pl. 2. Hippolyte Lalaisse, *Young Paludieres in Work Costumes,* 1844–1846. Chromolithograph, 38x 20 cm (15 x 7.9 in). Published by Editions Charpentier, Nantes. Musée de Bretagne, Rennes. Public Domain. http://www.collections.musee-bretagne.fr/ark:/83011/FLMjo115380.

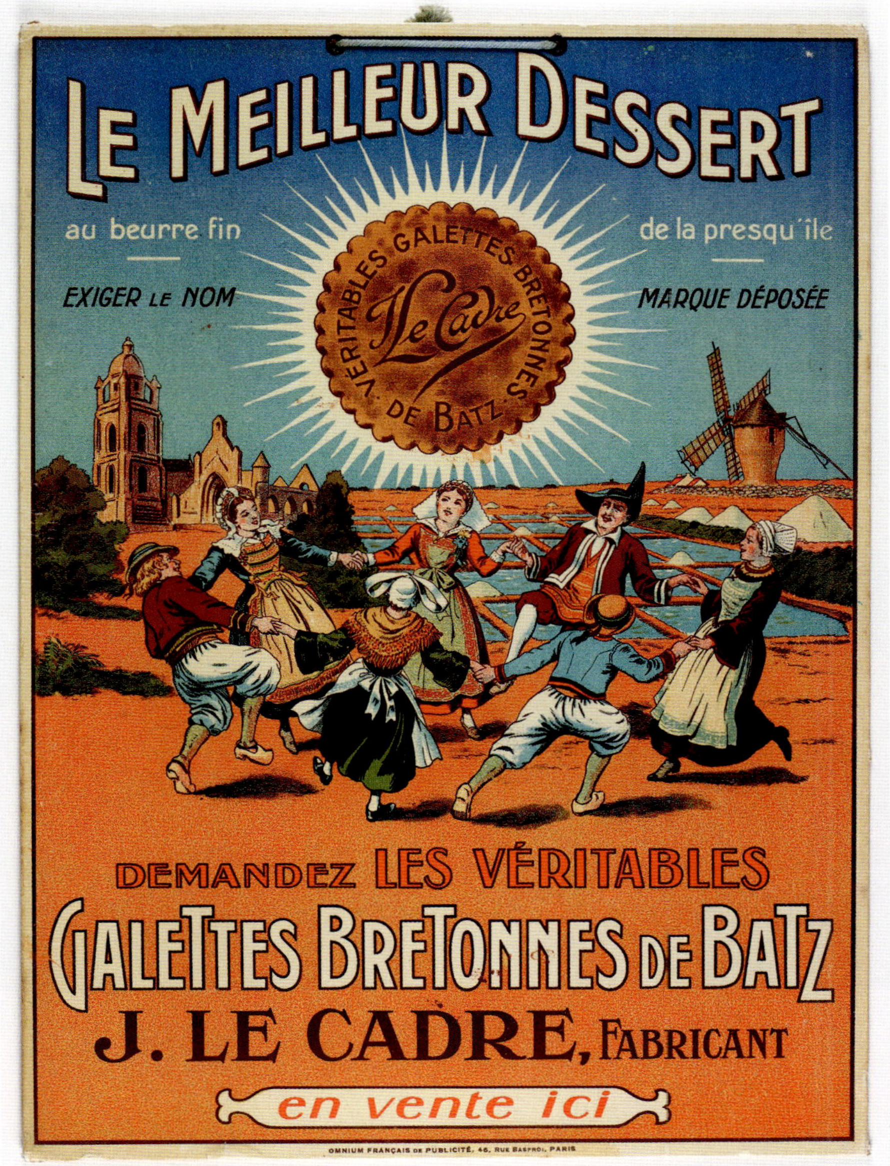


Pl. 3. Advertisement for Batz Biscuits, depicting dancing paludiers, early 20th century. Chromolithograph, 38 x 27.5 cm (15 x 10.8 in). Public Domain. http://www.collections.musee-bretagne.fr/ark:/83011/FLMjo226522.

Pl. 4. Joseph Nicéphore Niépce, *Point de vue du Gras*, c. 1826. Heliograph. Harry Ransom Center, University of Texas at Austin. Public Domain.

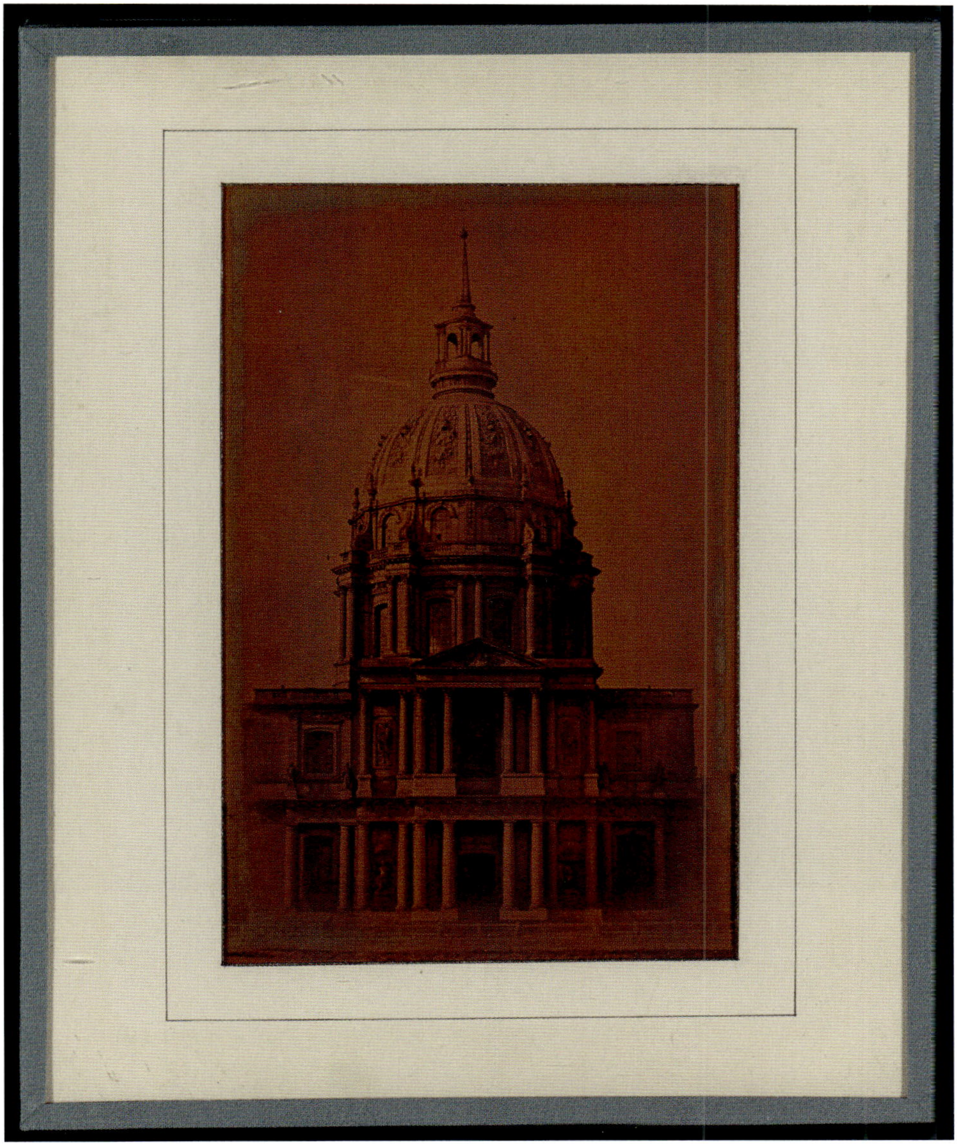

Pl. 5. Hippolyte Fizeau, *[Dôme des Invalides]*, c. 1840–43. Photogalvanic copper. The J. Paul Getty Museum, Los Angeles. 84.XT.265.5. Public Domain.

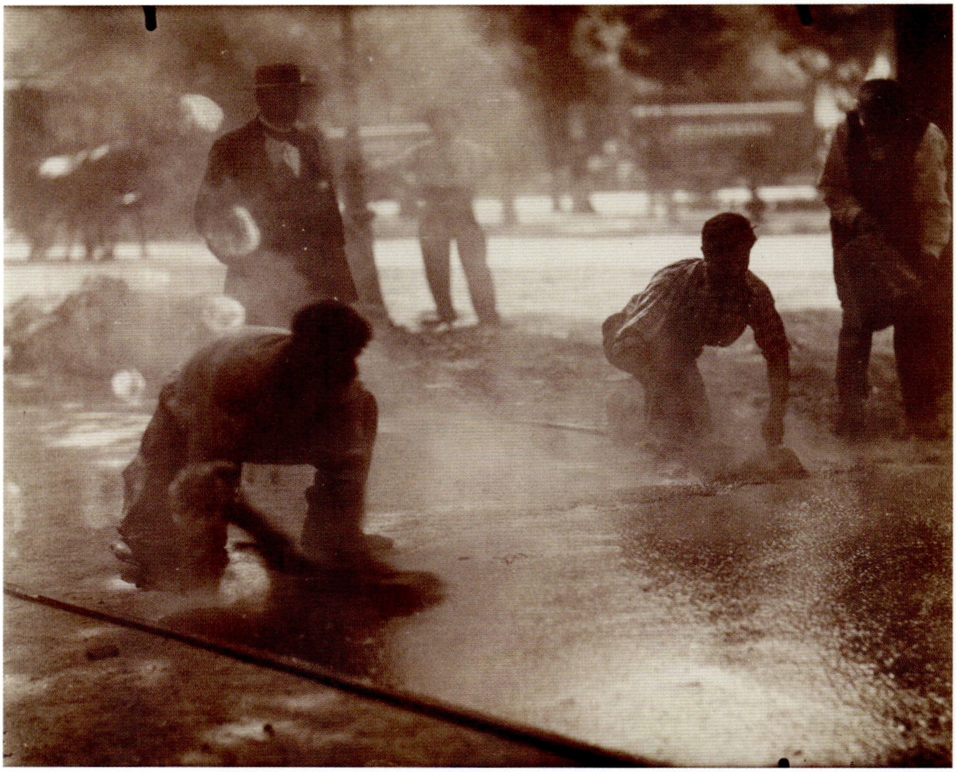

Pl. 6. Eugène Atget, *Asphalters*, c. 1899–1900. Gelatin silver printing-out-paper print, 17.5 x 21 cm (6.9 x 8.3 in). Museum of Modern Art, 140.150. Source: Scala Archives.

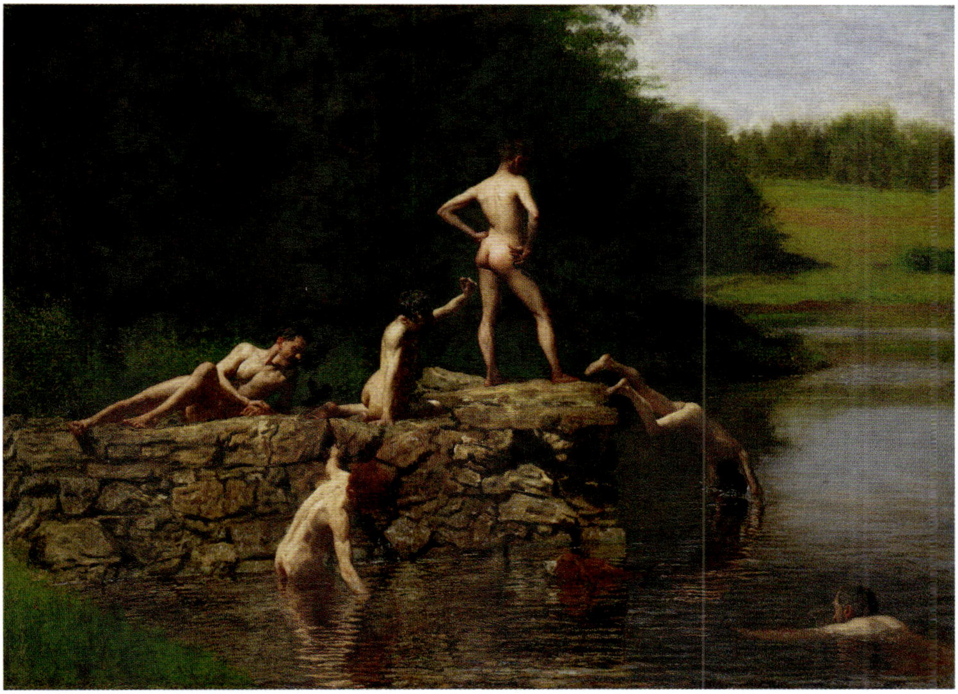

Pl. 7. Thomas Eakins, *Swimming*, 1885. Oil on canvas, 69.6 x 92.5 cm (27 3/8 x 36 3/8 in). Amon Carter Museum of American Art, Fort Worth, Texas: Purchased by the Friends of Art, Fort Worth Art Association, 1925; acquired by the Amon Carter Museum of American Art, 1990, from the Modern Art Museum of Fort Worth through grants and donations from the Amon G. Carter Foundation, the Sid W. Richardson Foundation, the Anne Burnett and Charles Tandy Foundation, Capital Cities/ABC Foundation, Fort Worth Star-Telegram, The R. D. and Joan Dale Hubbard Foundation and the people of Fort Worth. 1990.19.1.

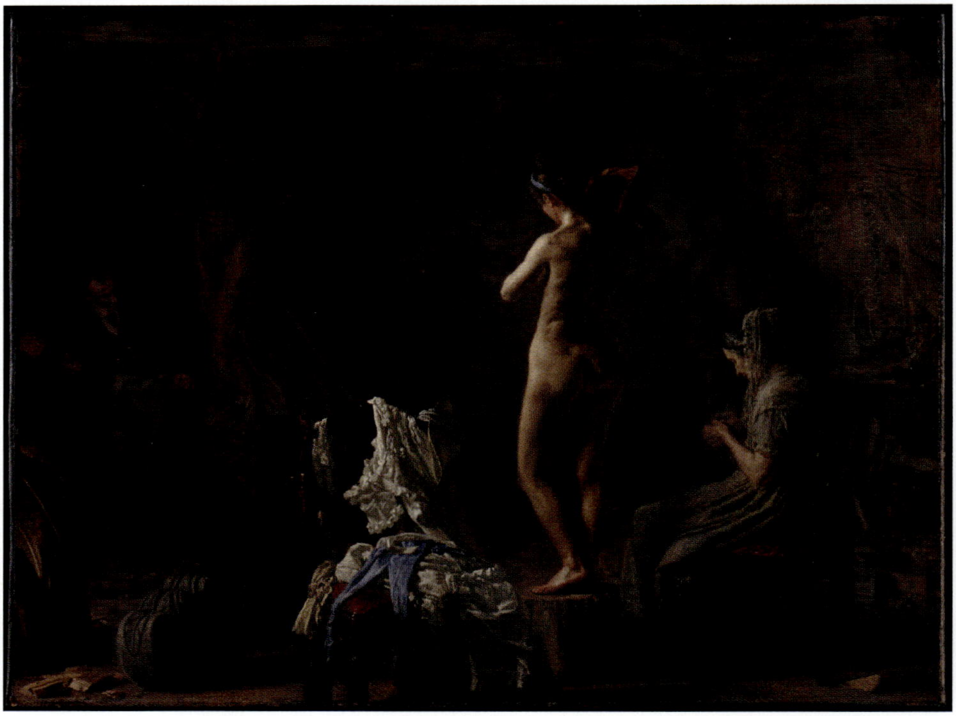

Pl. 8. Thomas Eakins, *William Rush Carving His Allegorical Figure of the Schuylkill River*, 1876–1877. Oil on canvas, 51.1 x 66.4 cm (20 1/8 × 26 1/8 in). Philadelphia Museum of Art: Gift of Mrs. Thomas Eakins and Miss Mary Adeline Williams, 1929. 1929-184-27. Public Domain.

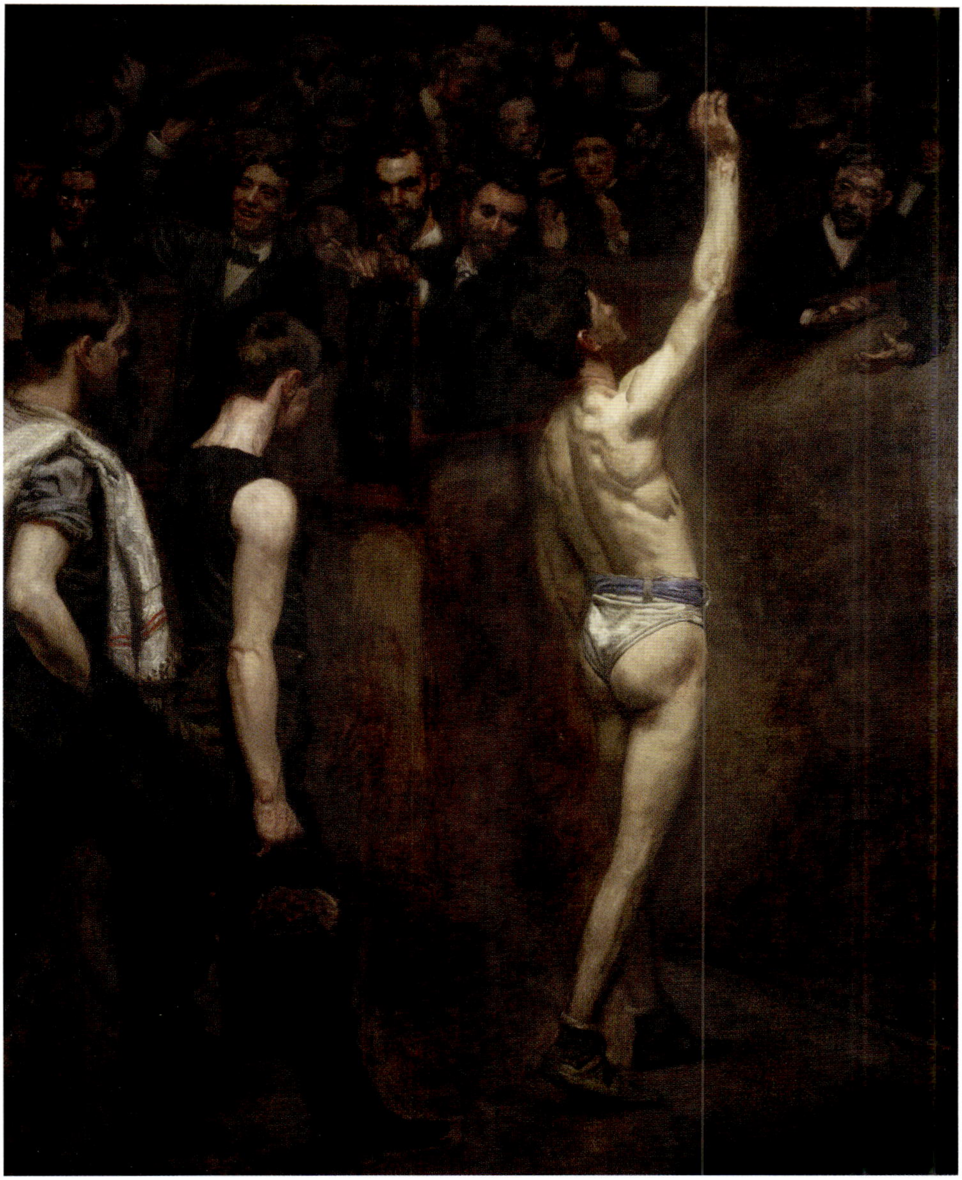

Pl. 9. Thomas Eakins, *Salutat*, 1898. Oil on canvas, 127 cm x 101.6 cm (50 in. x 40 in). Addison Gallery of American Art, Phillips Academy, Andover, MA: Gift of anonymous donor, 1930.18. Public Domain.

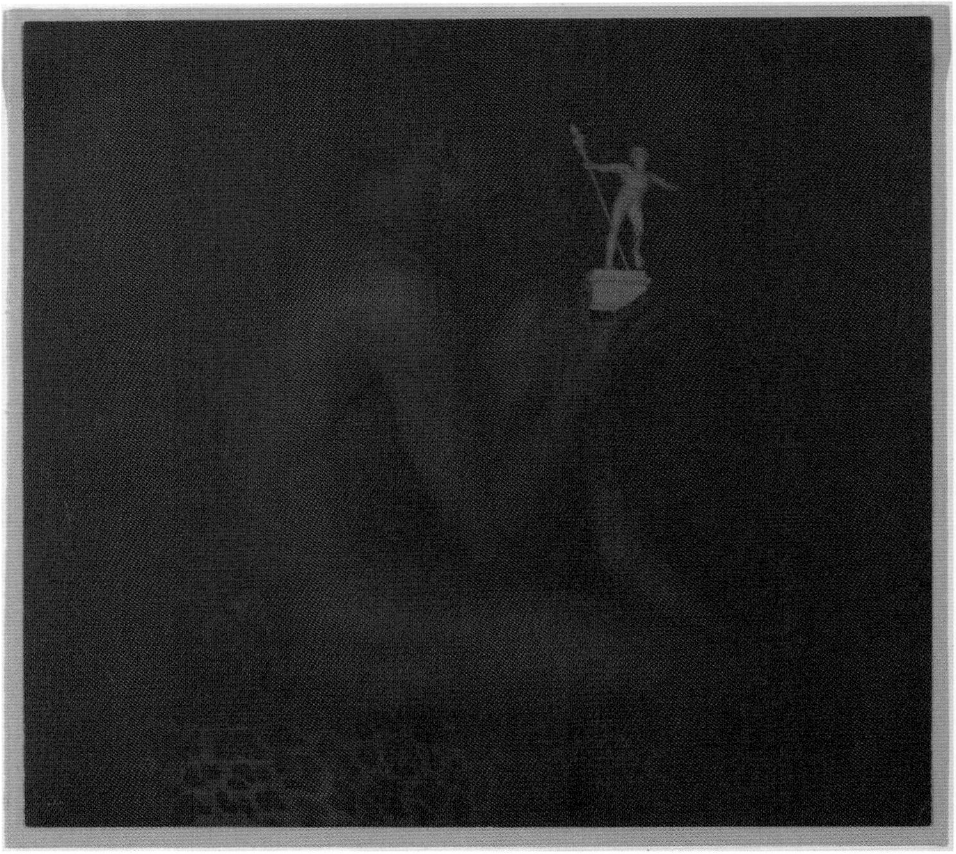

Pl. 10. F. Holland Day, *Ebony & Ivory*, 1897. Alfred Stieglitz Collection, The Metropolitan Museum of Art, New York. Source: Art Resource, NY.

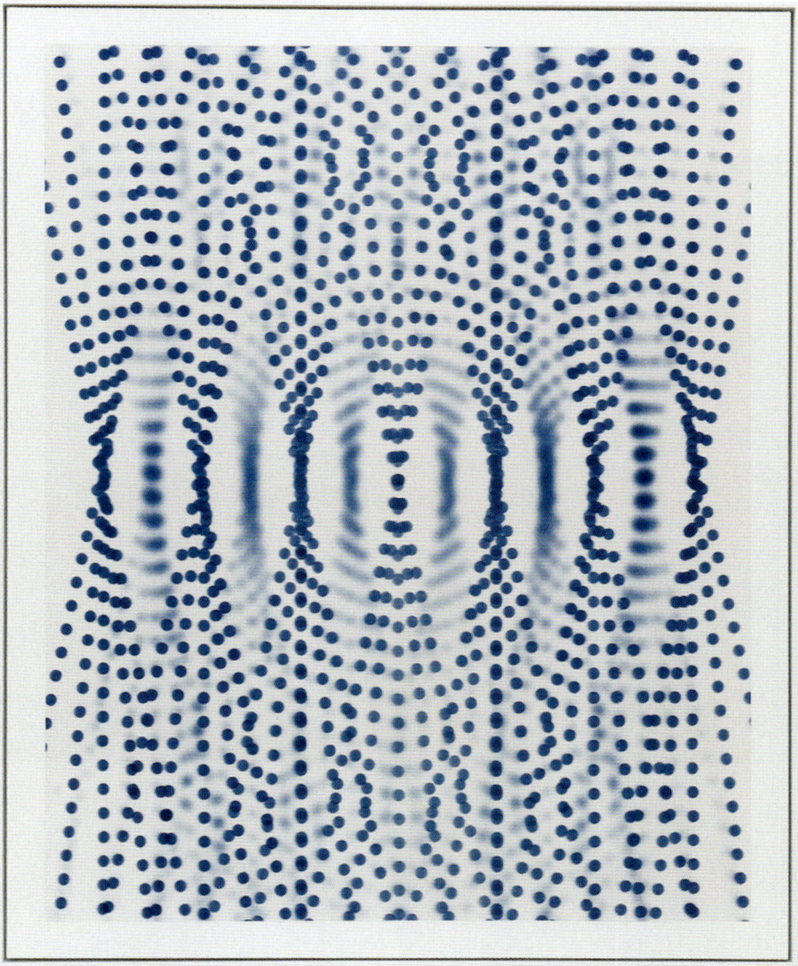

Pl. 11. John Opera, *Radial #8*, 2018. Cyanotype, acrylic and vinyl paint on canvas in artist's frame, 154.9h x 124.5w x 5d cm (61h x 49w x 2d in).

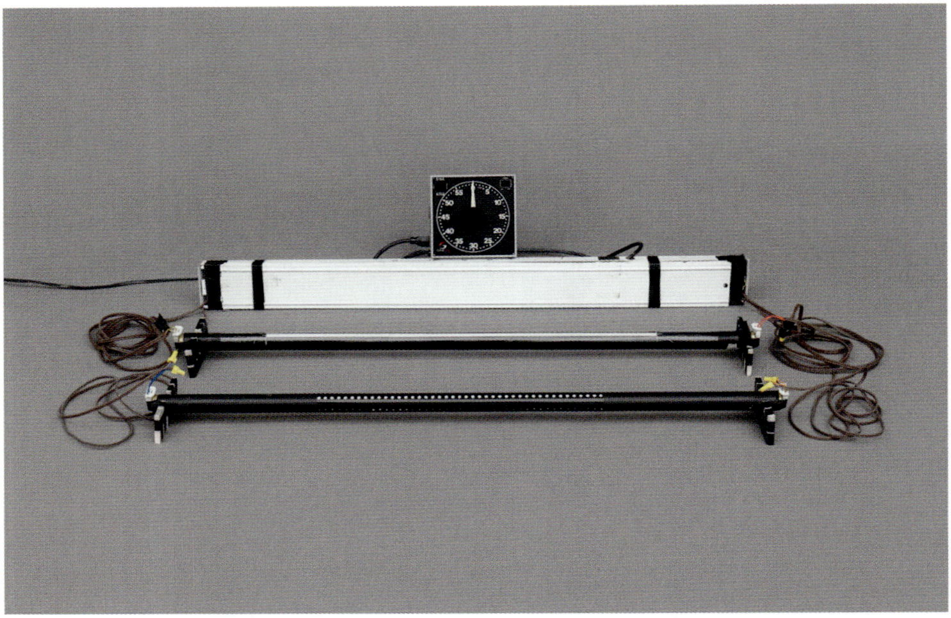

Pl. 12. Photographic Exposure Tool. Metal fluorescent fixture, custom manufactured actinic lightbulbs, custom ballast, electrical wiring, and GraLab darkroom timer, dimensions variable. Photo: John Opera, 2017.

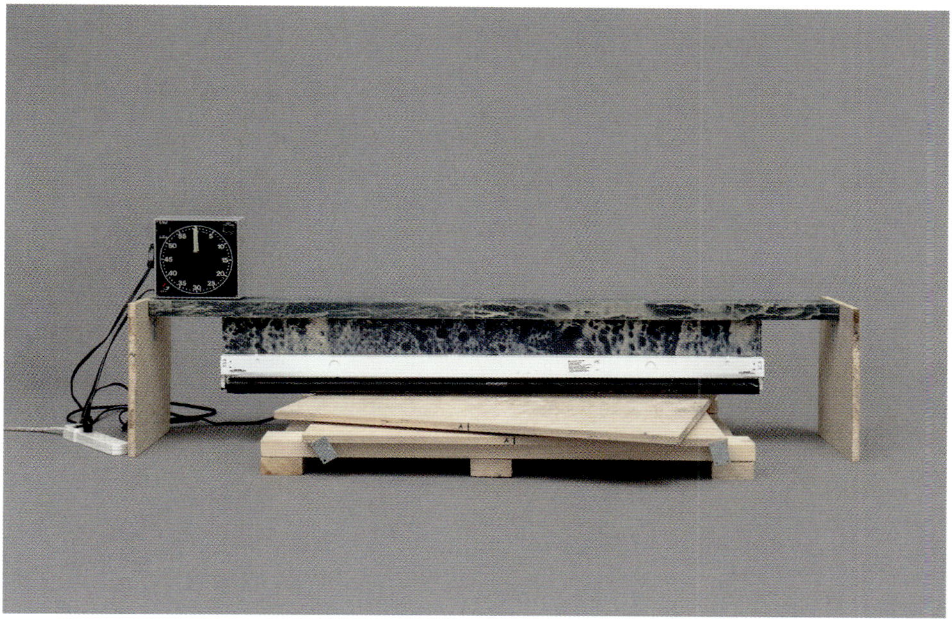

Pl. 13. Fixed-Position Photographic Exposure Tool with Turntable. Wood, turntable mechanism, metal fluorescent fixture, custom manufactured actinic lightbulbs, custom ballast, electrical wiring, and GraLab darkroom timer, 55.9h x 152.4w x 61d cm (22h x 60w x 24d in). Photo: John Opera, 2017.

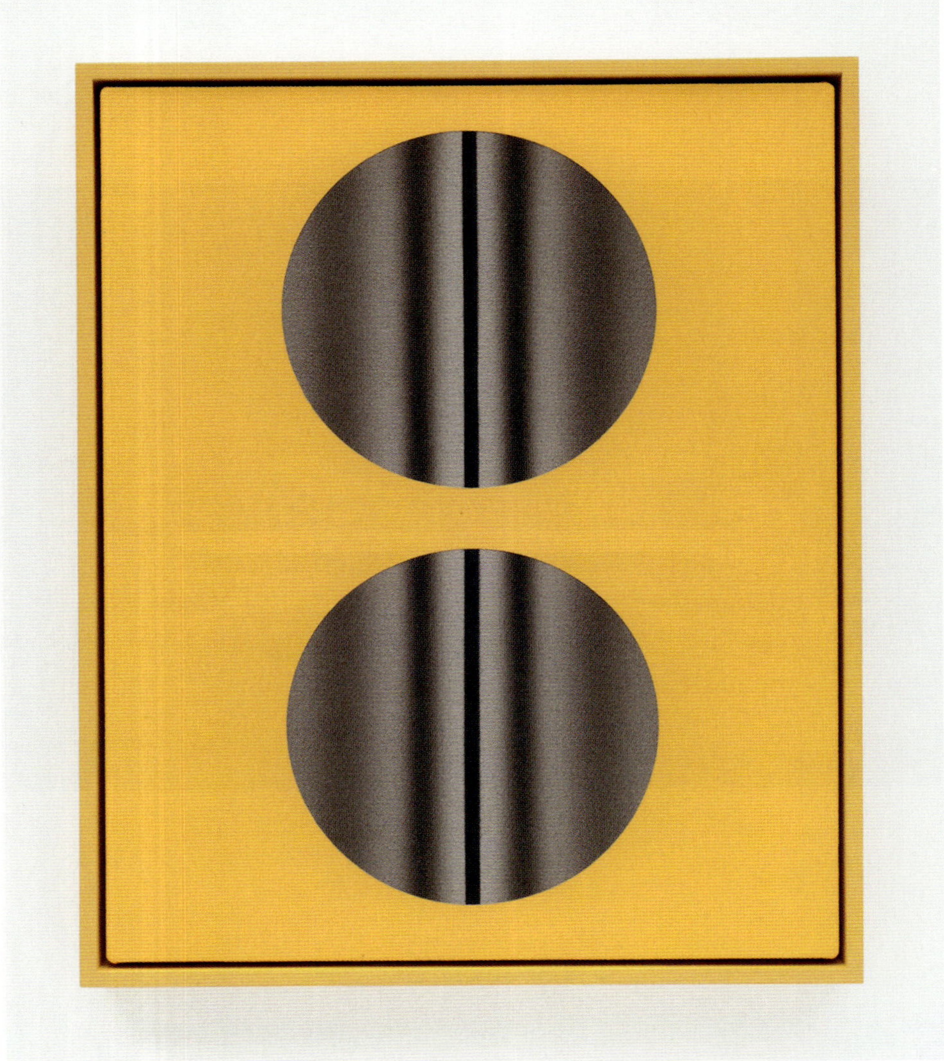

Pl. 14. John Opera, *Double Lens (yellow with lines)*, 2018. Cyanotype, acrylic, and flashe on canvas in lacquered artist frame, 53.3 x 43.2 cm (21 x 17 in).

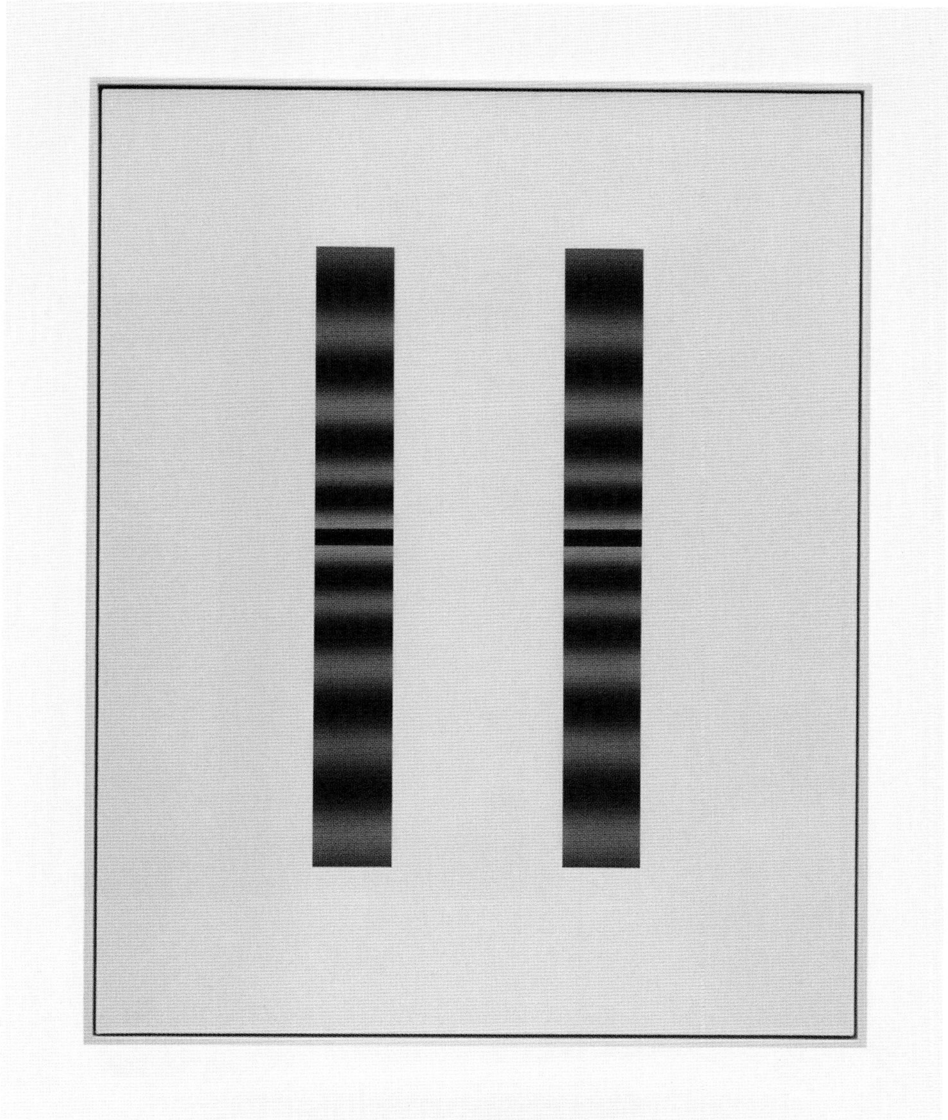

Pl. 15. John Opera, *Double Slit (blue-blue)*, 2017. Cyanotype, acrylic, and flashe on canvas in lacquered artist frame, 116.8 x 91.4 cm (46 x 36 in).

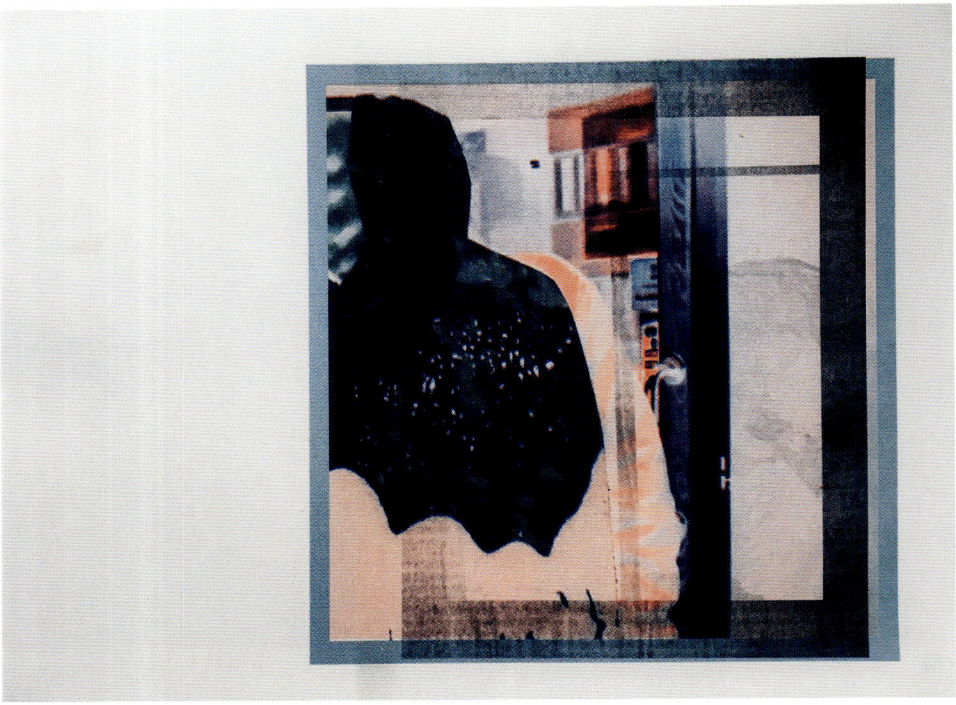

Pl. 16. Stine Behrendtzen, *Riso*, 2020. Multimedia collage, multiple layers.

# Contributors

**Kris Belden-Adams** is Associate Professor of Art History at the University of Mississippi, and specializes in the history and theory of photography. She is the author of *Photography, Temporality, Modernity: Time Warped* (2019, Routledge) and *Photography, Eugenics, 'Aristogenics': Picturing Privilege* (2020, Routledge). She also is the editor and contributor of two chapters to the volume *Photography and Failure: One Medium's Incessant Entanglement with Mishaps, Flops, and Disappointments* (Bloomsbury Academic Press, 2017), and the co-editor of the forthcoming volume *'These Are Our Stories': Global Expressions of 'Other' Histories, Narratives, and Identities in Photographic Albums* with Mary Trent.

**Geoff Bender** is Assistant Professor of English and English Education at the State University of New York, College at Cortland, where he also teaches gender studies. Recent essays have been published or are forthcoming in the *Hawthorne Review*, *Text & Image*, *Educational Considerations*, *English Teaching: Practice & Critique*, and *Henry James' Travel: Fiction & Non-Fiction* (Routledge, 2019). His current book project, *Beautiful Men: Cutting the Androgynous Figure over the Long Nineteenth Century*, explores the visual and verbal rhetorics of the masculinities of the period.

**Maura Coughlin**'s research focuses on ecological histories and visual representations of coastal communities in Atlantic France. Her recent publications include a co-edited book, *Ecocriticism and the Anthropocene in Nineteenth-Century Art and Visual Culture* (Routledge, 2019) and articles on the marine painter Elodie La Villette and the Brittany-based photography of the Geniaux brothers. She is Professor of Visual Studies in the Department of English and Cultural Studies at Bryant University in Smithfield, RI, where she teaches courses in art history and the environmental humanities.

**David LaRocca** is the author, editor, or co-editor of a dozen books. He edited *The Thought of Stanley Cavell and Cinema*, *Inheriting Stanley Cavell*, and a suite of books in film-philosophy: *The Philosophy of Charlie Kaufman*, *The Philosophy of War Films*, and *The Philosophy of Documentary Film*. His articles have appeared in journals such as *Afterimage*, *Cinema*, *Conversations*, *Epoché*, *Estetica*, *Liminalities*, *Post Script*, *Transactions*, *Film and Philosophy*, *The Senses and Society*, *The Midwest Quarterly*, *Journalism, Media and Cultural Studies*, *The Journal of Aesthetic Education*, and *The Journal of Aesthetics and Art Criticism*. He was Harvard's Sinclair Kennedy Traveling Fellow in the United Kingdom and participated in an NEH Institute, a workshop with Abbas Kiarostami, Werner Herzog's Rogue Film School, and the School of Criticism and Theory at Cornell. He has taught philosophy and cinema and held visiting research or teaching positions at Binghamton, Cornell, Cortland, Harvard, Ithaca College, the School of Visual Arts, and Vanderbilt.

**Jacob W. Lewis** received his PhD from Northwestern University and teaches art history at the University of Rochester. He has published essays on 19th-century photography in several catalogues and anthologies, including *Is Paris Still the Capital of the Nineteenth Century?* (Ashgate/Routledge, 2016) and *Photography and Failure* (Bloomsbury, 2017). Currently, he is co-editing an anthology of essays titled *Ubiquity: Photography's Multitudes* (Leuven) and is working on a manuscript on early photography, class politics, and conceptions of everyday life titled *Photography's Genre: Art and the Everyday in Nineteenth-Century France*.

**Mary Marchand** is Professor of English at Goucher College, where she directs the American Studies Program. Her recent research has focused on the origins of forensic science and the far-reaching implications of biometric technologies.

**Rasmus R. Simonsen** is Senior Lecturer of communication design & media at the Copenhagen School of Design and Technology. His research and teaching focus on how different aesthetic and technological domains intersect to create new critical dialogues. He has published articles in a number of journals – including *Leviathan: A Journal of Melville Studies*, *ESQ*, *Children's Literature*, *Journal for Critical Animal Studies*, and *Design and Culture*. In 2016, he co-edited a collection of essays entitled *Critical Perspectives on Veganism* (Palgrave).

**Zachary Tavlin** teaches in the Liberal Arts Department at the School of the Art Institute of Chicago. His work can be found in *Diacritics, ESQ, Wallace Stevens Journal, English, Continental Philosophy Review*, and many other venues.

**Christa Holm Vogelius** is a Mads Øvilsen Fellow in Art History at the University of Copenhagen, where she is working on a monograph on Jacob Riis and housing reform. She received her PhD in 19th-century American literature from the University of Michigan, and has published on photography, poetics, and gender studies.

# Index

## Q



## R

## S



## T



## V